Jim Burns's work represents his integrity, intelligence, and his heart for kids. The *Uncommon* high school group studies will change some lives and save many others.

stephen arterburn
Bestselling Author, *Every Man's Battle*

Jim Burns has found the right balance between learning God's Word and applying it to life. The topics are relevant, up to date and on target. Jim gets kids to think. This is a terrific series, and I highly recommend it.

les j. christie
Chair of Youth Ministry, William Jessup University, Rocklin, California

There are very few people in the world who know how to communicate life-changing truth effectively to teens. Jim Burns is one of the best. These studies are biblically sound, hands-on practical and just plain fun. This one gets a five-star endorsement.

ken davis
Author and Speaker (www.kendavis.com)

I don't know anyone who knows and understands the needs of the youth worker like Jim Burns. The *Uncommon* high school group studies are solid, easy to use and get students out of their seats and into the Word.

doug fields
Senior Director of HomeWord Center for Youth and Family @ Azusa Pacific University
Simply Youth Ministry (www.simplyyouthministry.com)

The practicing youth worker always needs more ammunition. The *Uncommon* high school group studies will get that blank stare off the faces of the kids at your youth meeting!

jay kesler
President Emeritus, Taylor University, Upland, Indiana

In the *Uncommon* high school group studies, Jim Burns pulls together the key ingredients for an effective series. He captures the combination of teen involvement and a solid biblical perspective with topics that are relevant and straightforward. This will be a valuable tool in the local church.

dennis "tiger" mcluen
Executive Director, Youth Leadership (www.youthleadership.com)

Young people need the information necessary to make wise decisions related to everyday problems. The *Uncommon* high school group studies will help many young people integrate their faith into everyday life, which, after all, is our goal as youth workers.

miles mcpherson
Senior Pastor, The Rock Church, San Diego, California

This is a resource that is user-friendly, learner-centered and intentionally biblical. I love having a resource like this that I can recommend to youth ministry volunteers and professionals.

duffy robbins
Professor of Youth Ministry, Eastern University, St. Davids, Pennsylvania

The *Uncommon* high school group studies provide the motivation and information for leaders and the types of experience and content that will capture high school people. I recommend it highly.

denny rydberg
President, Young Life (www.younglife.org)

Jim Burns has done it again! This is a practical, timely and reality-based resource for equipping teens to live life in the fast-paced, pressure-packed adolescent world of today.

rich van pelt
President, Compassion International, Denver, Colorado

Jim Burns has his finger on the pulse of youth today. He understands their mindsets and has prepared these studies in a way that will capture their attention and lead them to greater maturity in Christ.

rick warren
Senior Pastor, Saddleback Church, Lake Forest, California
Author of *The Purpose Driven Life*

high school group study

jim burns

general editor

living out Jesus' teachings

Published by Gospel Light
Ventura, California, U.S.A.
www.gospellight.com
Printed in the U.S.A.

Originally published as *The Word on The Sermon on the Mount* by Gospel Light in 1996.

ISBN 978-0-8307-6385-6

To order copies of this book and other Gospel Light products in bulk quantities,
please contact us at 1-800-446-7735.

dedication

To Craig Deane,
From youth group kid to coworker in youth ministry!
Your ministry, your lifestyle and your friendship are truly an inspiration.
Thank you for wiring the stereo!
God is using you in a hundred wonderful ways.
You are loved and appreciated.
Jim

Being confident of this, that he who began a good work in you will carry it on to completion until the day of Christ Jesus.

PHILIPPIANS 1:6

contents

how to use the *uncommon* group bible studies

Each *Uncommon* group Bible study contains 12 sessions, which are divided into 3 stand-alone units of 4 sessions each. You may choose to teach all 12 sessions consecutively, to use just one unit, or to present individual sessions. You know your group, so do what works best for you and your students.

This is your leader's guidebook for teaching your group. Electronic files (in PDF format) of each session's student handouts are available for download at **www.gospellight.com/uncommon/ living_out_Jesus_teachings.zip.** The handouts include the "message," "dig," "apply," "reflect" and "meditation" sections of each study and have been formatted for easy printing. You may print as many copies as you need for your group.

Each session opens with a devotional meditation written for you, the youth leader. As hectic and trying as youth work is much of the time, it's important never to neglect your interior life. Use the devotions to refocus your heart and prepare yourself to share with kids the message that has already taken root in you. Each of the 12 sessions are divided into the following sections:

starter

Young people will stay in your youth group if they feel comfortable and make friends in the group. This section is designed for you and the students to get to know each other better.

message

The message section will introduce the Scripture reading for the session and get students thinking about how the passage applies to their lives.

dig

Many young people are biblically illiterate. In this section, students will dig into the Word of God and will begin to interact on a personal level with the concepts.

apply

Young people need the opportunity to think through the issues at hand. This section will get students talking about the passage of Scripture and interacting on important issues.

reflect

The conclusion to the study will allow students to reflect on some of the issues presented in the study on a more personal level.

meditation

A closing Scripture for the students to read and reflect on.

unit I
priorities

It is a rare occasion when I am speechless. Cathy has told me throughout our marriage that I talk too much. She's right! However, there has been a few times when I was so struck with awe and amazement that I was reduced to absolute silence with a tear or two running down my cheek. I think of the first time I held my children, or standing in St. Peter's Basilica in Rome, or my mother's passing from earth to eternity, or when our pastor announced, "You are now man and wife." For me, that same sense of amazement and awe fills my soul when I read the words of Jesus in the Bible—especially in His famous "Sermon on the Mount."

My hope is that when you finish these sessions, you and your group members will have a richer faith and a deeper understanding of the core teachings of Christ. No one can study Jesus' Sermon on the Mount without having a profound respect for the Man from Galilee who gave us these words and, more importantly, lived His life according to them. I believe that all who study His message will have the same response as those first listeners had more than 2,000 years ago: "When Jesus had finished saying these things, the crowds were amazed at his teaching, because he taught as one who had authority, and not as their teachers of the law" (Matthew 7:28-29).

William Barclay introduced this most important message in this way:

> The Sermon on the Mount is greater than we think. Matthew in his introduction wishes us to see that it is the official teaching of Jesus; that it is the opening of Jesus' whole mind to His disciples; that it is the summary of the teaching which Jesus habitually gave to His inner circle. The Sermon on the Mount is nothing less than the concentrated memory of many hours of heart to heart communion between the disciples and their Master.

My prayer is that your heart and your students' hearts will burn with a desire to be silent before the Lord and hear Him speak through these powerful words of Christ.

setting the right priorities

Follow my example, as I follow the example of Christ.
1 CORINTHIANS 11:1

Are you a full-time professional youth worker? Are you a Sunday School volunteer for your church and youth ministry? Or is this your first time preparing a Bible study for teens and you're scared to death? Regardless of the amount of experience you have in ministering to young people, chances are you're a busy person. As you try to balance your life with work, friends, family, social events, your favorite sitcom, working out, attending youth ministry meetings, and, yes, preparing Bible study lessons like this one, it can be easy to lose perspective on why you're doing what you're doing.

This is why studying the beatitudes in Jesus' Sermon on the Mount is so important. Christ's words provide a reminder about *why* you're doing what you're doing. They allow you to pull off the busy highway of life for a spiritual rest area where you can be refreshed and renewed in your faith.

In youth ministry, there is always the temptation to do more and more at the cost of spending less and less time with God—to make one more phone call, schedule one more appointment, or create one more event. Yet Jesus' teachings in the beatitudes call us to look past our "doing" and really consider who we are in Christ. They inspire us to first "be" in Christ and to rest in Him.

To truly make a difference in young people's lives, we need godly characters carved in the image of Christ. We need to be pilgrims before we are event programmers. We need to be followers before we are leaders. Teenagers respond to the changed lives of adults who sincerely and authentically love them with the love of Christ. That's something no program or event can ever do.

So, before you begin to prepare for this lesson, take a few minutes to ask God for a refreshing and new perspective of His Word. Ask Jesus to make the beatitudes a reality in your life.

Let us often remember, my dear friend, that our sole occupation in life is to please God. What meaning can anything else have?

BROTHER LAWRENCE

setting the right priorities

starter

THE FIGHT: Ahead of time, ask an older male volunteer to read the following story. Introduce the illustration by mentioning that this is a true story that was told by an old colonel who served in the Austrian Army during World War I.

> I was commanded to march against a little town on the Tyrol and lay siege to it. We had been meeting stubborn resistance in that part of the country, but we felt sure that we should win because all of the advantages were on our side. My confidence, however, was arrested by a remark

from a prisoner we had taken. "You will never take that town," he said, "for they have an invincible leader."

"What does the fellow mean?" I inquired of one of my staff. "And who is this leader of whom he speaks?"

Nobody seemed able to answer my question. So, just in case there should be some truth in the report, I doubled preparations.

As we descended through the pass in the Alps, I saw with surprise that the cattle were still grazing in the valley and that women and children—yes, and even men— were working in the fields. I thought to myself, *Either they are not expecting us, or this is a trap to catch us.* As we drew nearer the town, we passed people on the road. They smiled and greeted us with a friendly word, and then went on their way.

Finally, we reached the town and clattered up the cobble-paved streets—colors flying, horns sounding a challenge, arms in readiness. Women came to the windows or door-ways with little babies in their arms. Some of them looked startled and held their babies close, and then went quietly on with their household tasks without panic or confusion.

It was impossible to keep strict discipline, and I began to feel rather foolish. My soldiers answered the questions of children, and I saw one old warrior throw a kiss to the little golden-haired tot on the doorstep. "Just the size of Lisa," he muttered. There was still no sign of an ambush. We rode straight to the open square that faced the town hall. Here, if anywhere, resistance surely was to be expected.

Just as I reached the hill and my guard was drawn up at attention, an old white-haired man, who by his insignia I surmised to be the mayor, stepped forth, followed by 10 men in simple peasant costume. They were all dignified and unabashed by the armed force before them—the most terrible soldiers of the great and mighty army of Austria.

The old man walked down the steps straight to my horse's side, and with hand extended, cried, "Welcome, brother!" One of my aides made a gesture as if to strike him down with his sword, but I saw by the face of the old mayor that this was no trick on his part.

"Where are your soldiers?" I demanded.

"Soldiers?" he replied in wonderment. "Why, don't you know we have none?" It was as though I had asked where were his giants or where were his dwarfs.

"But we have come to take this town," I said.

"Well," he replied, "no one will stop you."

"Are there none here to fight?"

At this question, the old man's face lit up with a rare smile that I will always remember. Many times later, when I was engaged in bloody warfare, I would suddenly see that man's smile—and, somehow, I came to hate my business.

His words were simply, "No, there is no one here to fight. We have chosen Christ for our leader, and He taught men another way."

After the reading has concluded, take a few minutes to discuss the following questions:

- How did the town respond to the arrival of the Austrian Army in their midset?
- How did the town's response affect the army?
- How do you think the mayor's response to the challenge to fight affected the outcome of the day?

Conclude by stating that as this story shows, when we adopt Jesus' teachings and apply them to our lives, we can never see things the same way.

message

The people Jesus encountered were hungry to hear what He had to say. Crowds followed Him as He traveled from town to town, hanging on His words and watching the way He lived. At one point, Jesus went up to a mountainside and began teaching the people what has become known as the "Sermon on the Mount." He began by explaining the types of individuals whom God considers "blessed."

Now when Jesus saw the crowds, he went up on a mountainside and sat down. His disciples came to him, and he began to teach them. He said:

"Blessed are the poor in spirit, for theirs is the kingdom of heaven.

"Blessed are those who mourn, for they will be comforted.

"Blessed are the meek, for they will inherit the earth.

"Blessed are those who hunger and thirst for righteousness, for they will be filled.

"Blessed are the merciful, for they will be shown mercy.

"Blessed are the pure in heart, for they will see God.

"Blessed are the peacemakers, for they will be called children of God.

"Blessed are those who are persecuted because of righteousness, for theirs is the kingdom of heaven.

"Blessed are you when people insult you, persecute you and falsely say all kinds of evil against you because of me. Rejoice and be glad, because great is your reward in heaven, for in the same

way they persecuted the prophets who were before you" (Matthew 5:1-12).

1. Those who are "poor in spirit" (Matthew 5:3) put their trust in Christ. They do not seek the things of this world but the things of God. What do these people receive? To whom do people who live in the kingdom of heaven belong?

    _____

    _____

    _____

    _____

2. Those who "mourn" (verse 4) are truly sorry for their sins and for the suffering in the world. They lead lives that, from the world's point of view, are difficult. What does this verse say the reward is for these people?

    _____

    _____

    _____

    _____

3. In verse 5, Jesus commends those who are "meek." These individuals are similar to the poor in spirit, in that humility is an earmark of their lives. The meek do not seek to get their way or achieve status for themselves but allow God to care for their needs. What will the meek receive?

    _____

    _____

    _____

4. The next group of people whom Jesus describes are "those who hunger and thirst for righteousness" (verse 6). These people actively seek to obey God so they can have a close relationship with Him. What will these people receive?

_____

_____

_____

_____

5. What is "mercy"? What is the result of showing mercy?

_____

_____

_____

_____

6. In verse 8, Jesus refers to the "pure in heart," which describes people who love God with all of their heart. God is welcome in every corner of their lives and nothing stands in the way of their loving Him. What will the pure in heart receive?

_____

_____

_____

_____

7. "Peacemakers" (verse 9) are not interested in self-ambition. What do peacemakers receive? Who do people see when they look at a peacemaker's life?

_____

_____

_____

_____

8. "Those who are persecuted because of righteousness" (verse 10) refers to people who won't compromise their relationship with God. Why does Jesus say these individuals can rejoice (see verses 11-12)?

_____

_____

_____

_____

_____

dig

This passage in Matthew 5:1-12 is commonly called the "beatitudes." One way to look as this section of Scripture is to think of Jesus' teachings as "be attitudes," or character qualities that define a person who reflects Christ in his or her life. Each of the beatitudes begins with the word "blessed," which in the Greek means "fortunate." It implies that the person described is to be congratulated and that his or her life is to be admired. It does not refer to the person's psychological state of mind or his or her feelings. It simply means that he or she is a model to be held up and followed.

1. What qualities do the individuals whom Jesus describes in Matthew 5:1-12 have in common?

_____

_____

_____

_____

_____

2. How do the qualities that Jesus lifts up as commendable differ from the qualities that the world admires?

    _____
    _____
    _____
    _____
    _____

3. What do you observe about the order in which Jesus mentions each character quality in the beatitudes?

    _____
    _____
    _____
    _____
    _____

4. From the world's point of view, why is it surprising that the meek will inherit the earth?

    _____
    _____
    _____
    _____
    _____

5. How do the words "hunger" and "thirst" describe a genuine desire to know God?

    _____
    _____
    _____
    _____

6. How does our merciful treatment of others affect our lives?

_____

_____

_____

_____

7. What does it mean to "see God"?

_____

_____

_____

_____

8. What do you think the people might have felt when they heard Jesus say these words in Matthew 5:10-12?

_____

_____

_____

_____

apply

As you read these descriptions of people whom Jesus calls blessed, take a moment to think about the areas in which you would like to grow more into a "beatitude" believer.

1. In the following list, next to each trait rate your level of commitment from 1 to 10, with 1 being a long way to go and 10 being approaching Christlikeness.

   ___ Poor in spirit: *I realize I am helpless without Christ; therefore, I place my complete trust in Him.*

___ Mourn: *I am truly sorry for my sin and for the suffering in the world.*

___ Hunger and thirst for righteousness: *I desire a relationship with God more than money, people, success or anything else.*

___ Mercy: *I hurt for others, feel what they feel, think their thoughts, and experience their pain.*

___ Pure in heart: *I have pure motives and reasons for all my actions. I don't dwell on impure thoughts.*

___ Peacemaker: *My goal is for all my relationships with others to be completely peaceful.*

___ Persecuted for righteousness: *I obey Christ regardless of criticism, loneliness, rejection or fear.*

2. Now consider what it would take for you to reflect Jesus in every area of your life. What would you need to do to become more of a disciple of Christ? (Check all that apply.)

❑ Obey Him more.

❑ Meditate on His Word.

❑ Start a new life with Him by asking Him to make me His child.

❑ Trust Him more completely.

❑ Choose one beatitude and make a commitment to ask God to help me improve in that area.

❑ Find Christlike friends.

❑ Weigh the costs and pay the price.

3. When you belong to God, you live a life that is free from this world's standards and one that serves as an example

of Christ to others. How would you describe your relationship with God?

_____

_____

_____

4. Which of the beatitudes is the most difficult for you personally to follow? Why?

_____

_____

_____

_____

5. What beatitude is the most apparent in your life? Why?

_____

_____

_____

_____

6. What does a person's life look like when he or she completely trusts in Jesus?

_____

_____

_____

7. How does dealing with sin in your life affect your relationship with God?

_____

_____

_____

_____

8. Why is it impossible to live up to the beatitudes without
    God's help?

    _____

    _____

    _____

    _____

    _____

reflect

We are all works in progress, and there is always room for us to
grow. Often we strive to grow through our own efforts, but we
can only make temporary progress this way. The beatitudes show
us that when we put aside our agendas, our pride, our self-pity
and our inadequate feelings and choose to trust that God is powerful enough to comfort us, protect us and grow us in Him, we
will be truly blessed.

1. What things stand in the way of you having a more open
    and vulnerable relationship with God?

    _____

    _____

    _____

    _____

2. What risks are required for you to trust God?

    _____

    _____

    _____

    _____

3. In what area of your life do you need to be more obedient to what Christ is calling you to do?

    _____

    _____

    _____

4. Who in your life can help you take the next step in living for Jesus?

    _____

    _____

    _____

5. What kind of person do you want to be? What kind of person do you think God wants you to be?

    _____

    _____

    _____

    _____

6. What does it mean to want God more than anything else in this world?

    _____

    _____

    _____

7. How could an influx of mercy in your school or community make a tremendous impact for Christ?

    _____

    _____

    _____

    _____

8. Why is it difficult to find "pure" motives and actions to-
    day? How could having this characteristic affect your rela-
    tionships with others?

    _____

    _____

    _____

    _____

9. What would it look like to be a peacemaker in your school?

    _____

    _____

    _____

    _____

10. How could persecution—when people insult you and say
    bad things about you because you are a follower of Christ—
    serve as an opportunity for you to reflect God's love to
    others and show them His nature?

    _____

    _____

    _____

    _____

meditation

Blessed are those whose ways are blameless, who walk
according to the law of the Lord. Blessed are those who keep
his statutes and seek him with all their heart—they do no
wrong but follow his ways.

PSALM 119:1-3

session 2

choosing to make
a difference

Not only so, but we also glory in our sufferings, because we know that
suffering produces perseverance; perseverance, character; and character, hope.
And hope does not put us to shame, because God's love has been poured out into
our hearts through the Holy Spirit, who has been given to us.

ROMANS 5:3-5

Disappointment is a reality in youth ministry that most of us
don't want to talk about too much. It's always easier to discuss
the exciting things that God is doing—where the next camp or retreat is going to be or how well a certain event went at the church.
Disappointment is also something of which we might not have
received much training. However, knowing that teenagers will let
us down from time to time can help us better accept what is just
one of the frustrating realities of ministry.

So, what does disappointment have to do with teaching young people that they can make a real difference in the world? The good news is that even though young people (and adults) from time to time will drop the ball, fall short, make mistakes and ultimately disappoint us, by God's grace, we are all still called to make a difference for Christ in the world. Furthermore, even when *we* disappoint others, God's grace can still fill in the cracks in our character.

There is a subtle temptation in youth ministry to focus on performance instead of process. Young people can—and *will*—make mistakes. The challenge of youth ministry is to walk alongside teens as they "work out" their faith in Christ. The trick is to not let our disappointment get in the way of remembering that developing faith is generally a long and difficult process.

Remember that it is by God's grace that Jesus calls us to be "the salt of the earth" and "the light of the world" (Matthew 5:13-14). Your students will shine their light brighter when they understand that they are under the grace of God and not a legalistic law of performance. Even your light will shine brighter as you rest in God's grace . . . in spite of the disappointments you may face.

*We are told to let our light shine, and if it does, we won't need
to tell anybody it does. Lighthouses don't fire cannons to call attention
to their shining—they just shine.*

D. L. MOODY

choosing to make a difference

starter

RHYME TIME: Give each group member a copy of the following handout and a pen or pencil. (Note that you can download this sheet in pdf form at **www.gospellight.com/uncommon/living_ out_Jesus_teachings.zip**). Tell the group that the left-hand column contains a word clue that they will need to use to figure out the two-word rhyming answer. The first letter in each rhyming-word answer has been given to make this a little easier!

Clue		Answer
1.	A distant light in the night sky	F _ _ S _ _ _
2.	A royal hawk-like bird	R _ _ _ _ E _ _ _ _

3.	A white-colored spike	P _ _ _ N _ _ _
4.	A covering for a log	W _ _ _ H _ _ _
5.	An enjoyable jog	F _ _ R _ _
6.	A distant automobile	F _ _ C _ _
7.	A tiny insect that makes honey	W _ _ B _ _
8.	What you would call an amphibian on a street	R _ _ _ T _ _ _
9.	A label you would find attached to a sack	B _ _ T _ _
10.	A lemon-colored dessert	Y _ _ _ _ _ _ J _ _ _ - _
11.	A tidy place where you would sit down	N _ _ _ S _ _ _
12.	The primary road in a town	M _ _ _ L _ _ _
13.	A hair condition people have when they wake up	B _ _ H _ _ _
14.	A sliced acorn, walnut or almond	C _ _ N _ _
15.	A run-down or aged-looking antler	W _ _ _ H _ _ _ _
16.	A notch or cut in a branch	S _ _ _ _ N _ _ _
17.	A place where you would find a sweeping device	B _ _ _ _ R _ _ _
18.	A rake-like tool you would use on a ski slope	S _ _ _ H _ _
19.	What you would find if a work of art was left in direct sunlight for too long	F _ _ _ _ P _ _ _ _
20.	A false pond or other large body of water	F _ _ _ L _ _ _

Allow 10 minutes or so for everyone to complete the handout, and then call time. Go through the answers listed at the end of this session and award a small prize to the person who has the most correct responses.

message

Throughout the Gospels, we find that Jesus often used "word pictures" or parables to help His listeners understand important truths about how God wanted them to lead their lives. Instead of barraging His listeners with deep theological arguments and weighty-sounding speeches, Jesus used simple stories and illustrations from their daily lives that they could easily understand. Today, we will look at one such passage.

> *You are the salt of the earth. But if the salt loses its saltiness, how can it be made salty again? It is no longer good for anything, except to be thrown out and trampled underfoot. You are the light of the world. A town built on a hill cannot be hidden. Neither do people light a lamp and put it under a bowl. Instead they put it on its stand, and it gives light to everyone in the house. In the same way, let your light shine before others, that they may see your good deeds and glorify your Father in heaven* (Matthew 5:13-16).

1. What two images does Jesus use to describe His followers?

   ----

2. Before people had refrigerators, they used salt to keep meat from rotting. Keeping this in mind, what do you think Jesus meant when He said, "You are the salt of the earth" (verse 13)?

   ----

3. What might cause Christians to lose their "saltiness"?

    _____

    _____

    _____

4. What does Jesus say about this type of person?

    _____

    _____

    _____

5. In ancient Israel, many towns were built on steep hills, not
    in the valleys. The people did this because it was easier to
    defend a town if it was situated on a hill. What else does Je-
    sus say about a town that is placed on a hill (see verse 14)?

    _____

    _____

    _____

6. Jesus goes on to say that no one lights a lamp and places
    it under a bowl, because that diminishes the light it gives
    (see verse 15). By using these two examples, what is Jesus
    telling His followers they need to do to change the world?

    _____

    _____

    _____

7. What does Jesus say will happen when you "let your light
    shine before others" (verse 16)?

    _____

    _____

    _____

8. In Philippians 2:14-15, Paul says, "Do everything without grumbling or arguing, so that you may become blameless and pure, 'children of God without fault in a warped and crooked generation.' Then you will shine among them like stars in the sky." What types of things do Christians need to do to reflect God's love to others?

    _____

    _____

    _____

    _____

dig

Throughout the Bible, we find other examples in which God used both salt and light to illustrate important principles to His people. Let's take a closer look at some of these passages in Scripture.

1. Read Job 6:6. Based on this verse, what was one important function of salt?

    _____

    _____

    _____

    _____

2. Turn to 2 Kings 2:19-22. What was the people's problem in this story? How did God use Elisha to help them?

    _____

    _____

    _____

    _____

3. What did salt represent in the miracle that Elisha performed?

    ----

4. From these passages, we see that salt was something that made food "savory" and that it also represented something with "purifying" properties. In what ways does this represent how believers in Christ are to live in the world?

    ----

5. The importance of light is obvious. After all, without it we wouldn't be able to see anything! However, in the Bible light represents much more than just something that keeps us from stumbling in physical darkness. Read John 8:12. What does Jesus say about Himself in this verse?

    ----

6. What do you think Jesus meant when He said that if we follow Him, we would also have "the light of life"?

    ----

7. In 1 John 1:5, we read, "God is light; in him there is do darkness at all." Why must we as Christians reflect this light?

    ----

8. When we let our "light shine before others" (Matthew 5:16), what gift are we giving to others? What does this tell us about the need to share our faith—the light of Christ—to a world filled with spiritual darkness?

    ----

apply

1. In Mark 9:50, Jesus states, "Salt is good, but if it loses its saltiness, how can you make it salty again?" Think about this verse for a moment. If you are "salt," how would you say your relationship with Christ is currently?

    _____

    blah   tasteless   mild   seasoned   spicy   very tasty

2. What is one thing you need to do today to add more "salt" to your Christian diet?

    ----

3. Jesus is clear that if you want to make an impact for God in this world, people have to see His light in you and recognize

there is something different about the way you live your life.
When it comes to shining for Christ, how are you doing?

- ❑ I shine brightly all the time.
- ❑ I flicker a bit now and then.
- ❑ I feel dark and cold.
- ❑ I need a new spark!
- ❑ I burn brighter every day.
- ❑ I shed light for God's glory.
- ❑ I need a few other candles for help.

4. Let's say you are a Christian and on the junior varsity bas-
    ketball team at your school. Your teammates are friendly
    and fun, but they have a warped sense of humor, often use
    foul language, and like to talk about sex. They tell you
    filthy jokes and invite you to parties where there is drink-
    ing and sexual promiscuity. What are some ways you can
    apply the salt-and-light principle in this situation?

    ----

5. Now let's say you are a person who is active in your church
    youth group. You like to read your Bible, have your daily
    quiet time with God, and hang around your fellow Christian
    students all day at school. In fact, you can't think of even *one*
    friend you have who is not a Christian. What are some of the
    challenges this would present in shining your light for God?

    ----

6. In 2 Corinthians 6:14, Paul writes, "Do not be yoked together with unbelievers. What do righteousness and wickedness have in common? Or what fellowship can light have with darkness?" Does this mean that you should never have any association with non-believers? If not, what is Paul saying in this verse?

_____

_____

_____

_____

7. Where do you find the balance in your life between witnessing to those who don't believe in Christ and staying out of situations where you would be tempted to sin?

_____

_____

_____

_____

8. What would you do if Jesus came to you today and said, "I want you to be My light to your family, your friends and your school. Will you shine for Me?"

_____

_____

_____

reflect

Billy Graham, the well-known evangelist, once said, "The evangelistic harvest is always urgent. The destiny of men and nations is always being decided. Every generation is strategic. God will hold us responsible as to how well we fulfill our responsibilities to this age and take advantage of our responsibilities."[1]

1. In what ways have you seen God using you to reach your generation for Him?

   _____

   _____

   _____

   _____

2. What can you do to better fulfill your God-given responsibilities?

   _____

   _____

   _____

   _____

3. Think about a person you admire for the way he or she boldly shares his or her faith for Christ. What is it about that person you most admire?

   _____

   _____

   _____

   _____

4. What traits in that person could you model to be salt and light for God?

   _____

   _____

   _____

   _____

5. Why is it so difficult at times to share the good news of Christ with others?

6. What are some simple ways that you could put the salt-and-light principle into practice at school?

7. What are some ways you can share the light of Christ not only with your words but also with your actions?

8. Why is it important to forgive yourself when you stumble and fail at representing Christ to this world? What do you think God wants you to do in these situations?

meditation

But if we walk in the light, as he is in the light,
we have fellowship with one another, and the blood
of Jesus, his Son, purifies us from all sin.

1 JOHN 1:7

Starter Answers: (1) far star, (2) regal eagle, (3) pale nail, (4) wood hood, (5) fun run, (6) far car, (7) wee bee, (8) road toad, (9) bag tag, (10) yellow Jell-O, (11) neat seat, (12) main lane, (13) bed head, (14) cut nut, (15) worn horn, (16) stick nick, (17) broom room, (18) snow hoe, (19) faint paint, (20) fake lake.

Note
1. Billy Graham, *Quote, Unquote* (Wheaton, IL: Victor Books, 1977), p. 102.

session 3

living in obedience
to God's laws

Anyone who loves me will obey my teaching. My Father will love them,
and we will come to them and make our home with them.

JOHN 14:23

The word "obedience" has negative connotations in many people's minds. Obedience requires submitting to the authority of
another, and for many people that can be a difficult course to follow. Our culture today favors power, strength, individuality and
confidence, and while none of those things are necessarily bad,
one trait that is typically not prized is humility.

Jesus understood the importance and power of obedience. He
was obedient to His Father and humble in everything He said and
did, even to the point of "becoming obedient to death . . . on a
cross" (Philippians 2:8). Jesus understood God's laws and took

them to heart, and He clearly designed His teachings on oaths, adultery, murder and divorce to help His listeners win at life.

These teachings are a few of the fundamentals that God has outlined for His children's own wellbeing and protection. Just as a football team must follow certain rules and stay within the painted lines on a field, God has given His Word to show us how to live within the freedom and safety of His commands. He has set boundaries not to restrict our freedom but to protect it.

How many students in your youth ministry have been hurt by broken marriage oaths, adultery and divorce? Countless marriages have failed because of the decisions of some parents not to follow God's fundamental commands for life. Young people need to be reassured that God's commands are given for their wellbeing. That's just one of the reasons why your ministry is so important!

This session will provide a good reminder to you and your group about the *purpose* of God's commands. It will provide you with the opportunity to talk with your students about sensitive topics such as adultery, divorce and the importance of keeping commitments. The session is also filled with great ideas on how to coach young people to stay "inbounds" for God and realize that the only way to win at life is by winning God's way.

Every great person has first learned how to obey,
whom to obey, and when to obey.
WILLIAM WILLARD

living in obedience to God's laws

starter

JESUS SAYS: To get your group members thinking about the concept of obedience to God, play a modified game of "Simon Says." Begin by having all the students line up opposite you. Tell the group that you will be reading a statement that may or may not begin with the words "Jesus says." If they think the statement is actually something Jesus said in the Bible, they should hop on their right foot. Tell them they will be out if they incorrectly identify a statement that Jesus didn't say or if they act without first hearing the words "Jesus says." (To make this a bit easier, you might want to have a helper to watch which group members are out.) Here are some ideas for statements that *are* from Christ:

- Jesus said, "Love your enemies and pray for those who persecute you" (Matthew 5:44).

- Jesus said, "You cannot serve both God and money" (Matthew 6:24).
- Jesus said, "Unless you change and become like little children, you will never enter the kingdom of heaven" (Matthew 18:3).
- Jesus said, "Go and make disciples of all nations" (Matthew 28:19).
- Jesus said, "Whoever wants to be my disciple must deny themselves and take up their cross and follow me" (Mark 8:34).
- Jesus said, "The Son of Man did not come to be served, but to serve, and to give his life as a ransom for many" (Mark 10:45).
- Jesus said, "Ask and it will be given to you; seek and you will find; knock and the door will be opened to you" (Luke 11:9).
- Jesus said, "I am the gate" (John 10:9).
- Jesus said, "I am the good shepherd" (John 10:11).
- Jesus said, "I am the way and the truth and the life" (John 14:6).
- Jesus said, "I am the true vine" (John 15:1).
- Jesus said, "You will receive power when the Holy Spirit comes on you" (Acts 1:8).
- Jesus said, "Here I am! I stand at the door and knock" (Revelation 3:20).

Here are ideas for some statements that are *not* from Christ:

- Jesus said, "The love of money is the root of all kinds of evil." (Paul said this in 1 Timothy 6:10).
- Jesus said, "Haste makes waste." (This is commonly attributed to Benjamin Franklin.)
- Jesus said, "Do to others what they did to you." (This is a not-quite-correct interpretation of Jesus' words in Luke 6:31).

- Jesus said, "Cleanliness is next to godliness." (This is an ancient proverb that first appeared in English in the writings of Sir Francis Bacon.)

- Jesus said, "Are not two sparrows sold for a dollar?" (Jesus said for "a penny" in Matthew 10:29).

- Jesus said, "Lazarus, tear down this wall." (Ronald Reagan said, "Mr. Gorbachev, tear down this wall" in 1987.)

- Jesus said, "Everyone should be quick to listen, slow to speak and slow to become angry." (James said this in James 1:19).

- Jesus said, "Nazareth! Can anything good come from there?" (Jesus' disciple Nathanael actually said this about Christ in John 1:46.)

Be sure to mix up your statements and add in some that don't begin with the words "Jesus says." Your group members will likely find this a challenging game. When you are finished, discuss the following questions: (1) What made this game difficult? (2) Was it difficult to follow the rules? (3) Why do you think God gives us rules to follow?

message

Throughout the Gospels, we find the title *rabbi* (or "teacher") given to Jesus. His disciples call Him by this title (see Mark 9:5; 11:21), as do the Pharisees (a religious group of the time; see John 3:1-2), the common people (see Mark 10:51; John 6:24-25), and even the teachers of the law (see Matthew 8:19). The word *rabbi* in the first century referred to men who studied and knew God's law (the Torah) and teachers who had authority. Both of these characteristics applied to Christ.

the law and the prophets

In the next portion of the Sermon on the Mount, Jesus reveals how He represents the fulfillment of the law that God originally gave to Moses.

> *Do not think that I have come to abolish the Law or the Prophets; I have not come to abolish them but to fulfill them. For truly I tell you, until heaven and earth disappear, not the smallest letter, not the least stroke of a pen, will by any means disappear from the Law until everything is accomplished. Therefore anyone who sets aside one of the least of these commands and teaches others accordingly will be called least in the kingdom of heaven, but whoever practices and teaches these commands will be called great in the kingdom of heaven. For I tell you that unless your righteousness surpasses that of the Pharisees and the teachers of the law, you will certainly not enter the kingdom of heaven* (Matthew 5:17-20).

1. What was Jesus' view of the Old Testament laws and the prophets?

    _____

    _____

    _____

    _____

    _____

2. What role does obedience to God's law play in establishing the least and greatest in His eyes?

    _____

    _____

    _____

    _____

laws against murder

In Exodus 20:1, God told Moses, "I am the LORD your God, who brought you out of Egypt, out of the land of slavery." God proceeded to give Moses a series of 10 laws for the Israelites to follow, which today are known as the Ten Commandments. The Sixth Commandment was, "You shall not murder" (verse 13). It is to this law that Jesus next refers in His Sermon on the Mount.

You have heard that it was said to the people long ago, "You shall not murder, and anyone who murders will be subject to judgment." But I tell you that anyone who is angry with a brother or sister will be subject to judgment. Again, anyone who says to a brother or sister, "Raca," is answerable to the court. And anyone who says, "You fool!" will be in danger of the fire of hell.

Therefore, if you are offering your gift at the altar and there remember that your brother or sister has something against you, leave your gift there in front of the altar. First go and be reconciled to them; then come and offer your gift (Matthew 5:21-24).

1. What three types of "attitude murder" does Jesus mention in this passage?

   _____

   _____

   _____

   _____

2. What does Jesus say should take place before worship?

   _____

   _____

   _____

   _____

3. What are the results of uncontrolled anger?

_____

_____

_____

_____

laws against adultery

In Exodus 20:14, God told His people, "You shall not commit adultery." This was the Seventh Commandment, which Jesus addresses next.

> *You have heard that it was said, "You shall not commit adultery." But I tell you that anyone who looks at a woman lustfully has already committed adultery with her in his heart. If your right eye causes you to stumble, gouge it out and throw it away. It is better for you to lose one part of your body than for your whole body to be thrown into hell. And if your right hand causes you to stumble, cut it off and throw it away. It is better for you to lose one part of your body than for your whole body to go into hell (Matthew 5:27-30).*

1. How does Jesus define adultery?

_____

_____

_____

_____

2. In what ways is Jesus' definition even stricter than the original law?

_____

_____

_____

_____

laws against divorce

In Deuteronomy 24:1, God told the Israelites that if "a man marries a woman who becomes displeasing to him because he finds something indecent about her," that man could write her "a certificate of divorce." Jesus has this command in mind when He expands on God's law concerning divorce.

> *It has been said, "Anyone who divorces his wife must give her a certificate of divorce." But I tell you that anyone who divorces his wife, except for sexual immorality, makes her the victim of adultery, and anyone who marries a divorced woman commits adultery* (Matthew 5:31-32).

1. What is Jesus' view of divorce? How does it differ from the people's understanding of that time?

   _____

   _____

   _____

   _____

2. What do you think Jesus is trying to say about the sanctity of marriage?

   _____

   _____

   _____

   _____

laws against taking oaths

In biblical times, taking oaths was serious business. Vows represented solemn and sacred commitments to God, and there were dire consequences for those who broke them. This is why God told His people in Deuteronomy 23:21, "If you make a vow to the LORD your God, do not be slow to pay it, for the LORD your God will certainly demand it of you and you will be guilty of sin." But look at Jesus' next words concerning taking oaths:

> *Again, you have heard that it was said to the people long ago, "Do not break your oath, but fulfill to the Lord the vows you have made." But I tell you, do not swear an oath at all: either by heaven, for it is God's throne; or by the earth, for it is his footstool; or by Jerusalem, for it is the city of the Great King. And do not swear by your head, for you cannot make even one hair white or black. All you need to say is simply "Yes" or "No"; anything beyond this comes from the evil one (Matthew 5:33-35).*

1. What do you think Jesus meant by "swearing"?

   _____

   _____

   _____

   _____

2. Why do people feel the need to swear or promise something by taking an oath?

   _____

   _____

   _____

   _____

dig

For Jesus, obeying His Father's will was of utmost importance. God had sent Jesus to this earth to fulfill a mission—the redemption of humankind—and in doing so bring about the fulfillment of the laws He had given to the Israelites.

1. In Psalm 119:1-3, the psalmist writes, "Blessed are those whose ways are blameless, who walk according to the law of the LORD. Blessed are those who keep his statutes and seek him with all their heart—they do no wrong but follow his ways." What is the psalmist's attitude about God's laws?

    _____

    _____

    _____

2. Does the psalmist view God's laws as restrictive? Why or why not?

    _____

    _____

    _____

3. Read Ezekiel 20:11. What was God's motive for giving people laws?

    _____

    _____

    _____

    _____

4. Turn to Romans 3:20. Can anyone live up to God's standards under the law? According to this verse, what does the law show us?

    _____

    _____

    _____

5. In Matthew 5:22, Jesus states that anyone who calls a fellow
    disciple *"Raca"* will be answerable in court. *Raca* was an Ara-
    maic word of contempt that meant "senseless," "vain" or
    "empty-headed." What statement was Jesus making about
    how we should treat one another by connecting this act
    with murder?

    _____

    _____

    _____

    _____

6. What does Jesus instruct a person to do who is making a
    gift to God but then remembers that a fellow disciple is
    holding something against him or her?

    _____

    _____

    _____

    _____

7. In Matthew 5:29-30, Jesus used a powerful illustration to
    show how people should deal with sin in a drastic manner.
    In making this statement Jesus is not advocating self-mu-
    tilation—for even a blind person can lust. How would you
    put these verses into modern language?

    _____

    _____

    _____

    _____

8. Many wonderful people—both parents and kids—have been through hurtful divorces. What steps can you take that might help keep divorce out of your own future marriage?

    _____

    _____

    _____

9. In Matthew 19:3-6, when Jesus is asked whether it is lawful for a man to divorce his wife, He responds, "Haven't you read . . . that at the beginning the Creator 'made them male and female,' and said, 'For this reason a man will leave his father and mother and be united to his wife, and the two will become one flesh'? So they are no longer two, but one flesh. Therefore what God has joined together, let no one separate." What point do you think Jesus is making about God's original design for marriage?

    _____

    _____

    _____

apply

Let's take a closer look at what Jesus says in this portion of the Sermon on the Mount as it relates to anger, lust, marriage and oaths.

1. In Matthew 5:21-26, Jesus makes some strong statements about *anger*. People express anger in different ways. Which response best describes your method of venting anger? (Check the appropriate responses.)

    ❑ Yelling and screaming
    ❑ Sarcasm and criticizing

   ❑   Getting even with the person who made you mad
   ❑   Silent withdrawal or depression
   ❑   Physical outbursts
   ❑   Physical illness
   ❑   Destroyed self-image
   ❑   I have never been angry (denial)

2. What can you do to better manage your anger?

     _____

     _____

     _____

3. If we are to take Jesus' words seriously, we have to repair any damaged relationships with others before we attempt to worship God. Is there someone in your life with whom you need to restore a broken relationship? What steps do you need to take to patch up that relationship?

     _____

     _____

     _____

4. In Matthew 5:27-30, Jesus addresses the problem of *lust*. Which response best describes your reaction when you hear Jesus speaking about lust? (Check the appropriate responses.)

   ❑   I have no response, because it's not an issue for me.
   ❑   I get nervous because I know He's talking about me!
   ❑   I feel guilty because I've had lustful thoughts.
   ❑   I am anxious to ask forgiveness one more time.
   ❑   I am motivated to find support from other Christians.
   ❑   I want to read God's Word to clear my mind.

5. Why is it difficult for those who struggle with lust to talk with other Christians about their problem?

6. Jesus makes His views on *divorce* clear in Matthew 5:31-32. In what ways might divorce reveal the hardness of our hearts?

7. How does Jesus' teaching contrast with today's view on marriage and divorce?

8. How will love relationships between two Christians who put God first in their lives be stronger than those of people who do not invite God to be a part of their relationships?

9. Read James 5:12. How does this verse echo Jesus' words in Matthew 5:37? To what result does James say that taking oaths will lead?

10. Read James 5:12. How does this verse echo Jesus' words
in Matthew 5:37? To what result does James say talking
oaths will lead?

_____

_____

_____

_____

_____

reflect

In Jesus' day, the Pharisees prided themselves on keeping God's
law. Unfortunately, they became so devoted to keeping the letter
of the law that they missed the fact that Jesus—the fulfillment of
the law—was in their very midst. While they looked good and
righteous on the outside, they were lacking on the inside. In some
ways, they were like the man in the following story:

> A man went into a fried chicken place and bought several
> chicken dinners for himself and his date. As he was leaving,
> the young woman at the counter inadvertently gave him
> the proceeds for the day—a whole bag of money (much of
> it cash) instead of fried chicken.
>
> After driving to their picnic site, the man and his date
> sat down to enjoy some chicken together. It was then the
> man discovered he had received a lot more than chicken—
> more than $800, in fact. The man didn't hesitate. He quickly
> put the money back in the bag, got back into the car with
> his date, and drove all the way back to the restaurant.
>
> By the time the man arrived, the manager was frantic.
> The man looked at the manager and said, "I want you to

know that I came by to get a couple of chicken dinners, but I wound up with all this money. Here, please take it back."

The manager was thrilled. "I'm going to call the newspaper," he said, picking up his digital camera and taking a picture of the man. "People like you are rare, and the world needs to know that honesty and integrity still exist in the world! Your picture will be in tomorrow's edition!"

"Oh, no, no, no, don't do that!" the man stammered. "You see, the woman I'm with is not my wife . . . she's uh, somebody else's wife."[1]

1. How does this man's behavior illustrate someone who seems to be living a moral life on the outside but really is not a trustworthy person?

_____

_____

_____

_____

2. For all their morality, the Pharisees had an issue with pride. This is why Jesus said to them, "You brood of vipers, how can you who are evil say anything good? For the mouth speaks what the heart is full of" (Matthew 12:34). What is Jesus saying about the importance of having what is on the outside match the inside?

_____

_____

_____

_____

3. How do Jesus' words in this portion of the Sermon on the Mount make obedience to Him more challenging than merely obeying the law?

_____

_____

_____

_____

_____

4. In this section of Scripture, Jesus is calling His followers to enter into a deeper level of obedience to Him. Where would you place yourself on the obedience scale?

_____

Completely lacking   Off and on   Consistent and steady

5. In what ways does adultery or divorce break our relationship with God?

_____

_____

_____

_____

_____

6. How can one find forgiveness in the midst of divorce and/ or adultery?

_____

_____

_____

_____

7. In John 14:21, Jesus says, "Whoever has my commands and keeps them is the one who loves me. The one who loves me will be loved by my Father, and I too will love them and show myself to them." According to this verse, how should we show God we love Him?

    _____

    _____

    _____

    _____

    _____

8. There are times when Christians say, "If only God would reveal more of Himself, I would obey Him." According to this passage, why is the opposite true?

    _____

    _____

    _____

    _____

    _____

9. Read 1 Corinthians 1:30. What is the ultimate source of our righteous behavior?

    _____

    _____

    _____

    _____

    _____

meditation

You also died to the law through the body of Christ,
that you might belong to another, to him who
was raised from the dead, in order that we might bear
fruit for God. For when we were in the realm of the flesh,
the sinful passions aroused by the law were at work
in us, so that we bore fruit for death. But now, by dying
to what once bound us, we have been released from
the law so that we serve in the new way of the Spirit, and
not in the old way of the written code.

ROMANS 7:4-6

Note

1. Adapted from Charles Swindoll, *Growing Deep in the Christian Life* (Portland, OR: Multnomah Press, 1986), pp. 159-160.

loving the unlovable

If your enemy is hungry, feed him; if he is thirsty, give him something to drink.
In doing this, you will heap burning coals on his head.

ROMANS 12:20

Teaching teenagers a Bible study on loving their enemies is relatively easy in comparison to motivating them to actually do it. Perhaps that's why James said few of us should aspire to be teachers (see James 3:1)!

Who are the "unlovables" in your life right now? Who are the kids or adults who drive you crazy? Who are the people you feel like grabbing by the collar and screaming, "If you do that one more time, I'm gonna knock you into next week"? What types of personalities annoy you like a mosquito on your face? Or, worse, who are your enemies—those bile-producing adversaries with whom you lock horns in mortal combat?

One of the biggest challenges your students will ever face is learning how to love their enemies. An enemy is the last thing most of us would want to have, and loving an enemy is the last thing most of us would want to do. Loving the unlovable people in our lives requires a motivation and strength that comes from God. How else could we possibly do it?

There will always be people in our lives who just bug us. If we're really honest with ourselves and truthful with God, we have no real desire to love or be with people who irritate us. That's why we need God's grace to do what we can't do in our own strength. He can give us the humility and grace to love others in spite of ourselves.

Loving our enemies is the true evidence of a transformed life. It is the proof of a real conversion in our human nature. That's the direction this lesson is pointing us—in the direction of loving others as Jesus does.

The best way to destroy your enemy is to make him your friend.
ABRAHAM LINCOLN

loving the unlovable

starter

THE SALESPERSON: Of course, a good test of our love for others is how we treat those who bug us . . . like annoying salespeople. So, for this starter exercise, choose three group members to play the part of potential salespeople. Take them out of the room and explain to them that they will be selling a product to the group. They need to do their best to answer *all* the questions they are asked. The catch is that the salespeople will not know what product they are selling!

Now tell the rest of the group that each salesperson will be selling toilet paper. The group can ask any question they want about this product. Also tell them that the salespeople have no idea that the product they are selling is toilet paper—so they should not use the specific word "toilet paper" when they ask questions.

message

In the previous session, we discussed how Jesus stated that He did not come to "abolish the Law or the Prophets . . . but to fulfill them" (Matthew 5:17). In the next section of the Sermon on the Mount, Jesus continues to elaborate on various Old Testament laws and demonstrate how He is the fulfillment of them. In the process, He gives the people a whole new concept on what it means to love others.

a new understanding of revenge

After speaking about laws against murder, adultery, divorce and oaths, Jesus offers His followers a new—and startling—perspective on how they should treat their enemies and those who want to do harm to them.

> You have heard that it was said, "Eye for eye, and tooth for tooth." But I tell you, do not resist an evil person. If anyone slaps you on the right cheek, turn to them the other cheek also. And if anyone wants to sue you and take your shirt, hand over your coat as well. If anyone forces you to go one mile, go with them two miles. Give to the one who asks you, and do not turn away from the one who wants to borrow from you (Matthew 5:38-42).

1. What instructions did Jesus give to His followers on how to deal with those who did evil against them?

     _____

     _____

     _____

     _____

2. What did Jesus tell them to offer a person who sued them and took their shirts?

   ----

3. Notice that Jesus gives His followers three examples: (1) the person who slaps them on the cheek, (2) the one who sues them, and (3) the person who forces them to go a mile. What is Jesus' basic message or theme in each of these examples?

   ----

4. In what ways do these responses go against human nature?

   ----

loving your enemies

After breaking down the Old Testament laws on revenge, Jesus goes on to address the heart of the matter—how we should show love to those who hate us and those who persecute us.

> *You have heard that it was said, "Love your neighbor and hate your enemy." But I tell you, love your enemies and pray for those who persecute you, that you may be children of your Father in heaven. He causes his sun to rise on the evil and the good, and sends rain on the righteous and the unrighteous. If you love those who love you,*

what reward will you get? Are not even the tax collectors doing that? And if you greet only your own people, what are you doing more than others? Do not even pagans do that? Be perfect, therefore, as your heavenly Father is perfect (Matthew 5:43-48).

1. What does Jesus mean when He says, "Love your enemies"?

    _____

    _____

    _____

2. Notice that Jesus says God "causes his sun to rise on the evil and the good." Do you think this is fair? Why or why not?

    _____

    _____

    _____

3. How does Jesus want His followers to stand out from the crowd? What actions on their part will show that they belong to Him?

    _____

    _____

    _____

    _____

4. Why is it logical for Jesus' statements "love your enemies" (verse 44) and "be perfect . . . as your heavenly father is perfect" (verse 48) to be together in the same paragraph?

    _____

    _____

    _____

dig

To understand how startling these new commands on not taking revenge and loving your neighbors would be to a Jewish audience, we have to take a look at some of the Old Testament laws that Jesus was using to frame the discussion.

1. Leviticus 24:19-20 states, "Suppose someone hurts his neighbor. Then what he has done must be done to him. A bone must be broken for a bone. An eye must be put out for an eye. A tooth must be knocked out for a tooth. He must be hurt in the same way he hurt someone else." Imagine that you had grown up learning this law by heart. How would you react to Jesus' teaching on this passage?

    _____

    _____

    _____

    _____

2. Jesus' command on not taking revenge seems passive and weak in nature—almost as if you are to allow anyone to do harm to you. However, how does "turning the other cheek" actually require an attitude of *strength* on your part?

    _____

    _____

    _____

    _____

3. Proverbs 20:22 states, "Don't say, 'I'll get even with you for the wrong you did to me!' Wait for the Lord, and he will

save you." Why is this so difficult to do when you have been wronged?

_____

_____

_____

4. In what ways does loving your enemies led to better results than taking revenge against everyone who wrongs you?

_____

_____

_____

5. Read Acts 7:59-60. What did Stephen do when the religious leaders were putting him to death?

_____

_____

_____

6. How did Stephen model Jesus' words in Matthew 5:44?

_____

_____

_____

7. Often, it is difficult to know exactly who is being affected by our actions to take a stand for Christ. Read Acts 8:1. Who was present at Stephen's execution? In what ways do you think Stephen's prayer affected him?

_____

_____

_____

8. Turn to 1 Corinthians 4:12-13. How did Paul come to apply Jesus' words to his own life and to his instruction to others?

    _____

    _____

    _____

    _____

apply

Jesus' statements in Matthew 5:38-48 are some of the most profound and radical verses in the Bible. They are also among the most difficult to live out!

1. Think about a person who just annoys you. Now consider Jesus' words about loving that person and reacting with kindness when he or she does something that really gets under your skin. How does this make you feel? Circle the response that best applies to you.

    ❑   Amused. No one could possibly love *that* person.
    ❑   Overwhelmed. How am I supposed to do this?
    ❑   Exited. What a great opportunity to love others!
    ❑   Challenged. This is tough, but I think I can do it with God's help.
    ❑   Guilty. I know I should be doing better at this than I am.
    ❑   Encouraged. If God says I can do it, I know He will show me the way!

2. So, can anyone *really* follow these commands of Jesus—principles that go so completely against our natural responses

when others do us harm? Read the following story and answer the question that follows.

Angus was a Scottish prisoner during World War II in a
camp filled with Americans, Australians and Britons. The
camp had become an ugly scene. A dog-eat-dog mentality
had set in. Allies would steal from each other and cheat each
other. Men would sleep on their packs, and yet have them
stolen from under their heads. Survival was everything.

The law of the jungle prevailed . . . until the news of Angus's death spread throughout the camp. No one could believe big Angus had succumbed. He was strong—one of
those whom they had expected to be the last to die. Actually, it wasn't the fact of his death that shocked the men,
but the reason he died. It took a while for them to piece together the story.

The Scottish soldiers took the buddy system seriously.
They called their buddy their "mucker," and they believed
that it was literally up to each of them to make sure their
mucker survived. Angus' mucker, however, was dying. Everyone had given up on him—everyone but Angus. He had made
up his mind that his friend would not die.

Someone had stolen his mucker's blanket, so Angus had
given one of his own, telling the man that he had "just come
across an extra one." Likewise, at every meal, Angus would
get his rations and take them to his friend. He would stand
over him and force the man to eat, again stating that he
was able to get "extra food." Angus did anything and everything to see that his buddy got what he needed to recover.

However, as Angus's mucker grew stronger, Angus
grew weaker, until one day he slumped over and died. The

doctors discovered that he had died of starvation complicated by exhaustion. He had given everything he had—
even his own life.

The ramifications of Angus's acts of love and unselfish-
ness had a startling impact on the compound. As word cir-
culated, the feel of the camp began to change. Suddenly,
the men began to focus on their fellow soldiers. They began
to pool their talents. Soon the camp had an orchestra full of
homemade instruments and a church called Church Without Walls that was so powerful that even the Japanese
guards attended. The men began a university, a hospital,
and a library. The place was transformed—and all because
one man named Angus gave all he had for his friend.[1]

Loving others is tough under normal circumstances, but
what situation was present in this story that made Angus's actions all the more striking?

_____

_____

_____

_____

3. How could your commitment to living out God's love
   transform your world?

_____

_____

_____

_____

4. Now let's flip this around and look at what happens when
   people choose to give in to their feelings of retribution and

their need for revenge. Read the following story and answer the questions that follow.

Newton, Massachusetts—If you're a spurned lover or a frustrated employee, Nan Berman has some advice: Don't get mad; get even. Berman has a business called Enough Is Enough, billed as "Creative Revenge for Today's World." Berman has mailed a three-foot dead bluefish to an unfaithful husband in California and delivered a burned and messy suit to a lawyer who implied his girlfriend was "unsuitable."

The most common requests, however, are for 13 dead roses sent in a black box ($25) and 13 black balloons tied together by a single black rose ($30). Other "insults to suit the occasion" include a real stuffed shirt ($25) for pompous employers and drinking glasses with cigarette butts on the bottom for smokers.

Berman says: "Twenty years ago, people didn't speak up the way they do now. But since the '60s, people have expressed themselves. With me, you really have a way to vent things out." The 43-year-old Berman started Enough Is Enough after she spent a year driving a florist delivery truck for a boss who was "the grumpiest and most unpleasant person ever born."

Berman promises her customers anonymity. "I want to stress that we'll do anything, as long as it's legal," she says.[2]

Berman says that her business gives people a "way to vent things out." Is this a healthy or unhealthy way to vent anger? Explain.

How would you feel about using Berman's service?

_____

_____

_____

In what ways is Berman's service really a no-win situation for both parties?

_____

_____

_____

5. When someone wrongs you, is your first reaction to demand "an eye for an eye," or do you "turn the other cheek"? Explain.

_____

_____

_____

6. When you do wrong against God through your actions, does He take revenge against you, or does He give you godly discipline? What is the difference between the two? Why is one loving and the other not?

_____

_____

_____

_____

7. In Romans 5:10, Paul writes, "Once we were God's enemies. But we have been brought back to him because his Son has died for us. Now that God has brought us back, we are even more secure. We know that we will be saved be-

cause Christ lives." How should knowing that God has forgiven us for our sins compel us to show His love to those who have wronged us?

_____

_____

_____

8. Jesus said, "Be perfect, therefore, as your heavenly father is perfect" (Matthew 5:48). What kind of perfection was Jesus talking about?

_____

_____

_____

reflect

Now that you've looked at Jesus' words as they relate to forgiving others and loving your enemies, it's time to evaluate how you are doing in these areas.

1. When you look at Jesus' command to "turn the other cheek," what does that specifically mean to you?

_____

_____

_____

2. What is the most difficult part of "turning the other cheek" for you?

_____

_____

_____

3. What makes someone an enemy in your life?

_____

_____

_____

4. Read Luke 9:51-56. What was the disciples' attitude toward their enemies?

_____

_____

5. Why did Jesus rebuke them?

_____

_____

_____

6. Turn to Jeremiah 11:18-20. Was Jeremiah right for asking God to take vengeance on his enemies? Why or why not?

_____

_____

_____

7. Does asking God to deal with your enemies mean you are taking revenge against them? Why or why not?

_____

_____

_____

8. What individuals come to mind when you hear the words, "Love your enemies"? Take a step of courage and list the initials of those people below.

_____

_____

_____

9. What specific steps can you take to love those enemies?

_____

_____

_____

Take a moment to look over your list of enemies, and pray for each person. Ask God to soften your heart toward them and their hearts toward you and God. Don't be surprised to see major changes in your relationship with your enemy!

meditation

A new command I give you: Love one another. As I have loved you, so you must love one another.

JOHN 13:34

Notes
1. Adapted from Tim Hansel, *Holy Sweat* (Waco, TX: Word Books, 1987), pp. 146-147.
2. Adapted from Stephen Paroloni, editor, *Headline News Discussion Starters* (Loveland, CO: Group Books, 1990), p. 92.

unit II
motives

My mom died from cancer several years ago. It was not a pleasant experience. Mom was a hero in my life, yet her influence had little to do with her beauty, her intelligence or her sense of humor. It had more to do with her character. Mom had pure motives.

Mom was sick in bed for several months before she died. I would go over to her house almost every day. Usually, I would just sit in her room or get her something to eat. Dad would wait on her, wait on me, and watch ball games on TV.

One day, I was sitting in a chair in the bedroom with Mom when she looked up at me and said, "Jimmy, where's your dad?"

"He's in the living room watching a ball game, Mom," I answered. That's where he spent most of his time.

Mom looked up at me. "I never really liked baseball much," she said.

"Mom, you never liked baseball?" I asked. "Did you ever miss even one of my Little League, Pony League, junior high or high school baseball games?" I was absolutely shocked that she would say this after all those years of watching my and my brothers' games. She would sit with Dad for hours and watch ball games.

"No, Jimmy. I never much cared for that sport. I didn't go to the games to watch baseball. I went to support you."

Wow, after all these years, here she was telling me that she didn't even like the game. Her motive for watching ball games went far beyond enjoying the sport. It was the power of being there. She was present at those games for me.

I don't meet many people with pure motives these days. That is why this section of the Sermon on the Mount is so important. In these passages of Scripture, Jesus challenges us to live with a higher call and purer motives than the world. He talks about some where-the-rubber-meets-the-road issues such as handling money, judging others and worrying about material possessions. Jesus' teachings go against the grain of the culture and present an eternal perspective.

What a privilege we have to be able to place eternal truth from the mouth of Jesus in the lives of kids. Thank you for doing what you do—and thank you for the power of being there for the kids. Your very presence makes a difference, and your motives teach your students more than you will ever imagine.

testing our motives

Search me, God, and know my heart; test me and know my anxious thoughts.
See if there is any offensive way in me, and lead me in the way everlasting.
PSALM 139:23-24

"Why are you involved in youth ministry?" Ask any youth worker this question and you're bound to get a number of socially acceptable and spiritually correct answers based on apparently good and pure motives. "I want to see kids come to Christ." "I have a background of doing drugs, and I don't want teenagers to make the same mistakes I did." "My youth minister had a big impact on my life. I want to do the same for others." "No one else volunteered to work with the teenagers in our church."

However, what many of us won't so readily admit is that some of our motives are not so pure—that they do not always honor God. Is this shocking? Not really. If we're honest with one another, we have to admit that there is a dark side of ministry shadowed by impure motives, self-seeking ambition, misguided emotional needs and, at times, simplistic answers to complicated problems.

The truthful reality of living in a broken world is that everyone—whether Christian or not—must find a balance between the delicate scales of pure and impure motives. That's why this lesson is so important. As new creations in Christ, God is calling us to walk in truth with pure motives. To do so, we need the help of the Holy Spirit to sift through the inner lives of our hearts. We need God's grace to ferret out anything in our character that misrepresents the person God wants us to be. It's a process that begins with simple and beautiful prayers such as The Lord's Prayer.

Through Jesus Christ, we don't live under guilt or condemnation because of what our motives are or aren't. We have access to our heavenly Father, who gently purifies, clarifies and directs our hearts to ministering out of honest and authentic motives. That's what we really need. Honest!

People are always motivated by at least two reasons:
the one they tell you about and a secret one.

O. A. BATISTA

testing our motives

starter

LORD'S PRAYER PYRAMID: Divide the group into teams of six people. Give each team a Bible and ask them to find Matthew 6:9-13. Each person on the team will need to remember one part of this prayer, as follows:

Person 1: "Our Father in heaven, hallowed be your name . . ."

Person 2: "Your kingdom come, your will be done . . ."

Person 3: "On earth as it is in heaven."

Person 4: "Give us today our daily bread."

Person 5: "And forgive us our debts, as we also have forgiven our debtors."

Person 6: "And lead us not into temptation, but deliver us from the evil one."

Note: You can download this group study guide in 8½" x 11" format at **www.gospellight.com/uncommon/living_out_Jesus_teachings.zip.**

Give the teams two to three minutes to find the verse and assign the parts. When you say go, one at a time the teams will build a pyramid of three people on the bottom, two on the middle, and one on top. When everyone is in place, each person will recite the portion of the Lord's Prayer that was assigned to him or her. If the pyramid collapses or the teams get the prayer wrong, they forfeit their turn and the next team tries. Time the event and award a prize to the team who finishes with the fastest time. (*Note*: Make sure you take the necessary precautions to insure this is a safe activity.)

message

To the Jewish people in Jesus' day, there were three great pillars of spiritual life: (1) giving to the needy, (2) praying to God, and (3) partaking in fasting. While Jesus did not dispute the importance of these disciplines, what troubled Him was that so often people did the *right* things for the *wrong* reasons. In this next section of the Sermon on the Mount, He addressed these concerns and gave some radical teachings concerning these three important disciplines. In each case, He emphasized the importance of having the *right motives*.

proper motives in giving

In Deuteronomy 15:7, God told His people, "If anyone is poor among your fellow Israelites in any of the towns of the land the Lord your God is giving you, do not be hardhearted or tightfisted toward them." While many of the people followed this command, some did so out of improper motives. Here is what Jesus said about this:

Be careful not to practice your righteousness in front of others to be seen by them. If you do, you will have no reward from your Father in heaven.

So when you give to the needy, do not announce it with trumpets, as the hypocrites do in the synagogues and on the streets, to be honored by others. Truly I tell you, they have received their reward in full.

But when you give to the needy, do not let your left hand know what your right hand is doing, so that your giving may be in secret. Then your Father, who sees what is done in secret, will reward you (Matthew 6:1-4).

1. What does Jesus call people who draw attention to themselves when giving to the needy?

   _____

   _____

   _____

2. What does Jesus mean when He says that those who bring glory to themselves in their giving "have received their reward in full"?

   _____

   _____

   _____

3. Who ultimately gets the glory when you give "in secret"? How does this build humility into your life and give you the right motives?

   _____

   _____

   _____

proper motives in prayer

In Exodus 23:25, the Israelites were instructed to "worship the Lord your God." Prayer was an important part of the people's lives in ancient Israel. However, much like giving to the needy, some people were using prayer as a means to show how spiritual they were. Jesus addressed this problem next:

> And when you pray, do not be like the hypocrites, for they love to pray standing in the synagogues and on the street corners to be seen by others. Truly I tell you, they have received their reward in full. But when you pray, go into your room, close the door and pray to your Father, who is unseen. Then your Father, who sees what is done in secret, will reward you. And when you pray, do not keep on babbling like pagans, for they think they will be heard because of their many words. Do not be like them, for your Father knows what you need before you ask him.
>   This, then, is how you should pray:
>
> > Our Father in heaven, hallowed be your name,
> > your kingdom come, your will be done, on earth as it is in heaven.
> > Give us today our daily bread.
> > And forgive us our debts, as we also have forgiven our debtors.
> > And lead us not into temptation, but deliver us from the evil one.
>
>   For if you forgive other people when they sin against you, your heavenly Father will also forgive you. But if you do not forgive others their sins, your Father will not forgive your sins (Matthew 6:5-15).

1. In these verses, Jesus begins by giving His followers instructions on how to check their motives when they come

to God in prayer. What were the three ways Jesus said they should *not* pray?

Do not _____ (verse 5).

Do not _____ (verse 7).

Do not_____ (verse 8).

2. What did Jesus do after He taught them how not to pray?

   ....

   ....

   ....

3. Why do you think Jesus followed the prayer He gave to the people with the statement found in verses 14 and 15?

   ....

   ....

   ....

proper motives in fasting

When people fast, they temporarily give up something important to them—such as food—so they can give the time they normally devote to that thing for prayer. By experiencing the discomfort of sacrificing something for a period of time, people can better reflect of Jesus' ultimate sacrifice for them.[1] Unfortunately, like giving to the poor and praying to God, people in Jesus' time were using fasting to bring glory to themselves instead of to God. Jesus talked about this next:

When you fast, do not look somber as the hypocrites do, for they disfigure their faces to show others they are fasting. Truly I tell you, they have received their reward in full. But when you fast, put oil

*on your head and wash your face, so that it will not be obvious to
others that you are fasting, but only to your Father, who is unseen;
and your Father, who sees what is done in secret, will reward you*
(Matthew 6:16-18).

1. Notice that Jesus did not say *if* you fast—He assumed that
    His followers *would* fast. What does this tell you about the
    importance of fasting?

    _____

    _____

    _____

    _____

2. What similarities do you see in Jesus' words in this pas-
    sage and in His instructions on prayer in Matthew 6:5-8?

    _____

    _____

    _____

3. What promise do people receive who fast with the right
    motives?

    _____

    _____

    _____

dig

So much of our lives today are guided by secret motives. All too
often we make good decisions for the wrong reasons, and eventually we become extremely unhappy because of it. This is why Jesus
asks us to always test our motives.

1. In Matthew 6:2, the word Jesus uses for "hypocrite" was a term applied to stage actors. Ancient actors wore masks and hid their "true selves" behind a false identity. Keeping this in mind, what are people really doing when they give to the needy out of a desire to look righteous?

    _____

    _____

    _____

    _____

2. Jesus uses two exaggerations when giving instructions to the people on giving: (1) they shouldn't announce their gifts with "trumpets" or fanfare; and (2) they shouldn't let their left hand know what their right hand is doing when they give. Why do you think Jesus used these expressions to make His point?

    _____

    _____

    _____

3. In Jesus' time, the "pagans" would call on as many of their gods as possible in their prayers, reminding their deities of all the sacrifices they had done and why their gods were obligated to help them. The Romans were especially concerned about having knowledge of the "correct word formulas" to make sure their gods heard their prayers. How does this shed light on Matthew 6:5-8?

    _____

    _____

    _____

    _____

4. Notice that Jesus continually refers to God in this passage as "Father." What does this tell you about the relationship you should have with God? What does this say about not having to pray the "right formula" to get God to answer you?

    _____

    _____

    _____

    _____

5. Both Matthew and Luke provide a version of the Lord's Prayer. In Luke's version, the disciples asked Jesus to give them the prayer by stating, "Lord, teach us to pray, just as John [the Baptist] taught his disciples" (Luke 11:1). Why do you think the disciples wanted Jesus to provide them with a model for prayer?

    _____

    _____

    _____

    _____

6. What is the importance of Jesus beginning the Lord's Prayer by giving glory to God and asking for His will to be done? What does this say about what your attitude in prayer should be?

    _____

    _____

    _____

    _____

7. Many of the images Jesus used in the Lord's Prayer would have been familiar to His listeners. "Daily bread" would have

reminded them of how God provided for the Israelites in the wilderness. Poor peasants often had "debts" they had to pay back. Asking for God to not "lead them into temptation" would have reminded them of a common prayer in which they asked God to keep them from sinning. How would Jesus' use of these common images have helped the people to better understand His meaning?

----

8. How do children act when they want to convince their parents that they are really sick and need to stay home from school? How is this similar to the way hypocrites act when they are fasting (see Matthew 6:16)?

----

9. In ancient times, putting oil on your head and washing your face were typical ways of preparing yourself to face the day. What does this say about how you should act when fasting?

----

apply

It's so easy to let the truly important issues of life get out of focus. If you are like most people, you probably tend to put off dealing with the most significant priorities and spend the bulk of your time on the less important issues of life.

1. Write down the five most important people, things and/or activities in your life. Number them in order of importance to you, with 1 being the most important.

    _____

    _____

    _____

    _____

    _____

2. Now evaluate your list in light of what you believe would most glorify God. Do you think your priorities are pleasing to Him? Why or why not?

    _____

    _____

    _____

    _____

3. What decisions and action steps will you take to begin the process of putting these priorities in proper order?

    _____

    _____

    _____

4. The Lord's Prayer can help you to better understand the heart and soul of Jesus. What does this prayer in Matthew 6:9-13 tell you about God?

_____

_____

_____

5. What does this prayer tell you about what you should say to God? How does this prayer compare to the typical prayers you say to God?

_____

_____

_____

_____

6. In the space below, write each line of the Lord's Prayer in your own words.

Our father in heaven _____

hallowed be your name _____

your kingdom come _____

your will be done _____

on earth as it is in heaven. _____

Give us today our daily bread. _____

And forgive us our debts _____

as we also have forgiven our debtors. _____

And lead us not into temptation _____

but deliver us from the evil one. _____

7. As previously mentioned, fasting is an exercise in which you deprive yourself of the normal pleasantries of life for the sake of putting God first. Fasting is about more than

just not eating. In fact, you may need to fast from a boy-friend, a girlfriend, a car, a sport, partying or any other thing that has displaced God's rightful position in your life. What do you need to "fast" from in your life?

_____

_____

_____

_____

8. When it comes to giving up food or making other sacri-fices as a way of putting your focus on God, which of the following would be true?

   ❑   I would be interested in trying it.
   ❑   I'm not big on making sacrifices.
   ❑   I have never even considered trying it.
   ❑   I consider it part of my regular spiritual growth.
   ❑   It seems strange. I don't know about this "fasting" thing.

9. In Colossians 3:23, Paul writes, "Whatever you do, work at it with all your heart, as working for the Lord, not for hu-man masters." What does this tell you should be the mo-tivation for all your work?

_____

_____

_____

reflect

Now that you've looked at Jesus' words as they relate to giving, prayer and fasting, it's time to reflect on your own life and see where your priorities truly lie.

1. Read 2 Corinthians 9:6-8. What should your attitude be when giving?

   _____

   _____

   _____

2. Turn to Luke 21:1-4. Why is God more concerned with your priorities in giving than in the amount you give?

   _____

   _____

   _____

3. In John 14:14, Jesus says, "You may ask me for anything in my name, and I will do it." What does this tell you about the power of prayer?

   _____

   _____

   _____

4. What are some areas in your life where fasting would help you to get your priorities straight? (Remember that these areas are not necessarily evil—they just keep you from being all that God wants you to be).

   _____

   _____

   _____

5. How important in your spiritual life are giving, praying and fasting?

   _____

   _____

   _____

6. What are your motives for the following activities?

    Going to church: _____
    Praying: _____
    Giving: _____
    Helping others: _____

7. Are there any motives in your life that you now see the need
    to change? If so, what steps will you take to change them?

    _____

    _____

    _____

    _____

meditation

Am I now trying to win the approval of human beings, or of
God? Or am I trying to please people? If I were still trying to
please people, I would not be a servant of Christ.

GALATIANS 1:10

Note

1. Adapted from a definition by Reuben P. Job and Norman Shawchuck, A *Guide to Prayer*
   (Nashville, TN: The Upper Room, 1983), p. 9.

living in a
material world

*Be shepherds of God's flock that is under your care, watching over them—
not because you must, but because you are willing, as God wants you to be;
not pursuing dishonest gain, but eager to serve.*

1 PETER 5:2

A few years ago, there was a student named Scott whose father had died in a car crash when Scott was a little boy. The party responsible for the crash established a trust fund for the boy and his family. For the next 14 years, that money—which amount to a large sum at the time—accrued interest.

When Scott turned 18, he became legally responsible for all the money in his trust fund. By now, the fund was worth several hundred thousand dollars! Scott immediately went out and bought a new car. He bought his friends all sorts of expensive items—meals, movie tickets and trips. Scott had so much money that he didn't know what to do with it all. So he just blew it.

Scott ended up spending most of his money and didn't bother to invest or save it for a rainy day. Yet no matter how he spent the funds, chances are it didn't buy him much happiness. It certainly couldn't buy him the father he wished he could have had. Maybe that's a story you'll want to tell the students in your youth ministry as you work through this session on money to help them look deep and evaluate what is truly most important to them.

You and your students might be surprised how critical the subject of money was to Jesus. In fact, there are more verses in the Bible that talk about money, finances, investing and using our resources for God than there are for other well-known subjects like love, grace or forgiveness. God has a lot to say about money because He knows how quickly it can steal people's hearts.

You'll find plenty of money matters and questions about the true treasures of our hearts in this lesson. Your time and energy in preparing this lesson will serve as a great investment with eternal returns.

When I have any money I get rid of it as quickly as possible,
lest it find a way into my heart.
JOHN WESLEY

living in a material world

starter

MONEY QUIZ: So, how well do your students know their *dinero*? This quiz will test their knowledge about the currency they may use every day. Before you begin, make sure all coins and bills are put away to prevent any one person having an advantage over the other group members. Hand out one sheet of paper to each individual and ask the students to number the paper from 1 to 10. Now slowly read the following questions and give the students a few seconds to answer each one:

1. On a penny, which direction is Lincoln facing?
2. What is the name of the building that appears on the back of a nickel?

3. On a dime, what words appear to the lower left of President Roosevelt?

4. On the back of a half dollar coin, there is a picture of an eagle with a shield. What does the banner directly above the eagle say?

5. What words appear at the top of a one-dollar bill on the front side?

6. On the back of a one-dollar bill, what is the eagle holding in its claws?

7. In addition to the eagle, what other image appears on the back of a one-dollar bill?

8. Which President is on the two-dollar bill?

9. Every U.S. bill has two signatures on the front side. What are the offices these individuals hold?

10. How many times will you find the word "twenty" on the front of a twenty-dollar bill?

When you are finished, read the answers found at the end of this session. Explain to the group that during today's session, they are going to be looking a bit more closely at money to see what Jesus said about it.

message

Jesus spent a lot of time in the Gospels talking about money. In fact, the only subject He seems to have spoken about more was the kingdom of God. Why did Jesus focus so much on money? Perhaps it was because He knew how quickly wealth could steal and corrupt people's hearts. As we see in the next section of the Sermon on the Mount, Jesus was concerned about how His followers prioritized spending their funds.

Do not store up for yourselves treasures on earth, where moths and vermin destroy, and where thieves break in and steal. But store up for yourselves treasures in heaven, where moths and vermin do not destroy, and where thieves do not break in and steal. For where your treasure is, there your heart will be also.

The eye is the lamp of the body. If your eyes are healthy, your whole body will be full of light. But if your eyes are unhealthy, your whole body will be full of darkness. If then the light within you is darkness, how great is that darkness!

No one can serve two masters. Either you will hate the one and love the other, or you will be devoted to the one and despise the other. You cannot serve both God and money (Matthew 6:19-24).

1. In the previous section of the Sermon on the Mount, Jesus warned His followers not to have improper motives when giving, praying or fasting, as this would lead to them receiving "their reward in full" while here on earth. What does Jesus say about storing up heavenly treasures in this passage?

   _____

   _____

   _____

   _____

2. In Job 1:21, Job states, "Naked I came from my mother's womb, and naked I will depart." How does this statement agree with what Jesus says in this passage about the dangers of storing up treasures on earth?

   _____

   _____

   _____

   _____

3. What do you think Jesus meant when He said, "Where your treasure is, there your heart will be also"?

    _____

    _____

    _____

4. In Matthew 5:14, Jesus says to His followers, "You are the light of the world." What does light represent? What does darkness represent?

    _____

    _____

    _____

5. What does Jesus mean when He says the eye is the "lamp" of the body?

    _____

    _____

    _____

6. What could be the result of keeping your eyes focused on sinful things instead of godly things?

    _____

    _____

    _____

    _____

7. Why do you think Jesus refers to money or riches as a "master"?

    _____

    _____

    _____

8. Why is it impossible to serve both God and money?

    ....

    ....

    ....

dig

Throughout the Bible we find instruction on how we are to handle our money—and how we are to seek eternal rewards instead of earthly ones.

1. Read 1 Timothy 6:9-10. According to Paul, what is the problem with setting your motives on getting rich and having material wealth?

    ....

    ....

    ....

2. The Bible states that believers in Christ will receive eternal rewards when their lives on this earth are finished. In particular, Scripture states that believers will receive crowns. Look up each passage below and write down the type of crown it says Christians will receive.

Passage	Type of Crown
1 Corinthians 9:25	
1 Thessalonians 2:19	
2 Timothy 4:8	
1 Peter 5:4	
Revelation 2:10	

3. Read the Parable of the Rich Fool in Luke 12:13-21. Why does God call a person who focuses on storing up wealth a "fool"?

    _____

    _____

    _____

4. In Matthew 6:22, Jesus says that if your eyes are "healthy," your whole body will be filled with light. The Greek word for "healthy" that Jesus uses in this verse implies being generous. Given this, what is Jesus saying about having the proper motivations in life and always focusing on God?

    _____

    _____

    _____

5. In Acts 26:18, Paul states that his mission was to "open [people's] eyes and turn them from darkness to light, and from the power of Satan to God." How did Paul understand the eyes to be the "lamp of the body"?

    _____

    _____

    _____

    _____

6. Read 1 John 2:15-17. What three worldly sins does John mention? How do these sins relate to Jesus' words in Matthew 6:22-23?

    _____

    _____

    _____

7. In Matthew 7:24, the word Jesus uses for "money" is *Mammon*. This was a common Aramaic term for money or property, but in this passage Jesus treats it as if it were an entity that people worshiped—like a false god or a demon. What does this tell you about the power that money and wealth has to control your life?

    ----

8. In Luke 18, a rich young man asked Jesus what he had to do to obtain eternal life. When Jesus told Him to keep God's commandments, the man said he had done this since his youth. What did Jesus then tell the man to do (see verse 22)?

    ----

9. Given what you have learned in this session about the power of money, why did Jesus say it is hard "for the rich to enter the kingdom of God" (verse 24)?

    ----

apply

In this passage of the Sermon on the Mount, Jesus is talking about people's *attitudes* as they relate to wealth and material goods. As Paul said, it is the *love* of money that is evil, not necessarily money itself. In fact, many of the heroes in the Bible were wealthy—such as Abraham, Jacob and Job, to name just a few. The difference for followers of Jesus is that their goal in life is not about making more money, or saving more money, or even giving away more money. Their focus is on using the resources that God has given them to bring Him glory and serve others in His kingdom.

1. Read Luke 19:1-10. Back in Jesus' time, tax collectors were wealthy individuals who often profited by collecting more taxes from people than what was due. The Jews looked down them and felt they were traitors working for the Roman Empire. Zacchaeus was no exception. But what happened when he met Jesus?

    _____

    _____

    _____

    _____

2. How much did Zacchaeus say he would give back to the poor? Why do you think he didn't give *all* of his possessions back to the poor?

    _____

    _____

    _____

3. What had happened in Zacchaeus' heart that caused Jesus to say, "Today salvation has come to this house" (verse 9)?

    _____

    _____

    _____

4. In Acts 4:36-37, we read of a man named Barnabas who "sold a field he owned and brought the money and put it at the apostles' feet." Later, a man named Ananias and his wife, Sapphira, also sold a piece of their property. Read Acts 5:1-6. What did this couple do differently from Barnabas? What was the result?

    ---

5. Ananias and Sapphira wanted to be righteous like Barnabas—or at least *appear* righteous like him. What got in the way?

    ---

6. To whom did Peter say Ananias had lied? What did Peter mean by this?

    ---

7. Here is one way that you can view money:

    Money can buy medicine, but not health.
    Money can buy a house, but not a home.
    Money can buy companionship, but not friends.
    Money can buy entertainment, but not happiness.

Money can buy food, but not an appetite.
Money can buy a bed, but not sleep.
Money can buy a crucifix, but not a Savior.
Money can buy the good life, but not eternal life.[1]

How do these words and Jesus' statements in Matthew 6:19-24 influence your view on wealth and the things of this world?

8. In what ways are Jesus' teachings on money the opposite of what our society preaches?

reflect

Now that you've looked at Jesus' words as they relate to money and material wealth, it's time to reflect on your own life and see where your priorities lie.

1. What makes money such a "treasure" in people's eyes?

2. How do you feel about giving your money to those who are in need?

    ----

3. If you were to look at your bank statement, what would it reveal about what you truly treasure?

    ----

4. Do you give a percentage of your income to your church? Why or why not?

    ----

5. Do you feel God prompting you to look at how you spend your money or change some of your spending habits? If so, how will you change them?

    ----

6. Why do so few people treasure eternal rewards—those things that "moths and vermin" cannot destroy?

    ----

7. In your own words, what will it take for you to . . .

Make seeking spiritual treasure your first priority?

_____

_____

_____

Serve the Lord and not money?

_____

_____

_____

meditation

Whoever loves money never has enough; whoever loves
wealth is never satisfied with their income.

ECCLESIASTES 5:10

Starter Answers: (1) to the right, (2) Monticello, (3) "In God We Trust," (4) "E Pluribus Unum," ("Out of Many, One") (5) "Federal Reserve Note," (6) a branch and arrows, (7) a pyramid with an eye, (8) Thomas Jefferson, (9) Treasurer of the United States and Secretary of the Treasury, (10) twice—once in the denomination "twenty dollars" and again over the U.S. Treasury seal.

Note

1. Charles Swindoll, *Strengthening Your* Grip (Waco, TX: Word Books, 1982), pp. 84-85.

letting go
of anxieties

Anxiety weighs down the heart, but a kind word cheers it up.
PROVERBS 12:25

Have you noticed how worried and anxious teenagers are these days? A 12-year-old boy worries about wearing the wrong colors of clothes to school for fear that someone will think he is in a gang. A freshman girl in high school begins taking PSAT courses for fear of not getting into the right college. A scared senior thinks about cheating on a test for fear of not graduating. A 14-year-old girl worries how her mom is doing after her parents' divorce. Doesn't this sound familiar? You could certainly fill in the blanks with other stories of the teenagers you know who carry similar burdens.

But let's talk about *you* for a minute. What anxieties are you facing light now in your life? What struggles and burdens are you carrying? A difficult aspect of youth ministry is preparing and speaking about topics with which you are currently wrestling, such as worry, trust and faith. For instance, you may be between jobs right now and are anxious about how long you can make it before your funds dry up. Or you may be in conflict with another church staff member and you're constantly worrying about what you say and do in front of that person. Or you may have just balanced your checkbook and you're wondering why you're spending so much "free" time with teenagers when what you really need is a second job.

My prayer for you as you prepare this lesson is that you come to a deeper knowledge of God and His faithfulness as a provider. The Lord knows your every need. He sees inside your heart. He knows the troubled thoughts in your mind. He knows your checkbook balance. He never intended to tell His followers not to be worried or anxious without intending to give them His peace. His peace is something both you and your students need on a daily basis.

Anxiety is the result of doing our own thing in our
own timing and with our resources.
Lloyd John Ogilvie

letting go
of anxieties

starter

STRESS TRIP: This is a fun activity that will get your group members thinking about the topic of worry and what kinds of anxieties they are dealing with right now. Begin by asking everyone to get into a circle. Explain that you will begin the game by saying, "I'm going on a stress trip, and I'm bringing . . ." The person to your right will then have to think of something that he or she is worrying about right now. The only trick is that this has to be one word, such as "test," "homework," "tryouts," "money," "brother," or "parents." The next person in the circle will repeat the sentence, include the first person's item, and add one of his or her items to the list. The third person will repeat the first two items and add another item. The game will continue until a player can no longer remember all of the items in order.

message

In Jesus' time, there were many things that caused people to worry. The Israelites lived under the watchful rule of the Romans, who valued keeping the peace above all else. There were many factions among the people, and the Israelites never knew when uprisings might occur that would force the Roman troops to act. The Israelites were also dependent on rain and favorable weather to grow their crops. Disease was a normal part of life, and illnesses such as leprosy could make a person an outcast in society. Yet even in the midst of these very real problems, Jesus told the people not to worry.

> *Therefore I tell you, do not worry about your life, what you will eat or drink; or about your body, what you will wear. Is not life more than food, and the body more than clothes? Look at the birds of the air; they do not sow or reap or store away in barns, and yet your heavenly Father feeds them. Are you not much more valuable than they? Can any one of you by worrying add a single hour to your life?*
>
> *And why do you worry about clothes? See how the flowers of the field grow. They do not labor or spin. Yet I tell you that not even Solomon in all his splendor was dressed like one of these. If that is how God clothes the grass of the field, which is here today and tomorrow is thrown into the fire, will he not much more clothe you— you of little faith? So do not worry, saying, "What shall we eat?" or "What shall we drink?" or "What shall we wear?" For the pagans run after all these things, and your heavenly Father knows that you*

need them. But seek first his kingdom and his righteousness, and all these things will be given to you as well. Therefore do not worry about tomorrow, for tomorrow will worry about itself. Each day has enough trouble of its own (Matthew 6:25-34).

1. In the previous section of the Sermon on the Mount, Jesus addressed the issue of money and how it can become our master. How does Jesus use that discussion as a springboard to now talk about our worries and fears?

     _____

     _____

     _____

2. What is Jesus' first bold command in this passage (see verse 25)?

     _____

     _____

     _____

3. What example does Jesus use to show that God cares about our need for food?

     _____

     _____

     _____

     _____

4. What example does Jesus use to show God cares about our need for clothes?

     _____

     _____

     _____

5. What do you think Jesus is trying to say to us when He compares our needs with those of the birds and flowers?

    _____

    _____

    _____

6. What does Jesus say we lack when we worry (see verse 30)?

    _____

    _____

    _____

7. What does Jesus mean when He says that "the pagans" run after concerns such as what to eat, what to drink or what to wear? How should Christians be different?

    _____

    _____

    _____

8. What does Jesus say we should do instead of worrying about our needs (see verse 33)? What does God promise to do when we commit our needs to Him?

    _____

    _____

    _____

dig

In this passage, Jesus uses two common examples to show how God knows and cares about our every need. Let's examine each of these in more detail.

1. Read Psalm 104:10-15. How does God take care of the "beasts of the field" and the "birds of the sky"?

   _____

   _____

   _____

   _____

2. According to these verses, what does God do to provide food for people on earth?

   _____

   _____

   _____

   _____

3. Read Psalm 104:27-30. What do all the creatures of the earth look to God to do?

   _____

   _____

   _____

   _____

4. How do these verses show that everything that happens in this world is under the control of God?

   _____

   _____

   _____

   _____

5. In Matthew 6:26, Jesus states that the birds do not sow, reap or store up food in barns, yet they still survive because God feeds them. Jesus goes on to state, "Are you not

much more valuable than they?" What is Jesus implying by asking His followers this question?

----

6. In Luke 12:6-7, Jesus says, "Are not five sparrows sold for two pennies? Yet not one of them is forgotten by God. Indeed, the very hairs of your head are all numbered. Don't be afraid; you are worth more than many sparrows." What do these verses tell you about how much God values you?

----

7. In Matthew 6:28-29, Jesus says, "See how the flowers of the field grow. They do not labor or spin. Yet I tell you that not even Solomon in all his splendor was dressed like one of these." How does this passage show that God cares not just for our primary needs (like food and water) but also for our secondary needs?

----

8. People in Jesus' day valued their cloaks and considered them to be an essential item in protecting them from the elements. In fact, in Exodus 22:26-27, God instructed anyone who had taken a neighbor's cloak to return it by sunset so

that the person didn't have to face the cold night without it. But what does Jesus say in this passage about God's ability to take care us—even if we don't have a cloak?

_____

_____

_____

_____

9. What do you think Jesus means when He states, "Do not worry about tomorrow, for tomorrow will worry about itself" (verse 34)?

_____

_____

_____

_____

apply

The word "worry" comes from an Anglo-Saxon term that means "to choke" or "to strangle." This is a good description of what worry does to us! Worry won't take our problems away, but it will cause us to lose sleep, make us moody toward others, and run us down so we suffer from illnesses. Even more, worrying shows that we are unwilling to give the control of our lives to God and trust in Him to meet our needs.

1. What is one situation you are going through that is causing you to worry?

_____

_____

_____

2. What consequences are worrying about that situation caus-
    ing you physically?

    ....

    ....

    ....

    ....

3. What consequences are worrying about that situation caus-
    ing you in your relationships with others?

    ....

    ....

    ....

    ....

4. What consequences are worrying about that situation caus-
    ing you in your relationship with God?

    ....

    ....

    ....

    ....

5. Why is it so difficult to trust in the Lord in *all* situations
    and not be anxious?

    ....

    ....

    ....

6. Do you think worry a sin? Why or why not?

    ....

    ....

    ....

7. How does knowing that God even cares about the needs of birds and flowers help you to give all of your problems over to Him?

_____

_____

_____

_____

8. Do you believe God truly has the power to meet your needs? If so, what practical steps will you take today to trust in God to solve whatever problem you happen to be facing?

_____

_____

_____

_____

reflect

Imagine for a moment that you are among Jesus' disciples and you have just heard this important message on why you don't need to worry. As the following skit illustrates, you would probably have a few questions about Jesus' teaching! Read this short play to yourself or act it out as part of a group.

Cast: James, John, Peter, Philip and Matthew
Time: Jesus' day
Place: Walking on a road

James (whining): We sure have to walk a long way. What happens if our sandals wear out? Where are we going to find the money to buy new ones?

John: And what about our cloaks? Each of us has only one. What happens when a cloak gets a hole in it?

Peter: Weren't you Sons of Thunder listening to the Master today? Didn't He tell us not to worry about what we have to wear?

Philip: That's right. He said that even Solomon—the richest king Israel has ever known—didn't have clothing as beautiful as the way God clothes the flowers.

Peter: Right. I wish you two would listen to what the Master says instead of always worrying. Besides, if you want to worry about something, worry about food. It's getting late and we're nowhere near any town. How are we going to fill our bellies tonight?

Matthew: That's you to the core, Peter. Always worrying about your stomach. When have we ever gone hungry since being with the Master? But you still worry about food. If you're going to be like that, go back to fishing.

Peter: At least I had an honorable profession before joining Jesus. I wasn't a lousy tax gatherer, working for the Romans.

Philip: Knock it off, Peter. You may not have been a tax gatherer before you met Jesus, but you weren't the best person in the country. How many fights did you get into over nothing?

James: Besides, you aren't any better than John and me.

John: That's right. You don't listen any better than we do to what the Master says. Didn't He tell us just today not to worry about food?

Philip: They've got you there, Peter. Remember what He said about birds? God doesn't let them starve. He takes care of them.

Matthew: He even talked about how much more valuable we are than them. He said, "Five sparrows are sold for a few pennies . . ."

Peter: Trust a tax collector to know the price of every-thing!

Matthew: Better than only knowing about scaling fish and fixing nets.

Philip: Would you two stop bickering? How do you think Jesus would feel if He heard you two? Keep it up and you'll make the Pharisees look good.

Peter: What do you mean?

Philip: Don't they say one thing and do another? That makes them hypocrites. You two are acting exactly the same way, saying Jesus is your Master and then be-having the way you do. It's disgusting. Worrying and fighting over every little thing, when the only impor-tant thing to worry about is what is going to happen to us tomorrow. After all, we are going to be in a new place, and you never know what might happen there!

James (to John): Maybe Philip needs a taste of his own medicine.

John: A little reminder of the Master's words.

Philip: What are you two going on about?

Matthew: Don't you remember that Jesus said, "Do not worry about tomorrow, for tomorrow will worry about itself?"

Peter: Yeah, and He said that each day has enough trouble of its own.

Philip: Okay, okay, I get it. Well, I guess we all need to stick close to Jesus to understand what He says and put His words into practice.

1. How do you relate this skit to your own life?

2. Why do you think people worry?

3. What do you know about God that will help you when you are worried or afraid?

4. How did God show His love for people in the Bible? How has He shown His love for you?

5. What can you do to thank God for His love?

6. Imagine you were a bird of the air and God was looking at
    you. What do you think He would see? (Check one from
    the list below.)

    ❑   An eagle—flying strongly
    ❑   A chicken—running like crazy
    ❑   A baby bird—waiting to be fed
    ❑   An owl—wise and silent
    ❑   An ostrich—unable to fly
    ❑   A parrot—talking, talking, talking
    ❑   A crow—noisy and lazy
    ❑   A condor—different, rare and unique
    ❑   A sea gull—soaring to heaven
    ❑   A toucan—bright and colorful

7. What are some of the things that keep you grounded and
    unable to fly? (Check all that apply.)

    ❑   Doubting God
    ❑   Distrust of people
    ❑   A bad experience
    ❑   Unforgiven sin
    ❑   Laziness
    ❑   Distractions of the world
    ❑   Bitterness in relationships
    ❑   Lack of support
    ❑   Too much worry

8. Read Hebrews 11:1. What is the definition of "faith"?

    _____

    _____

    _____

    _____

9.   How does faith in God play an important part in your life?

_____

_____

_____

_____

10. What promises from this portion of the Sermon on the
     Mount can help you in your decision to live a life of faith
     and always trust in God?

_____

_____

_____

_____

meditation

And my God will meet all your needs according to the
riches of his glory in Christ Jesus.

PHILIPPIANS 4:19

judging others and ourselves

Do not show partiality in judging; hear both small and great alike.
Do not be afraid of anyone, for judgment belongs to God.

DEUTERONOMY 1:17

Isn't it amazing how the kids we would least expect to come to the Lord are the ones who often do? As youth workers, our judgments about some teenagers can sometimes be off track. Like anyone else, we're prone to make quick assumptions about them based on their style of dress, the way they cut their hair, what color they dye it, how many body piercings they have, and the number of tattoos on their arms or legs. We might *want* to judge all kids fairly, but if we're honest with ourselves, we often allow our human perceptions get in the way—especially if those kids are nothing like us.

Isn't that what judging others and making faulty assumptions is all about? We want people (even students) to be just like us. If they're not, we make a quick judgment, categorize the person, stereotype him or her and file the information in our mental catalog. As the bearers of righteousness and truth, we "know" what's right and wrong. Our perception, intuition and telescopic eyesight are so good that we are experts at discovering the tiny specks of dust in the eyes of others. We are masters at whacking others with our hypocritical judgment planks.

Jesus—the one and only true Judge—told us not to judge others. He knew we have a capacity to avoid taking responsibility for our own actions, attitudes and personal weaknesses. He knew how easy it is for us to see the errors in *others* rather than *ourselves*. This is why He gave us a better way. As we learn from His example, model the way He displayed grace and humility, and unconditionally love and accept the teens in our group, we will see young people's lives changed and transformed.

Always seek to be more like Jesus. Look beyond the outside appearances and actions. Judge not your teens, lest you be judged. Just love them!

Examine the contents, not the bottle.
THE TALMUD

judging others and ourselves

starter

YOU BE THE JUDGE: Begin this exercise by breaking the group members into teams of four to five people. Explain that you will read a scenario, and they must consider the evidence in their teams and make a judgment in the case. Once they render a verdict, you will read the next part of the scenario, and then they will have a chance to re-examine the evidence. Begin by reading the opening scenario.

opening scenario

A group not associated with First Church asked if it could hold its meeting at the church. The church granted permission, and the group assembled for a potluck dinner. The tabletops were lined with delicious food and the participants were anxious to dig in. In fact, one fellow was so hungry that he did just that—he dug into a bowl of salad with one hand, scooping a handful onto his plate. Across the table in the other line, a woman took offense at this man's behavior and told him off in front of everyone.

The pastor overseeing the gathering was alerted to the problem when the police entered the fellowship room. The woman had called them after she claimed the man had struck her. The police were there to take the man into custody.

> **Discussion:** Ask the teams to consider this evidence. Was it appropriate for the woman to call the police? Should the police arrest the man? Allow the teams to discuss their facts of the case and then present their findings to the group.

part two

It seems that the man did smack the woman. While the woman was telling him off, he simply gave her hand a smack.

> **Discussion:** Ask the teams to discuss whether this changes their previous decision.

part three

The man claims the woman who had brought the salad was moving through the line with him. She told the man that she had forgotten to bring any type of serving utensil and, with a laugh, she had reached into her salad with her hand and put her serving on her plate. She apparently told the man that if he wanted salad, he would just have to follow her lead and grab some. So he did. That was when the other woman across the table saw him and began the confrontation.

Discussion: Explain that with this piece of evidence, we have established that the man was not the first to put his hand into the salad, and that the salad's owner actually encouraged him to reach in. Of course, we still have the fact that the man slapped his accuser's hand. Ask the teams to discuss how these new facts affect their opinions.

part four

Another witness told the police that the woman who had been smacked had failed to mention that she had struck the man first. When the man put his hand into the salad bowl, she reached over as she was telling him off and slapped his hand a number of times. In fact, this witness says that the man did not smack her as much as hit her hand away to get her to quit hitting him.

Discussion: Explain that from this last piece of evidence, it now appears that this bizarre situation was a battle. Ask the teams to deliberate once more and decide who was ultimately at fault and why. If they were the police, how would they handle situation? How could the whole mess have been avoided?[1]

message

As this exercise shows, sometimes we can be too quick to make a judgment about a person. When that happens, we run the risk of offending the individual and damaging our relationship. Jesus had much to say about judging others in the Sermon on the Mount, which we will discuss next.

Do not judge, or you too will be judged. For in the same way you judge others, you will be judged, and with the measure you use, it will be measured to you.

Why do you look at the speck of sawdust in your brother's eye
and pay no attention to the plank in your own eye? How can you
say to your brother, "Let me take the speck out of your eye," when
all the time there is a plank in your own eye? You hypocrite, first
take the plank out of your own eye, and then you will see clearly
to remove the speck from your brother's eye (Matthew 7:1-5).

1. What warning does Jesus give to those who would judge
    others?

    _____

    _____

    _____

    _____

2. According to Christ, what happens to a judgmental person?

    _____

    _____

    _____

    _____

3. What example does Jesus use to show why we can often
    see the error in others but not in ourselves?

    _____

    _____

    _____

    _____

4. According to Jesus, who has the greater problem—us or
    the other person?

    _____

    _____

    _____

5. How does Jesus describe a person who judges in this way?

    _____

    _____

    _____

6. What does Jesus say we need to do to be able to take the speck out of our brothers' eye when we see it?

    _____

    _____

    _____

7. Why do you think it is easier to see problems in others than in ourselves?

    _____

    _____

    _____

8. Why do you think Jesus includes a teaching on judging others in the context of the Sermon on the Mount?

    _____

    _____

    _____

dig

In Luke 6:37-42, we real a parallel account of this portion of Scripture that gives us a few additional details that are not found in the passage in Matthew:

> *Do not judge, and you will not be judged. Do not condemn, and you will not be condemned. Forgive, and you will be forgiven.*

Give, and it will be given to you. A good measure, pressed down, shaken together and running over, will be poured into your lap. For with the measure you use, it will be measured to you. . . .

Can the blind lead the blind? Will they not both fall into a pit? The student is not above the teacher, but everyone who is fully trained will be like their teacher.

Why do you look at the speck of sawdust in your brother's eye and pay no attention to the plank in your own eye? How can you say to your brother, "Brother, let me take the speck out of your eye," when you yourself fail to see the plank in your own eye? You hypocrite, first take the plank out of your eye, and then you will see clearly to remove the speck from your brother's eye.

1. Both the Matthew and Luke accounts begin with Jesus' statement, "Do not judge, or you will be judged." What additional words does Luke include that are not found in Matthew's version?

   _____

   _____

   _____

2. How does Luke sum up the teaching in verse 38?

   _____

   _____

   _____

3. What point is Jesus making when He asks, "Can the blind lead the blind? Will they not both fall into a pit" (verse 39)?

   _____

   _____

   _____

4. What does Jesus mean when He says, "The student is not above the teacher, but everyone who is fully trained will be like their teacher" (verse 40)?

5. According to both accounts in Matthew and Luke, who is most responsible for the condemnation we receive when we judge others?

6. Read John 7:24. What additional instructions does Jesus provide on judging others?

7. Turn to Romans 2:1-4. How does Paul's statement agree with Jesus' words in the Sermon on the Mount?

8. In what ways does passing judgment on others show "contempt for the riches of [God's] kindness" (verse 4)?

apply

The Miranda Rights is a warning given to individuals whom the police have taken into custody. It is a procedure that law enforcement officials are required to follow to protect the presumed innocence of a person who is suspected of committing a crime. The warning is likely known by many of us because of the TV dramas that use it in police scenes. It reads as follows:

> You have the right to remain silent when questioned. Anything you say or do can and will be used against you in a court of law. You have the right to consult an attorney before speaking to the police and to have an attorney present during questioning now or in the future. If you cannot afford an attorney, one will be appointed for you before any questioning, if you wish. If you decide to answer any questions now, without an attorney present, you will still have the right to stop answering at any time until you talk to an attorney.

1. Imagine that you are in a spiritual court. How do you feel knowing that your words and actions will be reviewed at your spiritual hearing? (Check all that apply.)

   ❑ I'm in big trouble.
   ❑ I hope there wasn't a surveillance camera near me the last few days.
   ❑ I think it is time to ask for forgiveness.
   ❑ I think I'm good.
   ❑ I thank God for forgiveness.

2. If you take the words Jesus spoke in Matthew 7:1-5 seriously, what steps will you need to take to put those words into action?

_____

_____

_____

3. Is there anyone you have judged whom you need to ask for forgiveness? If so, what will you do to approach that person?

_____

_____

_____

4. How will this new understanding of Jesus' words influence your future behavior as it relates to judging your friends or family?

_____

_____

_____

5. How will it influence your future behavior as it relates to judging those who are in authority over you?

_____

_____

_____

_____

6. In Romans 13:1, Paul states, "Let everyone be subject to the governing authorities, for there is no authority except that which God has established. The authorities that exist have been established by God." What does this passage tell

you about respecting those in authority? Who has placed these individuals in those roles?

_____

_____

_____

7. How will this new understanding of Jesus' words in Matthew 7:1-5 influence your future behavior as it relates to judging other Christians?

_____

_____

_____

_____

8. In James 4:12 we read, "There is only one Lawgiver and Judge, the one who is able to save and destroy. But you—who are you to judge your neighbor?" Why is God as Lawgiver and Judge in a better position than you to judge people? What does this say about your "rights" to judge your neighbors?

_____

_____

_____

_____

reflect

"This might hurt a little." No one wants to hear these words, but the truth is that a little pain is often involved when it comes to adjusting our words and actions. It is not always easy—or painless—to remove the boards sticking out of our own eyes.

1. What are some of the areas in your life that need a little "eye surgery"?

    _____

    _____

    _____

    _____

2. How does a person go about "removing the plank" in his or her eye?

    _____

    _____

    _____

3. Why does Jesus consider judging others to be the act of a hypocritical person?

    _____

    _____

    _____

4. Which people in your life tend to receive most of your criticism? Why?

    _____

    _____

    _____

5. What will you do to address this problem and let those people know you love and accept them?

    _____

    _____

    _____

    _____

6. While self-reflection is good and healthy, continually blaming yourself for things in the past is an act of self-judgment. Why is this type of behavior harmful?

    _____

    _____

    _____

7. In 1 Thessalonians 5:11, Paul writes, "Therefore encourage one another and build each other up." What steps can you take to be more affirming and encouraging to others? How will this help you to be less critical of others' mistakes?

    _____

    _____

    _____

8. When you leave this world, how do you want people to remember you?

    _____

    _____

    _____

meditation

Do not let any unwholesome talk come out of your mouths,
but only what is helpful for building others up according to
their needs, that it may benefit those who listen.

Ephesians 4:29

Note

1. Adapted from Jim Burns, *Uncommon Object Lessons and Discussion Starters* (Ventura, CA: Gospel Light, 2010).

unit III
decisions

Here's what a typical Jim and Cathy Burns date looks like. We check the wallet for money, pick up the car keys, get into the car, pull out of the driveway, and drive down the street. "Where do you want to eat?" I ask Cathy.

"Oh, I really don't care," she replies. "Where do *you* want to eat?"

"It doesn't matter."

"Well, what kind of food do you want?"

"How about Mexican food?"

"Not Mexican."

"Do you feel like Italian? Fish? Burgers? How about Chinese food?"

"No, I don't think so."

"I know, let's go get a salad."

"I don't want a salad."

"Well, what do you want?"

"I don't care."

Sometimes we have to stop the car and *decide to decide*.

We sound a little like today's youth. The problem with this generation of students is not that they make *dumb* decisions, but that they don't make *enough* decisions. Such failure leads many wonderful and incredible people into big trouble.

This last section in this study is about decisions. You will teach your students how to make wise decisions—ones that they will live with for a lifetime.

Thanks for helping your group members "decide to decide" to put their trust in the Lord. I can't think of a more important job than what you are doing—helping kids make positive and eternal decisions.

And God smiled.

seeking God in prayer

Therefore confess your sins to each other and pray for each other so that you may be healed. The prayer of a righteous person is powerful and effective.

JAMES 5:16

A youth pastor once confessed that he and his team spent a lot more time in prayer during the early days of their youth ministry than they did when the group grew to a considerable size. It wasn't something he was particularly proud to admit, but it was the truth. He remembered meeting with a couple of his volunteer staff members and going down the roster of each student who had signed up for winter or summer camp. The team would pray for each student specifically *by name*.

However, as the ministry grew, the team became busier and busier. There were more students signing up at the last minute, more cabin assignments to make, more transportation details to finalize, and more volunteer staff meetings to schedule. The team became better at running camps, but their prayers for the Holy Spirit to work in their students' lives actually decreased. They found themselves becoming less dependent on God and more dependent on themselves. Without prayer, there just wasn't the same passion for God as there used to be.

There's an old saying that goes, "If the devil doesn't make you sin, he'll make you busy." The devil would love for us not to pray. In truth, what that youth pastor and his team experienced in their ministry wasn't unusual for most churches, youth ministries or even Christians. It wasn't that prayer was no longer important to them—after all, they still prayed. The problem was that their priorities had gotten off track, and prayer was no longer at the top of their list of important things to do.

When we pray, our primary purpose isn't to ask or receive from God but to be *with* God—to sit and wait and listen. Just as Jesus went to a solitary place early in the morning to be with and pray to His Father, so we are to increase our desire for meeting with and praying to the Lord. This lesson will serve as a great opportunity to talk about the priority of prayer in your youth ministry and the incredible difference that meeting with God can make in each of your student's lives.

Prayer does not change God, but changes him who prays.
Søren Kierkegaard

seeking God in prayer

starter

ASK, SEEK, KNOCK-KNOCK: For this activity, you will need to make one copy of the following handout for every person in your group (note that you can download this in pdf form at **www.gospel light.com/uncommon/living_out_Jesus_teachings.zip**). Tell your group members that the object of this game is for them to *seek* out another person and *ask* if that person's information matches one of the spaces on their sheet. If it does, the group members can write that person's name in the square. Note that they can only fill in the same person's name *once* on their sheets (or *twice* if you have a small group). When they are finished, they will need to find one person who knows a good "knock-knock" joke and write that in the final space on the sheet.

Note: You can download this group study guide in 8¹/₂" x 11" format at **www.gospellight.com/uncommon/living_out_Jesus_teachings.zip**.

This person was born in the month of February:	This person has a cat:	This person has a dog:
This person enjoys watching football on TV:	This person has read a play by Shakespeare:	This person is wearing something red:
This person is wearing brown shoes:	This person knows the Pledge of Allegiance:	This person likes Mexican food:
This person likes a musical band that you like:	This person likes the same flavor of ice cream as you:	This person has been to a foreign country:
Now find one person who knows a good "knock-knock" joke, and write that below:		

Transition to the message by stating that like this game, Jesus tells us to ask, seek and knock in prayer.

message

In Matthew 6:5, Jesus gave His followers a model prayer they could use to thank their heavenly Father for His blessings, ask for His will to be done on earth, request that He provide for their daily needs, and ask Him for forgiveness from their sins. In this next portion of the Sermon on the Mount, Jesus explains the power of this type of prayer and how God always seeks to bless His children.

Ask and it will be given to you; seek and you will find; knock and the door will be opened to you. For everyone who asks receives; the one who seeks finds; and to the one who knocks, the door will be opened.

Which of you, if your son asks for bread, will give him a stone? Or if he asks for a fish, will give him a snake? If you, then, though you are evil, know how to give good gifts to your children, how much more will your Father in heaven give good gifts to those who ask him! So in everything, do to others what you would have them do to you, for this sums up the Law and the Prophets (Matthew 7:7-12).

1. What three things does Jesus instruct His followers to do in verse 7?

    _____

    _____

    _____

    _____

    _____

2. What results does Jesus promise to those who do these things?

    _____

    _____

    _____

    _____

    _____

3. What do Jesus' words say about the power we have in prayer?

    _____

    _____

    _____

    _____

4. What two examples does Jesus use to show that God only
    wants the best for His children?

    _____

    _____

    _____

    _____

5. What does Jesus mean in verse 11 when He says that we
    are "evil"?

    _____

    _____

    _____

    _____

6. What point is Jesus making by comparing the gifts hu-
    man parents give to their children to the gifts that God
    gives to His children?

    _____

    _____

    _____

    _____

7. In verse 12, Jesus states what has become known as the
    Golden Rule: "Do to others what you would have them do
    to you." Why is this such an important rule for people to
    follow in order to get along?

    _____

    _____

    _____

8. What do you think Jesus meant when He said, "For this sums up the Law and the Prophets"?

_____

_____

_____

_____

_____

dig

Notice in this portion of the Sermon of the Mount that Jesus instructed us to "ask," "seek" and "knock" in prayer. This implies a form of persistence—we don't just say a prayer to God one time and then go on our way. God wants us to return to Him in prayer and seek out His direction for our lives.

1. Jesus tells a parable in Luke 11:5-10 that illustrates this concept of persistence in prayer. In this story, what problem does the person have who is knocking at the friend's door?

_____

_____

_____

_____

_____

2. What is the friend's response to the request?

_____

_____

_____

_____

3. What characteristics does the person have who is knocking at the door that ultimately convinces the friend to fulfill the request?

    _____

    _____

    _____

    _____

4. What is Jesus saying about prayer in this parable? What is He saying about God?

    _____

    _____

    _____

    _____

5. It is important to note that the words "ask," "seek" and "knock" in Matthew 6:7-8 are all written in the future present tense, which is best translated as "keep on asking," "keep on seeking," and "keep on knocking." How does this knowledge help you to better understand this passage?

    _____

    _____

    _____

    _____

6. Read Jeremiah 29:11-13. What type of plans does God have for us?

    _____

    _____

    _____

    _____

7. How does this show that God is a loving Father who gives *good* gifts to His children?

    _____

    _____

    _____

    _____

8. What should our understanding of this fact compel us to do (see verse 12)? What does God promise to do in response?

    _____

    _____

    _____

    _____

9. In Romans 6:23, Paul writes, "For the wages of sin is death, but the gift of God is eternal life in Christ Jesus our Lord." What does this passage say is the greatest gift that our heavenly Father ever gave to us?

    _____

    _____

    _____

    _____

apply

Mother Teresa once wrote, "Love to pray. Feel often during the day the need for prayer, and take trouble to pray. Prayer enlarges the heart until it is capable of containing God's gift of Himself. Ask and seek, and your heart will grow big enough to receive Him and keep Him as your own."

1. Do you find you have a "need for prayer" during the day? If not, why do you think this is the case?

   _____

   _____

   _____

2. What do you think keeps most believers from asking, seeking and knocking more often?

   _____

   _____

   _____

3. What would you say are the biggest roadblocks to prayer in your life?

   _____

   _____

   _____

4. Which of the following "ingredients" would best help you remove those roadblocks? (Check for the most appropriate response.)

   ☐   Praying on a more consistent basis.
   ☐   Scheduling time in my day to pray.
   ☐   Praying more with others.
   ☐   Keeping track of my prayers in a journal.
   ☐   Seeing more results from my prayers.
   ☐   Finding creative ideas for prayer.
   ☐   Studying the Bible and other books about prayer.
   ☐   Using Scripture to help me pray.
   ☐   Believing that God will answer when I pray.

5. Sometimes, one roadblock might be that you don't know
    exactly what to pray. Read Romans 8:26. What does Paul
    say you can do in such situations?

    _____

    _____

    _____

6. What is the greatest need you have right now that you
    want to give to God in prayer?

    _____

    _____

    _____

7. How does Jesus' promise in Matthew 7:7-12 assure you
    that God not only hears your request but is also con-
    cerned about your need?

    _____

    _____

    _____

    _____

8. In Matthew 21:22, Jesus says, "If you believe, you will re-
    ceive whatever you ask for in prayer." In Hebrews 11:1, we
    read, "Now faith is confidence in what we hope for and as-
    surance about what we do not see." What do these verses
    say is important for us to do when we approach God with
    our requests?

    _____

    _____

    _____

reflect

As you conclude this session, take a few moments to reflect on your own personal prayer life. Think about Jesus' words in this portion of the Sermon on the Mount and how they specifically apply to your life.

1. An important aspect of prayer is the realization that God is infinite—that He is not subject to any limitations in space, time, knowledge or power. In what ways have you been putting God in a "box" and not believing that He cares enough about your problems to answer your prayers?

    _____

    _____

    _____

    _____

2. In what ways have you doubted that God has the power to answer your needs?

    _____

    _____

    _____

    _____

3. How have Jesus' words in Matthew 7:7-12 changed your ideas about God?

    _____

    _____

    _____

    _____

4. In Romans 8:15, Paul writes, "For you did not receive the spirit of bondage again to fear, but you received the Spirit of adoption by whom we cry out, 'Abba, Father.'" In Jesus' time, "Abba" was a term of endearment that children often used for their father, similar to how kids today say "daddy" or "papa." What does this tell you about how you can approach God in prayer?

    _____

    _____

    _____

    _____

    _____

5. Where is the best place for you to pray?

    _____

    _____

    _____

    _____

6. When is the best time for you to pray?

    _____

    _____

    _____

    _____

7. What is the best method for your prayer time?

    _____

    _____

    _____

    _____

8. In the end, you can talk about prayer, study the concept and essentials of prayer, and even debate the various philosophies about prayer, but if you don't actually *pray*, you will never experience the power of prayer. Reread Matthew 7:7-12, and then take several minutes to pray. If you need some ideas on what to say, you can simply ask God:

    *   To take care of your family
    *   To help you in your daily life at school
    *   To give you opportunities to share your faith with friends
    *   To support your pastor and those in authority over you
    *   For His blessings on your church and community
    *   To help you be a person of character and integrity
    *   To give you the strength to follow Christ each day

    How would you like your prayer life to improve over the course of the next month? Over the course of the next year?

    _____

    _____

    _____

    _____

meditation

Rejoice always, pray continually, give thanks in all circumstances; for this is God's will for you in Christ Jesus.

1 THESSALONIANS 5:16-18

making the right
decisions

This day I call the heavens and the earth as witnesses against you
that I have set before you life and death, blessings and curses. Now choose life,
so that you and your children may live and that you may love the LORD
your God, listen to his voice, and hold fast to him.

DEUTERONOMY 30:19-20

Helping young people make good decisions is at the heart of youth ministry. Every decision a young person makes either shapes his or her character to be more like Christ's or conforms it to the pattern of this world. As teenagers make these choices, they begin to take a path that will either lead to them walking with God or following the crowd. The decisions that they make today will affect who they become tomorrow.

Your choice to be involved in the lives of young people is also an important decision that will make a difference for all eternity, because *you are making a critical difference in kids' lives.* You probably don't feel that way when it's 11 PM and you're still picking up popcorn after a crazy youth event. Or when your kids grumble, complain and never say a word of thanks.

Even as you sit down to prepare this Bible study, you probably realize that most of your group members will never understand the thought, time and energy you've spent to create something meaningful in God's Word for them to process. You are doing the unnoticed yet highly important kingdom work of helping kids enter through the narrow gate. Yet while you may not receive the thanks from your group, know that God sees what are doing, and that "your Father, who sees what is done in secret, will reward you" (Matthew 6:4).

May God encourage you today in a special way. May He confirm your ministry to teenagers. May He give you the vision and faith to hang in there when you feel like giving up. May He remind you always that your decision to love and be with kids will affect them for the rest of their lives.

Decision is a sharp knife that cuts clean and straight; indecision is a dull one that hacks and tears and leaves ragged edges behind it.

GORDON GRAHAM

making the right decisions

starter

YOU DECIDE: Before the session begins, gather the following items and display them on a table in the room: (1) the letter "O" written on a card, (2) a kernel of corn, (3) a ruler, (4) a pillow, (5) a spoon, (6) two banana peels, (7) a pair of scissors, (8) a dictionary, (9) a mirror, (10) an alarm clock, (11) a pitcher, (12) a match, (13) a nail, (14) shoe polish, and (15) a hot dog. Give each group member a copy of the following worksheet and a pen or pencil.[1] (Note that you can download this sheet in pdf form at **www.gospel light.com/uncommon/living_out_Jesus_teachings.zip.**) Explain that at the front of the room are a number of items they are to match to the "clues" given on their handouts. They are to write the name of the item next to the word it matches on the list.

1. Donut _____

2. The colonel _____

3. It's a foot _____

4. Headquarters _____

5. A stirring event _____

6. A pair of slippers _____

7. The peacemaker _____

8. Where love is found _____

9. A place for reflection _____

10. A morning caller _____

11. Seen at the ball game _____

12. Fire when ready _____

13. Drive through the wood _____

14. Bound to shine _____

15. Toasty canine _____

Allow 10 minutes or so for everyone to complete the activity, and then call time. Go through the answers listed at the end of this session and award a small prize to the person who has the most correct "decisions" as to which items matched.

message

Life is filled with numerous small decisions that can either take us to where we want to be or steer us seriously off track. In this next portion of the Sermon on the Mount, Jesus explains that the correct route we take in life won't necessarily be the easiest path that we could possibly choose.

Enter through the narrow gate. For wide is the gate and broad is the road that leads to destruction, and many enter through it. But small is the gate and narrow the road that leads to life, and only a few find it (Matthew 7:13-14).

1. What choice does Jesus tell His listeners to make before He even gives them the options?

   _____

   _____

   _____

   _____

2. What are the two options in life that Jesus describes?

   _____

   _____

   _____

3. What makes the wide gate so popular?

   _____

   _____

   _____

   _____

4. What does a person's life look like who chooses to go through the wide gate that leads to destruction?

   _____

   _____

   _____

   _____

5. What does a person's life look like who chooses to go through the narrow gate that leads to life?

6. Why do you think so few people find the road to life?

7. In Luke 13:24-25, Jesus says, "Make every effort to enter through the narrow door, because many, I tell you, will try to enter and will not be able to. Once the owner of the house gets up and closes the door, you will stand outside knocking and pleading." What does this tell you about the importance of the choices you make in your life right now?

8. What does this passage state is the reward for making the effort to go through the narrow door?

dig

In Jesus' time, there were different kinds of gates. There were wide gates, such as in the walls that surrounded the city of Jerusalem, that were large enough for people to go through with their animals and goods. Then there were narrow gates, such as in sheep pens, that were so small only one animal could go through at a time.

1. Read John 10:7-10. According to these verses, in what position does Jesus place Himself?

    _____

    _____

    _____

    _____

2. In biblical times, shepherds would close their sheep in their pen for the night and then stand guard over them. In this way, they functioned as the "gate" for their sheep. How does this relate to how Jesus watches over us?

    _____

    _____

    _____

    _____

3. What is the result of going through Jesus' gate?

    _____

    _____

    _____

4. What do the "thieves and robbers" represent? How do these individuals affect the choices we make?

5. What does the thief come to do? What did Jesus come to earth to do?

6. Read John 14:5-6. What question did Thomas ask of Jesus?

7. What does Jesus say are the results of taking the narrow way?

8. What is the only way that we can come to God the Father?

apply

Notice in this portion of the Sermon on the Mount that Jesus states that taking the narrow path is *difficult*, which implies it will involve a *cost* on our part.

1. In Luke 6:22, Jesus states, "Blessed are you when people hate you, when they exclude you and insult you and reject your name as evil, because of the Son of Man." What are some of the costs associated with taking the narrow way?

   _____

   _____

   _____

   _____

2. What can you see as the cost for the wide way?

   _____

   _____

   _____

3. What has it cost you personally to follow Christ?

   _____

   _____

   _____

4. What potential costs might be waiting for you as you continue to sacrifice to follow Christ?

   _____

   _____

   _____

5. In John 16:33, Jesus states, "In this world you will have trouble. But take heart! I have overcome the world." What two things does Jesus promise to those who make the difficult choice to follow Him?

    ---

6. Think about the types of choices you have made during your life. How would you say the majority of your decisions work out? (Check two of the following statements that best apply to you.)

    ❑   My decisions tend to lead me on the right track.
    ❑   My decisions tend to land me in a heap of trouble.
    ❑   My decisions turn out for the better eventually.
    ❑   My decisions tend to teach me about failure.
    ❑   My decisions are constantly returning to haunt me.
    ❑   I don't know . . . I tend to avoid making decisions.
    ❑   I prefer to others to make decisions for me.

7. Life is often filled with a series of small choices that lead to great consequences if we fail to take the proper steps. Consider the following story:

    One morning a vulture was hungry. As he was flying over the river, he saw the carcass of a dead animal floating down the river on a piece of ice. The vulture landed on the ice and began to gorge himself with this delightful meal. At one point he looked up to take a breath of air and noticed that he was 100 yards from a waterfall. However, instead of flying away, the vulture kept eating, though he kept his eye on the approaching waterfall. At 25 yards, he decided to take one last bite. Then, at 10 yards, he decided to take one last mouthful. With only a few feet to go before the falls, he decided he had eaten enough. He tried to fly, but found that his feet were now frozen to the ice. He tumbled to his death over the falls.

What important message does this story teach us about making decisions?

_____

_____

_____

_____

8. Do you think God really cares about the decisions you make? What have you read in the Bible that leads you to believe that way?

_____

_____

_____

_____

reflect

Many people are procrastinators when it comes to making decisions. Some have even allowed their procrastination to cause them to take the wide road that leads to destruction. Remember, not deciding to live for Jesus *is* a decision!

1. If you knew your life were going to end in a few weeks, what would you do differently?

   _____

   _____

   _____

   _____

2. What are the biggest decisions weighing on your shoulders right now?

   _____

   _____

   _____

   _____

3. What is one thing you would need to do to make better decisions?

   _____

   _____

   _____

4. What are the roadblocks in your life that are preventing you from making good decisions *right now*?

   _____

   _____

   _____

   _____

5. When it comes to practicing discipline, how would you rate yourself?

   _____

   Not so good   Doing okay   Doing really great

6. What are three areas in the following list that are the most difficult for you to discipline?

- ☐ Eating habits
- ☐ Handling money
- ☐ Thoughts
- ☐ Prayer life
- ☐ Speech
- ☐ Relationships
- ☐ Anger/moods
- ☐ Exercise
- ☐ Other: _____

- ☐ Sleep patterns
- ☐ Sexuality
- ☐ Humor
- ☐ Sarcastic tongue
- ☐ Study habits
- ☐ Church attendance
- ☐ Criticism of others
- ☐ Gossiping

7. Why is it often more difficult to recognize the small decisions you make each day that impact your integrity, such as cheating on a test or telling a "white" lie?

8. How do you think the enemy uses these small concessions to lead you down the wrong path?

9. Read James 4:7. How do you win the battle each day over temptation?

_____

_____

_____

_____

_____

meditation

Trust in the Lord with all your heart and lean not
on your own understanding; in all your ways submit to him,
and he will make your paths straight.

PROVERBS 3:5-6

Starter Answers: (1) the letter "O," (2) kernel of corn, (3) ruler, (4) pillow, (5) spoon, (6) two banana peels, (7) scissors, (8) dictionary, (9) mirror, (10) alarm clock, (11) pitcher, (12) match, (13) nail, (14) shoe polish, (15) hot dog.

Note

1. Adapted from Lyman Coleman, _Youth Ministry Encyclopedia_ (Littleton, CO: Serendipity House, 1985), p. 43.

bearing good fruit

Anyone who listens to the word but does not do what it says is like a man who looks at his face in a mirror and, after looking at himself, goes away and immediately forgets what he looks like. But the man who looks intently into the perfect law that gives freedom, and continues to do this, not forgetting what he has heard, but doing it-he will be blessed in what he does.

JAMES 1:23-25

Each and every day, young people are up against a legion of violent and promiscuous messages. No matter what the medium is—television, print, radio, film, the Internet—young people are surrounded by a seductive stream of false prophets. Teenagers are bombarded each day with message after message to do whatever feels right to them.

What makes youth ministry even more difficult is how you as a youth worker can stay pure in the midst of receiving the same messages. Whether you are paid or are a volunteer, like everyone else you are subject to temptation through what you hear and see. Society influences you just as much as it does young people. That is why this lesson on discerning good fruit from bad fruit and good prophets from bad prophets is so critical to for both *you* and *your young people's* relationship with God.

Just as a young David took on a huge, ugly, God-profaning Goliath with the Lord on his side, you as a youth worker can take on the messages you receive each day knowing that God will go before you into the battle. God is on your side. Your enemy is not Hollywood, television or the producers of the sick and twisted messages we hear and see every day. No, your enemy is Satan, and your mission is to pray for the Holy Spirit to transform hearts.

This lesson will provide a fantastic launching pad for you to discuss all the hot issues and topics that confront young people every day. You can be sure that the wisdom in God's Word will provide just what you need to walk in a way that honors Him. God's Word will supply you with the wisdom, discernment, protection, knowledge, understanding—everything the Holy Spirit uses—to produce good and lasting fruit in your life.

Of two evils, choose neither.
CHARLES SPURGEON

bearing good fruit

starter

TASTE TEST: Divide the group members into pairs, and give each pair a copy of the following test and a pen or pencil. (Note that you can download this sheet in pdf form at **www.gospel light.com/uncommon/living_out_Jesus_teachings.zip**). Explain that each of the answers to the questions is some type of food-related item. Have the group members complete the sheet with their partners.

1. "Hurry, dear. _____ be going."
2. Istanbul is in _____.
3. "I'm broke, man. Can you loan me a little _____?"
4. The _____achian mountains are beautiful in the fall.
5. The Parthenon is in the country of _____.

6. I have a _____ on my big toe.

7. The twentieth letter of the alphabet is _____.

8 _____ is found in the area of a circle.

9. "You are the _____ of the earth."

10. Two of a kind is a _____.

11. If you step on a tomato, you might _____ it.

12. I'll _____ you on the corner at 6:30 sharp."

13. "_____ on earth, goodwill toward men."

14. "He seems angry. What is his _____ with me?"

15. Kids always _____ their noses at foods that they don't like.

16. At Waikiki, you'll find many people _____ in the sun.

17. Adam and Eve were busy _____ Cain and Abel.

18. Every year, good gardeners will _____ their trees.

19. A rose is a very beautiful _____.

20. Christians celebrate the Lord's Day on _____.

Allow 10 minutes or so for everyone to complete the handout, and then call time. Go through the answers listed at the end of this session and award a small prize to the person who has the most correct responses.

message

Every day, we are bombarded with messages that tell us how we should act and what we should believe. How do we determine which messages are right and which are wrong? Jesus provides us with one way to tell the difference in this next portion of the Sermon on the Mount.

Watch out for false prophets. They come to you in sheep's clothing, but inwardly they are ferocious wolves. By their fruit you will recognize them. Do people pick grapes from thornbushes, or figs from thistles? Likewise, every good tree bears good fruit, but a bad tree bears bad fruit. A good tree cannot bear bad fruit, and a bad tree cannot bear good fruit. Every tree that does not bear good fruit is cut down and thrown into the fire. Thus, by their fruit you will recognize them (Matthew 7:15-20).

1. What is a "false prophet"?

   _____

   _____

   _____

   _____

   _____

2. What do you think Jesus means when He says these false prophets are like wolves in sheep's clothing?

   _____

   _____

   _____

   _____

3. How can you recognize these false prophets?

   _____

   _____

   _____

   _____

   _____

4. According to Jesus, why is it so vital for believers to know the difference between what bears good fruit and bad fruit?

_____

_____

_____

5. What happens to trees that bear bad fruit? Why is this necessary?

_____

_____

_____

_____

6. Why do you think Jesus included a warning on false prophets in the Sermon on the Mount?

_____

_____

_____

7. What are some of the reasons people follow popular leaders and celebrities?

_____

_____

_____

8. How can you evaluate a person's "fruit" and still remain consistent with Jesus' teaching in this passage?

_____

_____

_____

_____

dig

Jesus says that false prophets "come to you in sheep's clothing" (Matthew 7:15). The people of His day would have well understood this word picture, as they were very familiar with sheep and shepherds. The picture Jesus creates is of a wily and dangerous animal that is disguised as a sweet and non-threatening creature.

1. False prophets were a problem from the beginning of the Israelites' history. Read Deuteronomy 13:1-5. What test did God set up to help His people determine whether a prophet was from Him?

    ----

2. What did God command must happen to that "prophet or dreamer"? Why do you think He gave this strict command?

    ----

3. What was the danger in allowing this person to speak a false message among the Israelites?

    ----

4. False teachers were a problem in New Testament times as well. Read 1 Timothy 6:3-5. What test does Paul provide for believers to determine if a prophet is truly from God?

_____

_____

_____

_____

5. According to this passage, what bad fruit will these false teachers produce?

_____

_____

_____

_____

6. Now turn to 2 Peter 2:1-3. What do false prophets do?

_____

_____

_____

_____

7. How does Peter describe these individuals? What does he say has long been "hanging" over them?

_____

_____

_____

_____

8. James 3:1 states, "Not many of you should become teachers, my fellow believers, because you know that we who teach will be judged more strictly." What does this say to you about

your influence over others? Why must you be especially careful if you are in a place of authority over others?

----

apply

One of the problems in trying to determine teachers who preach messages contrary to God's will is that they don't come with a banner that says, "I am a false prophet!" In fact, the message they preach will likely seem good and productive. This is why Jesus warns that these "ferocious wolves" come in "sheep's clothing."

1. What disguises might false prophets wear today?

----

2. What makes false prophets so difficult to recognize in our modern world?

----

3. In John 15:5, Jesus said, "I am the vine; you are the branches. If you remain in me and I in you, you will bear much fruit; apart from me you can do nothing." What condition must believers follow in order to bear good fruit?

    _____

    _____

    _____

    _____

4. Can you bear good fruit outside of God's will? Why or why not?

    _____

    _____

    _____

    _____

5. Read Galatians 5:22-23. How can the traits that Paul lists help you determine the quality of a person's "fruit" or characteristics?

    _____

    _____

    _____

    _____

    _____

6. We all have people in our lives who are good influences and bad influences. Take a moment to think about who is influencing you and in what ways they are doing so. Then, in the chart on the next page, list these friends, family members, pastors, celebrities, teachers, or anyone else who influences your thoughts, beliefs and actions.

Name	How this Person Influences Me	Positive or Negative?
Susie Smith	She talks with me about God	Positive
Sam Jones	He invites me to parties/ peer pressure	Negative

7. What do you need to do to be better prepared to react to the false prophets in your life? (Check two answers that best apply to you.)

☐ Pray for God's discernment.
☐ Ask for advice from a godly person.
☐ Choose my friends more carefully.
☐ Learn more about was is true through God's Word.
☐ Give up some of the "false prophets" in my life.
☐ Speak up for God's truth more often.
☐ Take the idea of evil and false prophets more seriously.

8. What action steps can you take to ensure that you will bear good fruit?

----

reflect

As you conclude this session, take a few moments to reflect on the type of fruit that you are bearing in your life. Think about Jesus' words in this portion of the Sermon on the Mount and how they specifically apply to your life.

1. What are some of the good "fruit" (or characteristics) that you are displaying in your life?

----

2. What are some of the not-so-good fruit that you are displaying?

----

3. What are some of the good things going on in your relationship with Christ? What would you consider the not-so-good things?

----

4. What is the single most negative influence in your life right now?

_____

_____

_____

5. What is the single most positive influence in your life right now?

_____

_____

_____

6. In Matthew 12:33, Jesus says, "Make a tree good and its fruit will be good, or make a tree bad and its fruit will be bad, for a tree is recognized by its fruit." How can these words keep you from becoming complacent as a Christian?

_____

_____

_____

_____

7. In Matthew 13:3-4, Jesus tells a parable in which he states, "A farmer went out to sow his seed. As he was scattering the seed, some fell along the path, and the birds came and ate it up." According to verse 19, what type of person does this seed represent? How does Satan influence this person?

_____

_____

_____

_____

8. What can you do to protect yourself from those who
    would lead you away from God? What steps will you take
    to do these things today?

    _____

    _____

    _____

    _____

meditation

You did not choose me, but I chose you and appointed you so
that you might go and bear fruit—fruit that will last—and so
that whatever you ask in my name the Father will give you.

JOHN 15:16

Starter Answers: (1) lettuce, (2) turkey, (3) bread, (4) apple, (5) grease, (6) corn,
(7) tea, (8) pie (π), (9) salt, (10) pear, (11) squash, (12) meat, (13) peas, (14) beef,
(15) turnip, (16) bacon, (17) raisin, (18) prune, (19) flour, (20) sundae.

building on the true foundation

He is the Rock, his works are perfect, and all his ways are just. A faithful God
who does no wrong, upright and just is he.

DEUTERONOMY 32:4

Why does the Sermon on the Mount end with the crowds being amazed at Jesus' teachings? The only clue we are given is that Jesus "taught as one who had authority, and not as their teachers of the law" (Matthew 7:29). There was something different about the way Jesus presented the Scriptures to the people. They recognized this difference in Him and were impressed by it.

The people's acceptance of Jesus' authority reveals that there was a close relationship between the words He spoke and the way in which He lived His life. The people were amazed with Jesus and His words because He lived with integrity. Not only was the message Jesus was preaching transforming, but His life was as well.

There's a clear takeaway here for all of us who work with teenagers. Young people today are searching, but they're also skeptical. Yes, many of them have problems with authority, primarily because the authorities in their lives haven't done much to gain their respect. Teenagers today also aren't impressed with many religious leaders. They don't want to hear about developing a "true foundation" for their lives. They want to see that foundation alive and working in their leaders.

Young people today desperately want to believe in something greater than themselves, but they don't want to be embarrassed or made into fools. They want to be amazed. They want to live for a higher purpose. They want and need someone with authority to help them navigate the difficult and stormy seas of adolescence.

You have the awesome privilege of communicating the amazing words of Jesus to teens. As an authority in their lives, you don't have to be perfect . . . just authentic and real. You are just the person to model for them the true foundation that God has laid in your life.

Let us endeavor so to live that when we come to die
even the undertaker will be sorry.
ANONYMOUS

building on the true foundation

starter

WILL IT STAND: For this activity, you will need some masking tape, Popsicle sticks and a high-power fan. Divide the group members into two teams and give each team a strip of masking tape and a stack of Popsicle sticks. Tell the teams that they will be having a competition to see who can build the highest tower in five minutes. The catch is that once they have built their structure, you will be placing a high-power fan in front of it for 30 seconds to see how sturdy it is. The winner will be the team with the highest tower still standing *after that time*. The teams can only use the Popsicle sticks and masking tape that they have been given.

message

Jesus ends the Sermon on the Mount with a challenge to His followers to live out the teachings that He has just presented to them—to do the will of God their Father and build their lives on the firm foundation of His Word. His words are simple, His message is clear, and the truths He presents are powerful.

true and false disciples

In the previous sections of the Sermon on the Mount, Jesus explained how God desires to give those who seek Him good gifts (see Matthew 7:7-12), how those who want to follow God must go through the "narrow gate" (see verses 13-14), and how false prophets will attempt to lead them astray (see verses 15-20). Building on these points, Jesus now explains what distinguishes a true disciple from a false one:

> *Not everyone who says to me, "Lord, Lord," will enter the kingdom of heaven, but only the one who does the will of my Father who is in heaven. Many will say to me on that day, "Lord, Lord, did we not prophesy in your name and in your name drive out demons and in your name perform many miracles?" Then I will tell them plainly, "I never knew you. Away from me, you evildoers!"* (Matthew 7:21-23).

1. In this passage, Jesus refers to those who accept Him as a great teacher (who cry, "Lord, Lord") but who lack the commitment to follow Him. What does Jesus say about these types of people?

    _____

    _____

    _____

2. Hearing Jesus' words is not enough. What does a true follower of Christ do?

   _____

   _____

   _____

3. Why do you think Jesus places so much importance on
   obedience?

   _____

   _____

   _____

4. What does it mean "to do the will" of God the Father?

   _____

   _____

   _____

   _____

wise and foolish builders

Jesus concludes by leaving the people with a parable about two
men who build a house on different foundations:

> *Therefore everyone who hears these words of mine and puts them
> into practice is like a wise man who built his house on the rock. The
> rain came down, the streams rose, and the winds blew and beat
> against that house; yet it did not fall, because it had its foundation
> on the rock. But everyone who hears these words of mine and does
> not put them into practice is like a foolish man who built his house
> on sand. The rain came down, the streams rose, and the winds
> blew and beat against that house, and it fell with a great crash*
> (Matthew 7:24-27).

1. In what ways are those who both *hear* Jesus' words and *act* on them like the wise builder?

    _____

    _____

    _____

2. What are the benefits to that person of building his or her life on the solid foundation of God's Word?

    _____

    _____

    _____

    _____

3. In what ways are those who *hear* Jesus' words but do *not act* on them like the foolish builder?

    _____

    _____

    _____

    _____

4. What are the consequences to that person of building his or her life on the flimsy foundation of the world's standards?

    _____

    _____

    _____

    _____

dig

It is interesting that Jesus chose to conclude His message by noting that rain, wind and storms will come into every person's life. Followers of Christ are not exempt from pain and trouble. The question is what believers will *say and do* when those pressures arrive.

1. In Matthew 7:22, Jesus states, "Many will say to me on that day, 'Lord, Lord, did we not prophesy in your name and in your name drive out demons?'" What does Jesus mean when He refers to "that day"?

   _____

   _____

   _____

   _____

2. Is it possible to prophesy in Jesus' name and yet not be a true follower of Him? (See Numbers 22:1-12.)

   _____

   _____

   _____

   _____

3. Is it possible to drive out demons in Jesus' name and yet not be a true follower of Him? (See Acts 19:13-17.)

   _____

   _____

   _____

   _____

4. In 1 Corinthians 13:1, Paul states, "If I speak in the tongues of men or of angels, but do not have love, I am only a resounding gong or a clanging cymbal." How does this relate

to what Jesus said about those who are hearers of the Word but not doers of the Word?

_____

5. Jesus, like many of the Old Testament writers, compared wisdom and foolishness. Read Proverbs 12:15-20. What characteristics of wisdom are found in this passage?

_____

6. What characteristics of foolishness are found in this passage of Scripture?

_____

7. How does James 1:22 reinforce these words of Jesus?

_____

8. How does Matthew 7:24-29 provide a fitting conclusion to the Sermon on the Mount?

_____

apply

In Matthew 7:1-6, Jesus warned His followers not to judge others, for judgment belongs to God alone. Jesus now speaks of a coming time when God will judge those who claim to follow Him on whether they acted on His words. As Jesus states, many who call Him "Lord" neglect to truly make Him the Lord of their lives.

1. When it comes to calling Jesus Lord of your life, what are you really saying?

   ❏ "My Lord and my God."
   ❏ "My rescuer in a time of trouble."
   ❏ "My good buddy."
   ❏ "The same thing everybody else is saying."
   ❏ "My parents' Lord."
   ❏ "The cop in the sky."
   ❏ "The supreme being out there somewhere."
   ❏ "The great spoiler of fun."
   ❏ Other: "_____"

2. The word "lord" means "master." Jesus wants to be the master of your life. In what ways have you given this role over to Him?

   _____

   _____

   _____

3. In what areas of your life do you still need to allow Him total lordship?

   _____

   _____

   _____

4. What happens to you when the pressures of life come? To examine this question better, first think about what has caused worry, trouble or strain for you in the past. Check five items on the following list that you see as pressures in your life.

    - ❑ Death of someone close to you
    - ❑ Grades
    - ❑ Teachers
    - ❑ Money
    - ❑ Dating
    - ❑ Personal injury
    - ❑ Debts
    - ❑ College applications

    - ❑ Responsibilities
    - ❑ Illness of a loved one
    - ❑ School tasks
    - ❑ Friends
    - ❑ Moving
    - ❑ Holiday season
    - ❑ Family
    - ❑ Job
    - ❑ School tasks
    - ❑ Future

5. To what extent do you let the Lord be the foundation in your life during the storms? Circle the most appropriate answer on the following continuum, and then give the reason for your answer in the space provided.

Always	Most Often	Sometimes	Seldom	Never

    _____

    _____

    _____

    _____

    _____

6. Matthew 7:28-29 states the people were amazed that Jesus taught with such authority. How do you react to the au-

thority of Jesus in your life? Check one of the following phrases that best describes you.

- ❑   I am also amazed.
- ❑   He is the boss.
- ❑   I think He has to compete with me.
- ❑   My submission to His rule comes and goes.
- ❑   To be honest, He loses out to what I want to do most of the time.
- ❑   He seems to play second string on my team.

7. Dr. James Dobson tells a great story about a little obnoxious boy who was very disobedient. Read the following story and answer the question that follows.

Robert arrived in the dental office, prepared for battle.

"Get in the chair, young man," said the doctor.

"No chance!" replied the boy.

"Son, I told you to climb onto the chair, and that's what I intend for you to do," said the dentist.

Robert stared at his opponent for a moment and then replied, "If you make me get in that chair, I will take off all my clothes."

The dentist calmly said, "Son, take 'em off."

The boy forthwith removed his shirt, undershirt, shoes and socks, and then looked up in defiance.

"All right, son," said the dentist. "Now get in the chair."

"You didn't hear me," sputtered Robert. "I said if you make me get in that chair, I will take off all my clothes."

"Son, take 'em off," replied the man. Robert proceeded to remove his pants and shorts, finally standing totally naked before the dentist and his assistant.

"Now, son, get in the chair," said the doctor.

Robert did as he was told and sat cooperatively through the entire procedure. When the cavities were drilled and filled, he was instructed to step down from the chair.

"Give me my clothes now," said the boy.

"I'm sorry," replied the dentist. "Tell your mother that we're going to keep your clothes tonight. She can pick them up tomorrow."

Can you comprehend the shock Robert's mother received when the door to the waiting room opened, and there stood her pink son, as naked as the day he was born? The room was filled with patients, but Robert and his mom walked past them and into the hall. They went down a public elevator and into the parking lot, ignoring the snickers of onlookers.

The next day, Robert's mother returned to retrieve his clothes and asked to have a word with the dentist. However, she did not come to protest. These were her sentiments: "You don't know how much I appreciate what happened here yesterday. You see, Robert has been blackmailing me about his clothes for years. . . . If I don't immediately buy him what he wants, he threatens to take off all his clothes. You are the first person who has called his bluff, doctor, and the impact on Robert has been incredible."[1]

The dentist called the boy's bluff and the result was interesting, to say the least. What would happen if Jesus called your bluff if you were calling out, "Lord, Lord"? Circle the most appropriate answer.

❑   I would be caught living a lie.
❑   He would see me giving it my best.

❏   It depends on the time and the place.
❏   I would be happy to receive His insight.
❏   It would really scare me.

8. What is one way for you not only to say "Lord, Lord" in
    your life but to also go out and do His will?

----

reflect

As Jesus' closing parable in the Sermon on the Mount reveals,
each of us has a choice as to whether we are going to build our life
on the rock or on the sand. Read the following stories, and then
complete the ending by writing how the person either chose to
build his or her life on the solid foundation of Christ or the shift-
ing foundation of this world.

the story of bill

Bill's father was an alcoholic, and his mother was not a Christian.
All the rest of Bill's brothers and sisters (five, including Bill) had
basically partied through high school, gotten jobs that were less
than exciting, and were on the road to destruction. Bill was the
youngest. In truth, he didn't have a good role model in his entire
family. Yet for some reason, he seemed different. He wasn't the
partyer the others were, so far he had done well in school, and he
had a friend who was interested in taking him to church.

1. How will Bill's situation turn out if he chooses to give in to
    the temptations around him and build his life on the sand?

    _____

    _____

    _____

    _____

2. How will Bill's situation turn out if he chooses to follow
    God and build his life on the rock?

    _____

    _____

    _____

    _____

3. What would you say to Bill if you were his Christian friend?

    _____

    _____

    _____

4. Who in your life can you name who serves as an example
    of Christlike obedience?

    _____

    _____

    _____

the story of carrie

Carrie came from a Christian home. She had done all the "normal"
teenage rebellious stuff. She basically lived two separate lives—her

life at church and her life at school. Sometimes she felt guilty and was convicted about the worldly lifestyle she led at school, but she didn't really feel compelled to change. At a Christian camp, the speaker read these words from Jesus in Revelation 3:15-16: " 'I know your deeds, that you are neither cold nor hot. I wish you were either one or the other! So, because you are lukewarm—neither hot nor cold—I am about to spit you out of my mouth." Carrie knew she was lukewarm.

1. How will Carrie's situation turn out if she chooses to stay on the same course, lead a worldly lifestyle, and build her life on the sand?

2. How will Carrie's situation turn out if she chooses to follow God and build her life on the rock?

3. What sacrifices will Carrie have to make if she chooses this route?

4. What steps can you personally take to strengthen your
   foundation in Christ?

_____

_____

_____

_____

_____

meditation

For it is not those who hear the law who are
righteous in God's sight, but it is those who obey the
law who will be declared righteous.

ROMANS 2:13

Note
  1. Dr. James Dobson, *Straight Talk to Men and Their Wives* (Waco, TX: Word Books, 1980), pp. 58-60.

HOME HW WORD

WHERE PARENTS GET REAL ANSWERS

Get Equipped with HomeWord...

LISTEN
HomeWord Radio
programs reach over 800 communities nationwide with *HomeWord with Jim Burns* – a daily ½ hour interview feature, *HomeWord Snapshots* – a daily 1 minute family drama, and *HomeWord this Week* – a ½ hour weekend edition of the daily program, and our one-hour program.

CLICK
HomeWord.com
provides advice and resources to millions of visitors each year. A truly interactive website, HomeWord.com provides access to parent newsletter, Q&As, online broadcasts, tip sheets, our online store and more.

READ
HomeWord Resources
parent newsletters, equip families and Churches worldwide with practical Q&As, online broadcasts, tip sheets, our online store and more. Many of these resources are also packaged digitally to meet the needs of today's busy parents.

ATTEND
HomeWord Events
Understanding Your Teenager, Building Healthy Morals & Values, Generation 2 Generation and Refreshing Your Marriage are held in over 100 communities nationwide each year. HomeWord events educate and encourage parents while providing answers to life's most pressing parenting and family questions.

A Ministry with *Jim Burns*

In response to the overwhelming needs of parents and families, Jim Burns founded HomeWord in 1985. HomeWord, a Christian organization, equips and encourages parents, families, and churches worldwide.

Find Out More
Sign up for our FREE daily
e-devotional and parent e-newsletter
at HomeWord.com, or call 800.397.9725.

HomeWord.com

Small Group Curriculum Kits

Confident Parenting Kit

This is a must-have resource for today's family! Let Jim Burns help you to tackle overcrowded lives, negative family patterns, while creating a grace-filled home and raising kids who love God and themselves.

Kit contains:
- 6 sessions on DVD featuring Dr. Jim Burns
- CD with reproducible small group leader's guide and participant guides
- poster, bulletin insert, and more

Creating an Intimate Marriage Kit

Dr. Jim Burns wants every couple to experience a marriage filled with A.W.E.: affection, warmth, and encouragement. He shows husbands and wives how to make their marriage a priority as they discover ways to repair the past, communicate and resolve conflict, refresh their marriage spiritually, and more!

Kit contains:
- 6 sessions on DVD featuring Dr. Jim Burns
- CD with reproducible small group leader's guide and participant guides
- poster, bulletin insert, and more

Parenting Teenagers for Positive Results

This popular resource is designed for small groups and Sunday schools. The DVD features real family situations played out in humorous family vignettes followed by words of wisdom by youth and family expert, Jim Burns, Ph.D.

Kit contains:
- 6 sessions on DVD featuring Dr. Jim Burns
- CD with reproducible small group leader's guide and participant guides
- poster, bulletin insert, and more

Teaching Your Children Healthy Sexuality Kit

Trusted family authority Dr. Jim Burns outlines a simple and practical guide for parents on how to develop in their children a healthy perspective regarding their bodies and sexuality. Promotes godly values about sex and relationships.

Kit contains:
- 6 sessions on DVD featuring Dr. Jim Burns
- CD with reproducible small group leader's guide and participant guides
- poster, bulletin insert, and more

Tons of helpful resources for youth workers, parents and youth. Visit our online store at www.HomeWord.com or call us at 800-397-9725

Parent and Family Resources from HomeWord for you and your kids...

One Life Kit

Your kids only have one life – help them discover the greatest adventure life has to offer! 50 fresh devotional readings that cover many of the major issues of life and faith your kids are wrestling with such as sex, family relationships, trusting God, worry, fatigue and daily surrender. And it's perfect for you and your kids to do together!

Addicted to God Kit

Is your kids' time absorbed by MySpace, text messaging and hanging out at the mall? This devotional will challenge them to adopt thankfulness, make the most of their days and never settle for mediocrity! Fifty days in the Scripture is bound to change your kids' lives forever.

Devotions on the Run Kit

These devotionals are short, simple, and spiritual. They will encourage you to take action in your walk with God. Each study stays in your heart throughout the day, providing direction and clarity when it is most needed.

90 Days Through the New Testament Kit

Downloadable devotional. Author Jim Burns put together a Bible study devotional program for himself to follow, one that would take him through the New Testament in three months. His simple plan was so powerful that he was called to share it with others. A top seller!

Small Group Curriculum Kits

Confirming Your Faith Kit

Rite-of-Passage curriculum empowers youth to make wise decisions...to choose Christ. Help them take ownership of their faith! Lead them to do this by experiencing a vital Christian lifestyle.

Kit contains:
- 13 engaging lessons
- Ideas for retreats and special Celebration
- Solid foundational Bible concepts
- 1 leaders guide and 6 student journals (booklets)

10 Building Blocks Kit

Learn to live, laugh, love, and play together as a family. When you learn the 10 essential principles for creating a happy, close-knit household, you'll discover a family that shines with love for God and one another! Use this curriculum to help equip families in your church.

Kit contains:
- 10 sessions on DVD featuring Dr. Jim Burns
- CD with reproducible small group leader's guide and participant guides
- poster and bulletin insert
- 10 Building Blocks book

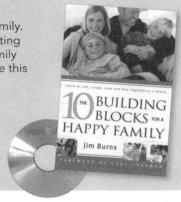

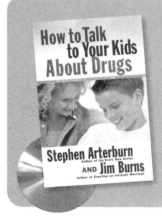

How to Talk to Your Kids About Drugs Kit

Dr. Jim Burns speaks to parents about the important topic of talking to their kids about drugs. You'll find everything you need to help parents learn and implement a plan for drug-proofing their kids.

Kit contains:
- 2 session DVD featuring family expert Dr. Jim Burns
- CD with reproducible small group leader's guide and participant guides
- poster, bulletin insert, and more
- How to Talk to Your Kids About Drugs book

Tons of helpful resources for youth workers, parents and youth. Visit our online store at www.HomeWord.com or call us at 800-397-9725

HOME WORD
WHERE PARENTS GET REAL ANSWERS

uncommon
leaders' resources

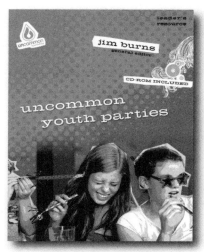

uncommon
youth parties
Jim Burns, General Editor
ISBN 978.08307.62132

uncommon missions
& service projects
Jim Burns, General Editor
ISBN 978.08307.57312

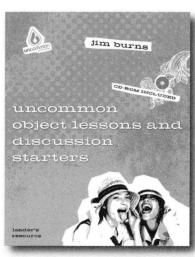

uncommon object lessons
& discussion starters
Jim Burns, General Editor
ISBN 978.08307.50986

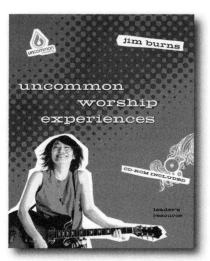

uncommon worship
experiences
Jim Burns, General Editor
ISBN 978.08307.54830

also available from
jim burns

dealing with
stress & crisis
Jim Burns, General Editor
ISBN 978.08307.62118

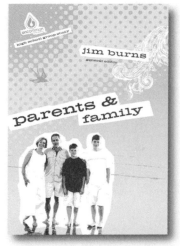

parents & family
Jim Burns, General Editor
ISBN 978.08307.50979

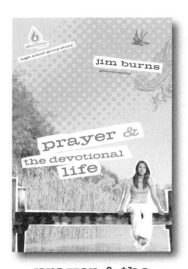

prayer & the
devotional life
Jim Burns, General Editor
ISBN 978.08307.54793

the new
testament
Jim Burns, General Editor
ISBN 978.08307.55660

uncommon
be extraordinary

Nurturing Habits of Mind *in* Early Childhood

Other ASCD publications by Arthur L. Costa and Bena Kallick:

Cultivating Habits of Mind (Quick Reference Guide)

Habits of Mind Across the Curriculum: Practical and Creative Strategies for Teachers

Learning and Leading with Habits of Mind: 16 Essential Characteristics for Success

Nurturing Habits of Mind *in* **Early Childhood**

Success Stories
from Classrooms
Around the World

Edited by
Arthur L. Costa *and* **Bena Kallick**

Alexandria, Virginia USA

Native peoples teach that the ultimate norm for morality is the effect that our choices have on persons living seven generations from now. If the results appear good for them, then our choices are moral ones; if not, they are immoral.

To our children, our grandchildren, and their children's children.

1703 N. Beauregard St. • Alexandria, VA 22311-1714 USA
Phone: 800-933-2723 or 703-578-9600 • Fax: 703-575-5400
Website: www.ascd.org • E-mail: member@ascd.org
Author guidelines: www.ascd.org/write

Ronn Nozoe, *Interim CEO and Executive Director;* Stefani Roth, *Publisher;* Genny Ostertag, *Director, Content Acquisitions;* Julie Houtz, *Director, Book Editing & Production;* Darcie Russell, *Editor;* Judi Connelly, *Associate Art Director;* Masie Chong, *Senior Graphic Designer;* Absolute Service, *Typesetter;* Mike Kalyan, *Director, Production Services;* Shajuan Martin, *E-Publishing Specialist*

PAPERBACK ISBN: 978-1-4166-2708-1   ASCD product #119017   n2/19
PDF E-BOOK ISBN: 978-1-4166-2710-4; see Books in Print for other formats.
Quantity discounts are available: e-mail programteam@ascd.org or call 800-933-2723, ext. 5773, or 703-575-5773. For desk copies, go to www.ascd.org/deskcopy.

Library of Congress Cataloging-in-Publication Data
Names: Kallick, Bena, editor. | Costa, Arthur L., editor.
Title: Nurturing habits of mind in early childhood : success stories from
    classrooms around the world / edited by Arthur L. Costa and Bena Kallick.
Description: Alexandria : ASCD, [2019] | Includes index.
Identifiers: LCCN 2018053310 | ISBN 9781416627081 (pbk.)
Subjects: LCSH: Early childhood education. | Cognition in children. |
    Learning, Psychology of.
Classification: LCC LB1139.23 .N86 2019 | DDC 372.21—dc23 LC record available at
    https://lccn.loc.gov/2018053310

28 27 26 25 24 23 22 21 20 19   1 2 3 4 5 6 7 8 9 10 11 12

Nurturing Habits of Mind *in* Early Childhood

Foreword

Maggie Dent

Nurturing Habits of Mind in Early Childhood: Success Stories from Classrooms Around the World is a long-overdue exploration of the wide-ranging possibilities, potentials, and benefits of introducing the wonderful Habits of Mind to our youngest learners. In my work as an educator and advocate in the early-years sector, as well as a passionate parent educator, I am excited that this book will elevate the importance of education in the early years as well as give educators a better understanding of the role that mindful thinking and questioning has in childhood.

As illustrated by the varied locales represented in this book—from the United States to Mexico, Australia, and New Zealand—the Habits of Mind approach is a comprehensive way for early childhood settings not only to implement a philosophical approach to learning and pedagogy, but also to create a mindful, respectful school culture. In such a culture, everyone—students, teachers, school leaders, and parents—is connected by shared values, positive expectations, and strong consistent modeling. The Habits of Mind offer a shared understanding of the language of learning.

The weaving of the Habits of Mind into the lives of all stakehold-ers, in a variety of cultural contexts, requires mindful thinking and collaboration, and that is one of the beauties of this approach. It can be woven into learning environments flexibly and in an emergent way that again shows how respectful and responsive it is to the rela-tionships that are at the core of early childhood education and care.

Acknowledging that students need to learn much more than just cognitive content, Habits of Mind embeds social and emotional learning into the day-by-day flow of the holistic educational journey, so that learners develop creative thinking, problem-solving skills, and resilience. Understandably, such an approach can seem daunt-ing, and so among the examples included in this book are those that explore the "getting started" phase, with messages from edu-cators on what helped and what was a challenge that needed to be addressed—ironically, by using Habits of Mind strategies. Messages and stories from families are also valuable, as they witness the posi-tive growth in their children's thinking and behavior.

The role that the Habits of Mind can play is more important than ever, as education has been disrupted by a focus on benchmark testing, which has come at a high cost: more student disengagement, higher levels of childhood anxiety and stress, teacher disillusion-ment and burnout, and a drop in the educational outcomes for many schools. The harmful denial of the importance of "soft skills" and the need for a more mindful approach to learning with our students are among the many reasons why this book is of such value. We can step forward knowing that shaping the minds of our youngest children with a respectful, well-researched approach that embraces the whole child must be a priority. Simply stated, we need to help children develop habits that will guide and nurture them throughout school and throughout their lives.

Young children learn so much from their key caregivers while they do the serious business of childhood—play. The Habits of Mind can become a helpful framework to embed the skills that enable

children to form meaningful relationships with family, educators, and their peers. In our digital landscape, I have serious concerns that children could lose the essential life skills needed to ponder deeply, be creative and magical, experience being brave, communicate their needs, and express themselves authentically.

This book is an inspirational, informative, and timely addition to the world of early childhood education. It will help those passionate educators who want to extend and enhance their current practice in a powerful, lasting way. The positive growth of an individual's sense of self in the early years is often left to instinct or chance. By becoming familiar with the Habits of Mind in the early years, children will build their thinking, communication, and inquisitiveness in a clearly guided manner that is embedded in the culture, community, and theory of action in their school. Creating lifelong learners who have the cognitive, emotional, and social competencies to navigate our ever-changing world needs to be a major focus in the early years, and the Habits of Mind will facilitate this aspiration.

Note: Maggie Dent is an Australian author, educator, and radio and TV commentator with a particular interest in the early years, adolescence, and resilience. She has been called Australia's Queen of Common Sense.

Acknowledgments

We express great appreciation to Genny Ostertag, Darcie Russell, and the editorial staff at ASCD for their skillful editorial refinement of the manuscript as well as their ongoing support and encouragement throughout the project.

We wish to acknowledge not only all the contributors to this book, but also all the teachers, administrators, support staff, and parents in all the communities around the world that have adopted and embraced the Habits of Mind. It is our hope that together we are making the world a more thoughtful, empathic, and peaceful place.

Introduction

Art Costa and Bena Kallick

A "habit of mind" means having a disposition toward behaving intelligently when confronted with problems. As educators, we are not only interested in how many answers students know, but also how they might behave when they do *not* know the answer. For example, when students are challenged by conditions that demand strategic reasoning, insightfulness, perseverance, creativity, and craftsmanship, we can help them learn to use the Habits of Mind (HOM) to facilitate their thinking. Habits of Mind are performed in response to questions, problems, and challenges to help find the answers to which are not immediately known.

The network of teachers and schools that practices Habits of Mind increases daily. We are honored that our research and work have been included in their daily practice. We are also highly appreciative of the educators who have contributed to this book. These educators have created and participated in HOM learning communities around the world and are eagerly sharing their experiences and successes with you. Their communities infuse HOM throughout the curriculum, use signs and signals throughout the school and in classrooms, invite and often train parents to use the habits, and

commit to the language and meaning of the habits to deepen, advocate, and sustain their use and meaning.

Indeed, using the Habits of Mind creates the potential for a transformational shift that opens learners' minds to possibilities as they become more effective thinkers and problem solvers. If we use the metaphor of an umbrella, the habits are the canopy of the umbrella and the ribs and spokes are strategies and tools that facilitate thinking. So, for example, a person must have the disposition and inclination to *think flexibly* before he can use the tool of creating a web of possibilities.

The images and descriptions in Figure 1 are a brief introduction to the 16 Habits of Mind. Each habit is specifically named as a set of behaviors—they all end with "-ing," implying that they are skills that we can always get better at performing. The shift from a fixed mindset to a growing mindset empowers today's learners to live with the volatility, uncertainty, complexity, and ambiguity that defines the world we live in. Despite changes, sometimes unanticipated, we can always think, problem solve, and work toward a better future.

Additional information about Habits of Mind, along with full definitions and descriptions, may be found in our previous book, *Learning and Leading with Habits of Mind* (Costa & Kallick, 2008).

Costa, A. L., & Kallick, B. (2008). *Learning and leading with habits of mind: 16 characteristics for success*. Alexandria, VA: ASCD.

Habits of Mind website is available at www.habitsofmindinstitute.org /resources/what-is-habits-of-mind/

Figure 1   **Habits of Mind**

Persisting: *Stick to it!* Persevering on a task through to completion; remaining focused; looking for ways to reach your goal when stuck; not giving up.

Managing impulsivity: *Take your time!* Thinking before acting; remaining calm, thoughtful, and deliberative.

Listening with understanding and empathy: *Understand others!* Devoting mental energy to another person's thoughts and ideas; making an effort to perceive another's point of view and emotions.

Thinking flexibly: *Look at it another way!* Being able to change perspectives, generate alternatives, consider options.

Thinking about thinking (metacognition): *Know your knowing!* Being aware of your own thoughts, strategies, feelings, and actions and their effects on others.

Striving for accuracy: *Check it again!* Always doing your best; setting high standards; checking and finding ways to improve constantly; searching for truth.

Questioning and posing problems: *How do you know?* Having a questioning attitude; knowing what data are needed and developing questioning strategies to produce those data; finding problems to solve.

Applying past knowledge to new situations: *Use what you learn!* Accessing prior knowledge; transferring knowledge beyond the situation in which it was learned.

Thinking and communicating with clarity and precision: *Be clear!* Striving for accurate communication in both written and oral form; avoiding overgeneralizations, distortions, deletions, and exaggerations.

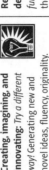

Gathering data through all senses: *Use your natural pathways!* Paying attention to the world around you; gathering data through all the senses: tasting, touching, smelling, hearing, and seeing.

Creating, imagining, and innovating: *Try a different way!* Generating new and novel ideas, fluency, originality.

Responding with wonderment and awe: *Have fun figuring it out!* Finding the world awesome and mysterious; being intrigued with phenomena and beauty.

Taking responsible risks: *Venture out!* Being adventuresome; living on the edge of your competence; trying new things constantly.

Finding humor: *Laugh a little!* Finding the whimsical, incongruous, and unexpected; being able to laugh at yourself.

Thinking interdependently: *Work together!* Being able to work with and learn from others in reciprocal situations; engaging in teamwork.

Remaining open to continuous learning: *There is so much more to learn!* Having humility and pride when admitting you don't know; resisting complacency.

Part I: Discovering and Exploring the Habits of Mind

What are the Habits of Mind and why are they important for young learners? These first few chapters will amaze you as you learn about what is happening in the developing minds and brains of preschool and early grades children—and why this is a critical time to introduce them to the habits.

As you become acquainted with the 16 Habits of Mind, we will give you insights and ideas about how to introduce them to your classroom, school, and community. It's an exciting, worthwhile adventure in helping young children learn about and interact with their world.

1

Brain Development in Children 2 to 7

Judy Willis

All experiences and interactions shape the human brain. The process of learning—including both building the brain's knowledge base and understanding information and experiences—is evidenced in the continual remodeling of the brain throughout life.

Despite the latest functional imaging brain scans, scientists cannot predict exactly what a given strategy or intervention will mean for an individual student. Functional magnetic resonance imaging (fMRI) measures changes in the metabolic activity and blood flow to areas of the brain that reflect the increased activity of cells in these regions. Because we know the functional anatomy related to regions and pathways through the brain, these images provide real-time pictures of how the brain responds in different conditions. Nevertheless, by understanding brain development during the critical years of early childhood and recognizing those interventions that best correlate with our growing insight, we can successfully enhance the positive influences of educators, parents, and other caregivers as they seek to promote children's highest potential brainpower and

realization of desirable goals (Knowland & Thomas, 2014). Thus, the vocabulary, actions, reflection, and modeling of the Habits of Mind at this age have a lifelong effect.

What's Happening in the Brain in Early Childhood

A long-held misconception contended that brain growth stops at birth, after which brain cells die throughout one's lifetime. Before neuroimaging was available to help us look at the workings of the brain, most neuroscientists believed that only young brains were plastic, or changeable. They believed not only that all the brain's memory-holding cells (neurons) were present at birth but also that all or most of the connections between these neurons developed in the first year of childhood and then became permanent. We now know that lifelong growth of the supporting and connecting cells enriching the communication between neurons, allied with associated increases in cognition and social-emotional skill sets, actively continues far beyond that first year.

The brain's most rapid growth occurs during gestation, when the production rate of neurons in the fetus reaches up to 250,000 per minute (Cowan, 1979). However, an intense second period of accelerated growth occurs between ages 2 and 7, followed by another rapid maturation phase extending through adolescence into the teen years.

In the first year or two after birth, most of the brain's development and activity is programmed for automatic, involuntary, reflexive, and reactive behaviors and information acquisition to ensure survival and fulfill children's basic needs. What makes this time of their lives and brain development so exciting is the accelerated rate and enhanced responsiveness with which they construct new connections between neurons. It's important to keep in mind, though, that each child develops at a unique pace. This chapter focuses on the rapid growth phase between ages 2 and 7, as their brains

dramatically establish the wiring conducive to information storage, understanding, and communication.

Although experience-responsive brain growth occurs throughout our lives, the brain structures respond particularly robustly to learning experiences, environment influences, and emotional interactions during these childhood years. With maturation, brain development shifts from its focus on survival, pleasure seeking, and pain avoidance to expanded networks guiding more goal-directed skills and management of our environment, behaviors, and emotions. The brain's structural changes with this maturation are reflected in children's accelerating understanding; skills; and cognitive, social, and emotional maturation. Understanding the cellular and structural changes going on in children's brains from ages 2 to 7 provides a foundation for promoting the construction of neural networks to help them reach their greatest potential.

Neuroplasticity generates these changes in neural networks in response to learning, enhanced by each new or repeated activation of the network. Brain development and intelligence are plastic. Internal and environmental stimuli constantly change the structure and neural networks triggered by response to physical, cognitive, or emotional experiences; ideas; memory activation; or sensory intake.

Neuroplasticity is one of the most exciting areas of research in the neuroscience of learning and the brain. Research reveals evidence that all brains have the potential to become better and all students smarter, especially with guidance and encouragement. The changes that take place over time represent the lifelong growth and augmentation of the connecting cells that support and allow communication between neurons. Thus, input, experience, and practice result in enhanced efficiency of information processing by boosting neuron-to-neuron communication, with increased growth of dendrites, axonal myelin, and synapses. Dendrites and axons are the wiring that connects neurons to each other. The point of contact

between the information-carrying outgoing axon and the dendrite that will carry information to the next neuron is called the synapse. Myelin is the axon power-boosting coating that is like a layer of insulation when the circuit is repeatedly used, making information travel faster and memory storage stronger.

Use It or Lose It

Part of what occurs during brain maturation is the use-it-or-lose-it phenomenon of *pruning*. As the most frequently used networks mature and develop more connections, myelin, and synapses, the least frequently used networks are pruned away. This process increases the brain's efficiency and strengthens those networks used most often. It also increases the brain's efficiency to allow more of its limited supply of oxygen and glucose to be available for the most active pathways.

Pruning intensifies during the third or fourth year of life, when it includes neurons not used as part of connecting circuits and small connections of neurons, axons, and dendrites receiving little activation. This process is visualized on imaging as thinning of the cortical gray matter strip, which forms the outermost part of the brain.

Because pruning depends on which information is used, the environment plays an increasingly important role in determining which connections are maintained or lost in children's brains. A give-and-take streamlining process takes place, as eliminating excess material allows more efficient processing. As the number of small, unused neuronal circuits decreases, the number of neural connections expands in response to use, and the brain develops into a much faster and more sophisticated organ. Because of this plasticity, teachers, parents, and caregivers become the brain changers who can promote learning by providing experiences that activate children's neural networks, allowing their brains to construct meaningful memories and knowledge.

Practice Makes Permanent

Memory can be thought of as the construction, expansion, and strengthening of neural networks in response to activation. Let's now consider what factors influence the construction of durable memory networks. Each time a network holding a memory is activated—perhaps the meaning of a word or a skill such as kicking a ball—the neuroplastic response is stimulated, strengthening the networks of connections among the neurons, each holding pieces of the memory. It is the mental manipulation of learning (practice, rehearsal, using information in new ways) that makes these networks grow stronger, faster, and more durable (Chang, 2015; Neumann, Lotze, & Eickhoff, 2016).

During their early years, children learn very quickly through experience. A child's natural curiosity drives investigation, careful observation (visual and auditory), and motivated memory construction. Reading favorite books to children is one example of how strong memories are built. These memories are embodied by children's accurate and enthusiastic verbal predictions of "what comes next." Information driven by curiosity, personal relevance, and association with pleasure or satisfaction is more likely to be remembered when it is carefully observed and revisited, particularly when it is experienced through multiple senses (Thomas, 2016).

New memories of information, tasks, and skills must be activated or practiced, or they will be pruned. Even if instruction—say, for decoding words during the last month of school—is successful, the same literacy skill may not carry over to the following school year. It takes practice, repetitive use of the pathway, and review to retain stored learning in neural networks. If students do no further work with the words for the intervening months, pruning will likely eliminate many of the constructed networks.

Regions of Brain Maturation During Childhood

The growth and pruning process that takes place in response to activation or use of the circuits continues through our lifetime. On a

larger developmental scale, whole regions of the brain follow a predictable, age-related, regional progression of growth and pruning described as *maturation*. The physical changes in a region undergoing its rapid maturation phase essentially consist of accelerated neuroplasticity. There is more vigorous pruning of the networks previously constructed but unused, and a more exuberant myelination of the networks that are activated and used most frequently.

The cerebral cortex is where the maturation process, with its phases of cognitive and emotional development, is most evident. The cerebral cortex comprises the outer layers of the brain. The outermost layer, *gray matter*, and below that a thicker layer, *white matter*, constitute the majority of the cerebral cortex. Gray matter consists of neurons, end branches of axons, dendrites, and synapses. White matter is so named because it contains bundles of myelinated axons. The white color of the myelin gives the region its lighter color.

The changes related to childhood brain maturation involve phases of increases in gray matter, followed by decreases overlying an ongoing accumulation of white matter (Shaw et al., 2006). Gray matter first goes through its most accelerated phase of maturation in the posterior and lower regions of the brain (directing the basic functions, such as digestion, and driving the rapid, reactive responses to perceived threat or unexpected change). Next to undergo rapid maturation, peaking between ages 3 and 5, are the sensory and motor control centers of the brain. This sequence seems logical, considering that younger children experience their world through their senses and continually build their motor skills to more successfully satisfy their needs and later their curiosity.

These peaks are followed by a more gradual reduction in gray matter over a period of years. Many of the connections and small networks constructed during the young child's early experiences are inconsistently reactivated (recalled, experienced, used) and thus pruned. The more accelerated phase of growth between ages 5 and 7

takes place in the higher cognitive and social-emotional processing regions of the prefrontal and temporal lobe cortices. Subsequently the frontal lobes display more active pruning and myelin formation as neural networks of executive function develop. This is the last and longest rapid maturation phase, extending through the teens into the early 20s (Gogtay et al., 2004).

As we age, the size of the cerebral cortex grows, augmented by learning and experience. The expansion of myelin and the ever-increasing extension of dendrites and synapses connecting neurons into circuits of related information amplify rapid and efficient communication between neurons in the maturing cortex. The thicker layering of myelin speeds the transmission of the electrical messages, enabling them to jump over sections of the axon (a process called *saltatory conduction*) rather than having to travel more slowly through its entire length (Shaw et al., 2006).

Activating Brain Networks During Their Accelerated Maturation

Considering that maturation in the brain increases its efficiency, it follows that the brain is more responsive to molding of its neural networks during children's rapid maturation periods of heightened neuroplastic response. Recognizing which regions are undergoing rapid maturation at a particular time should not limit learning experiences to these phases of brain development alone. The brain continues to be responsive throughout life. Nevertheless, such recognition can help promote awareness of types of experiences and environments that might be most fruitful at any given stage.

For example, between ages 3 and 5, during peaks of rapid maturation of the sensory and motor control centers of the brain, children are particularly engaged by sensory and motor experiences. Consider the eagerness preschoolers have for exploring objects

through multiple senses, exemplified by their tendency to jump into every puddle they pass. These are also "sweet spots" in time for experiencing the Habits of Mind. Later, as children's brains begin the more vigorous phase of growth in the prefrontal and temporal lobe cortices, the potential arises to promote neuroplastic growth in the regions associated with higher cognitive and social-emotional processing.

Development of the Neural Networks of Executive Functions

As noted earlier, the neural networks that direct executive functions develop in the prefrontal cortex and begin their extended maturation starting around age 5. These networks are what give children increasing voluntary control over their attention focus, inhibitory control, delay of gratification, emotional self-awareness and self-management, interpersonal relationships and empathy, goal-directed behavior, planning and prioritizing, critical thinking, judgment, reasoning, and flexibility of thinking and adaptability. All these executive functions contribute to a child's potential to achieve a fulfilling and joyful life.

Although this section focuses on the prefrontal cortex developing executive functions, other foundational experiences and exposures are strongly linked to success in school and life. For example, there is a strong association between parents' language use and interaction patterns and children's language development (Huttenlocher, Vasilyeva, Cymerman, & Levine, 2002).

Research supports the idea that the strength of children's executive functions serves as one of the best predictors of school readiness, including social-emotional and academic competence and the development of literacy and numeracy (Allan, Hume, Allan, Farrington, & Lonigan, 2014; Kim, Nordling, Yoon, Boldt,

& Kochanska, 2013). Using brain imaging and monitoring of the electrical signals produced by activated brain networks, we can see evidence of increased response in children's developing neural networks of executive functions when they are activated and used. For example, activation of the prefrontal cortex is seen in young children when they use the executive function networks for behavioral inhibition, such as suppressing an automatic response during delay of immediate gratification (Stevens & Bavelier, 2012).

Given the central role of executive functions in school readiness, and the correlation of early school success with later success in school and life, it is relevant to consider which executive functions are most strongly correlated with that readiness and how interventions could enhance the neuroplastic strengthening of these networks during early childhood. A study of 100 children ages 2 to 5 evaluated their performance on a variety of tasks that rely on executive functions in relation to academic and social school readiness. The findings indicated that the ability to delay gratification was a manifestation of developing social-emotional skills, such as self-regulation. Along with inhibitory control (the ability to filter irrelevant information), skills of self-regulation were prominent predictors of academic readiness (Mann, Hund, Hesson-McInnis, & Roman, 2017)—a finding that relates to such Habits of Mind as *managing impulsivity, thinking about thinking (metacognition),* and *listening with empathy.* This and other studies provide support for the importance of the development of social-emotional as well as academic competence in preparing children for school readiness, peer relationships, positive attitudes toward school, emotional self-management, and academic achievement (Blair & Razza, 2007; Mann et al., 2017; Razza & Raymond, 2015).

Additional studies evaluated neuroplastic growth and brain network strength in children burdened by delays, high stress, and low socioeconomic environments. These studies linked improvements in children's attention, cognition, and language to

interventions designed to increase activation of their executive function networks (Neville, Stevens, & Pakulak, 2013; Stevens, Lauinger, & Neville, 2009).

Because low-functioning foundational neural networks related to executive function and cognition can have extensive consequences for later learning, it is reasonable to promote the environments and experiences that are linked to promoting more successful development (Blair & Razza, 2007; Razza & Raymond, 2015). Recommendations for promoting activation of components of the executive function networks for all children during these early years—through facilitated play, games supporting inhibitory control, building empathy, and parental guidance—are a vital part of the content of this book. The rest of this section will suggest categories or characteristics of some interventions supporting the developmental opportunities in young children's brains.

Attention Focus and Goal-Directed Behaviors

The executive functions have numerous isolated aspects that can be activated with deliberate attention focus and plans or actions to achieve specific goals. The distinctions are useful both for research specificity and guidance for recognizing opportunities to promote the activation of these executive function networks. For example, *distraction inhibition* and *sustained focus* are built into games like Follow the Leader; Red Light, Green Light; and Simon Says. *Delay of gratification* is another self-control component; this skill set gained attention with the research by Walter Mischel and colleagues in the 1960s and '70s that has come to be known as the Marshmallow Test. After developing an initial play activity with the researcher, a 4- or 5-year-old child was shown a marshmallow and promised a reward of two marshmallows for waiting until the researcher came back (15 minutes later). The reported correlations 10 and more years later found that the children who could delay gratification and wait for the two marshmallows had (on average) higher SAT scores, more job satisfaction,

higher income, more stable marriages, and better health (Mischel, Ebbesen, & Raskoff-Zeiss, 1972; Mischel, Shoda, & Rodriguez, 1989).

Opportunities to help children build their delay of gratification or other impulse controls are abundant. They may simply consist of being aware of not wresting control away from children but rather helping them recognize the consequences of taking a toy away from a friend or not waiting their turn by recalling how they felt when they were the target of others' impulsive behaviors. Identifying the benefits of successfully delaying immediate gratification to achieve a goal (for example, by taking the time to look for things they need to bring home from the classroom instead of racing out the door when dismissed) has a similar impact. This skill set is what children need to persevere when facing the challenges and setbacks natural to the processes of developing literacy, building successful collaboration skills, and achieving emotional self-management.

As children reach preschool age, there are opportunities to help them recognize both their self-efficacy and goal-building strategies. Registering their progress and sustained efforts, rather than just the end products, is useful. When children are prompted to predict what they will need to do next or in an upcoming situation—for example, what type of voice they will use when they get to the library or what supplies they'll need to keep a new goldfish healthy—they activate goal planning.

Building skills to take on challenges, overcome obstacles, and persevere after mistakes is essential to developing the executive functions of sustained attention focus and goal-directed behaviors. Young children are just beginning to wire in these control systems, and they need opportunities to activate skills to increase their tolerance for frustration.

Conversations about "what if?" can promote children's thinking about strategies and opening themselves to alternatives. These questions could be asking them what they could do if they saw two

friends pushing to get to the same toy or to think about what has made them happy in past times when they were sad. Ultimately, providing more and more time for them to struggle before stepping in will promote their own resilience and self-directed control networks.

Judgment and Flexible Thinking

Building children's self-management as they develop their neural networks and skill sets allows them to be consciously aware of, and to control, their emotions and work toward goals. This skill will guide their future decision making, judgment, and peer relationships.

Opportunities to help activate their developing executive function networks for judgment and flexible thinking are most authentic and meaningful when integrated into their daily experiences and activities. These can start with choices about clothes to wear or food options and ultimately evolve to richer decisions about relationships as they consider how their behavior affects others.

Opportunities to promote flexible thinking (cognitive flexibility) can further activate developing neural networks related to executive function. When giving young children a new toy, instead of showing them the "right" way to use it, encourage them to first explore it independently. They will often sustain interest longer and find innovative ways to engage with it.

Guide children to recognize how differences can be positives when exploring unfamiliar playgrounds, new cities, or diverse cultures. They can experience information through multiple perspectives, such as the variety of translated versions of the Cinderella story as represented in other countries or putting themselves into the persona of several different characters in a book.

Emotional Self-management

We recognize that emotional development takes place throughout life. Notably, though, it is during the early years that the

increased sensitivity and responsiveness in the regions of the brain associated with higher cognitive and social-emotional processing serve all children especially well. Recall that the cortical networks most responsible for coordinating emotional responses in the pre-frontal, temporal, and parietal cortices are highly active in neuro-plastic growth and pruning during these years. The cross-connecting among these regions has distinctive relevance in emotional devel-opment. What we see is burgeoning wiring evolving in the myelin-ated communications between subcortical emotional response areas and those regions of the prefrontal cortex that make up systems for control of executive function. These "top-down" communication networks under construction in their brains are critical for success-ful emotional processing, rational thinking, judgment, goal-directed behaviors, interpretation of social or emotional cues, and decision making.

An example of one such development is the social interaction skills that begin to emerge around age 3 as children become more aware of and responsive to the gestures, facial expressions, and actions of others and begin to connect these interpretations to what the other person is feeling. This awareness reflects the development of stronger communication between the neural networks in the prefrontal cortex and those that direct emotional processing in the amygdala and related regions of the temporal lobe.

If the sensory input from a facial expression to the amygdala is simultaneously accompanied by strong emotions, such as plea-sure, happiness, fear, or anxiety, the previously neutral sensory input becomes identified with the emotion in an associational neural network. Those linkages, if reinforced, lead to more automatic or generalizable emotional interpretations of facial expressions. This example illustrates how children develop the emotional patterns or association learning that triggers the brain to respond to future similar input or experiences.

Because the reinforced associations children develop become solid neural response networks, it becomes critical to observe their responses and intervene if they are developing strong negative associations. This situation might emerge when associations are incorrect, hurtful, or limiting, and they can undermine children's future social and emotional foundations. Guidance and interventions can be framed around experiences that build children's understanding of and respect for others.

As they build empathy, children activate their communications for "top-down" executive management for reflection instead of automatic reactions. Helping them with opportunities to understand and incorporate other points of view will promote their facilities for building peer relationships with warmth and trust.

Using the example of building higher-order processing of emotions by increasing awareness of emotional cues, teachers can provide guided experiences, such as asking children to interpret the meaning of facial expressions as they read books and hear stories. When children are prompted to describe how a person with a clear facial expression is feeling, they are moving toward the goal of reflecting on other people's perspectives as guides to their interactions. By identifying emotions depicted in emojis, picture books, and stories, children can be primed to be more aware of and verbal about their own emotions. When they can identify their feelings, they will be more facile at accessing the neural networks needed to calm themselves or reflect before acting. Guided play with other children in which they take on the characters of people in different jobs, or of different ages or backgrounds, provides experiential opportunities for them to further expand their perspectives.

As children get older and develop more control over executive function, there are increased opportunities to promote more independent self-management of emotions through their peer interactions. Again, not jumping in with immediate solutions helps them to build

their skill sets of handling interpersonal conflicts constructively, allowing them the chance to experience their emotions and the consequences of their actions—good and bad.

Teaching children ways to calm themselves so they can better maneuver through their interactions with others takes time, guidance, and practice. However, these efforts provide profound value as children are exposed to ever-increasing stresses. We know that chronic stress can have a negative impact on areas of brain development critical to memory, attention, language, and cognition; and coping tools built early will reduce the impact of later stressors (Lupien, McEwen, Gunnar, & Heim, 2009).

Young children's emotional responses are still strongly influenced by the "bottom-up" feed from the emotionally reactive amygdala and their brain's instinctual drives to seek pleasure and avoid pain, real or imagined. Just suggesting strategies to ameliorate stress, such as counting to 10, deep breathing, or mindfulness, though perhaps useful in the moment, is inadequate to promote the strong, fast, and easily retrievable control networks that young children need to self-manage and override their immediate, involuntary reactions.

It takes guided experiences over time, providing frequent opportunities for children to stimulate these neural network control systems, for emotional self-awareness and self-management to be incorporated as Habits of Mind. The repeated practices of self-calming strategies, including mindful breathing, calming visualizations, and activating optimistic memories, will facilitate the neuroplasticity that builds the dendrites, anonal myelin, and synapses. With those strong, durable, easily retrievable neural networks, children will have automatic, rapid access to these valuable skills whenever they are needed.

* * *

As you read this book, you'll acquire tools to help children reach their highest potential as joyful learners by engaging their brains' neuroplasticity. As the important brain changers you are, you'll gain more awareness and the skill sets to promote those learning environments and experiences that activate children's neural networks. They will develop the tools needed to construct knowledge about themselves and their world and the Habits of Mind needed to embrace the challenges and opportunities that lie ahead.

Allan, N., Hume, L., Allan, D., Farrington, A., & Lonigan, C. (2014). Relations between self-regulation and the development of academic skills in preschool and kindergarten: A meta-analysis. *Developmental Psychology, 50b* (10), 2368–2379.

Blair, C., & Razza, R. P. (2007). Relating effortful control, executive function, and false-belief understanding to emerging math and literacy ability in kindergarten. *Child Development, 78,* 647–663.

Chang, Y. (2015). Reorganization and plastic changes of the human brain associated with skill learning and expertise. In M. Bilalić, R. Langner, G. Campitelli, L. Turella, & W. Grodd (Eds.), *Neural implementations of expertise* (pp. 56–62). Lausanne, Switzerland: Frontiers Media SA.

Cowan, W. (1979). The development of the brain. *Scientific American, 241*(3), 113–133.

Gogtay, N., Giedd, J., Lusk, L., Hayashi, K., Greenstein, D., Vaituzis, A., . . . Thompson, P. (2004). Dynamic mapping of human cortical development during childhood through early adulthood. *Proceedings of the National Academy of Sciences of the USA, 101*(21), 8174–8179.

Huttenlocher, J., Vasilyeva, M., Cymerman, E., & Levine, S. (2002). Language input and child syntax. *Cognitive Psychology, 45*(3), 337–374.

Kim, S., Nordling, J., Yoon, J., Boldt, L. J., & Kochanska, G. (2013). Effortful control in "hot" and "cool" tasks differentially predicts children's behavior problems and academic performance. *Journal of Abnormal Child Psychology, 41,* 43–56.

Knowland, V., & Thomas, M. (2014). Educating the adult brain: How the neuroscience of learning can inform educational policy. *International Review of Education, 60,* 99–122.

Lent, R., Azevedo, F., Andrade-Morales, C., & Pinto, A. (2012). How many neurons do you have? *European Journal of Neuroscience, 35*(1), 1–9.

Lupien, S. J., McEwen, B. S., Gunnar, M. R., & Heim, C. (2009). Effects of stress throughout the lifespan on the brain, behavior and cognition. *National Review of Neuroscience, 10*(6), 434–445.

Mann, T., Hund, A., Hesson-McInnis, M., & Roman, Z. (2017). Pathways to school readiness: Executive functioning predicts academic and social-emotional aspects of school readiness. *Mind, Brain and Education, 11*(1), 21–31.

Mischel, W., Ebbesen, E., & Raskoff-Zeiss, A. (1972). Cognitive and attentional mechanisms in delay of gratification. *Journal of Personality and Social Psychology, 21*(2), 204–218.

Mischel, W., Shoda, Y., & Rodriguez, M. (1989). Delay of gratification in children. *Science, 244*(4907), 933–938.

Neumann, N., Lotze, M., & Eickhoff, S. (2016). Cognitive expertise: An ALE meta-analysis. *Human Brain Mapping, 37*(1), 262–272.

Neville, H. J., Stevens, C., & Pakulak, E. (2013). Family-based training program improves brain function, cognition, and behavior in lower socioeconomic status preschoolers. *Proceedings of the National Academy of Sciences of the USA, 110*(29), 12138–12143.

Pakkenberg, B., Pelvig, D., Marner, L., Bundgaard, M., Gundersen, H. J., Nyengaard, J. R., & Regeur, L. (2003). Aging and the human neocortex. *Experimental Gerontology, 38*(1–2), 95–99.

Razza, R., & Raymond, K. (2015). Executive functions and school readiness: Identifying multiple pathways for school success. In S. Robson & S. F. Quinn (Eds.), *Routledge International Handbook of Young Children's Thinking and Understanding* (pp. 133–149). New York: Routledge.

Shaw, P., Greenstein, D., Lerch, J., Clasen, L., Lenroot, R., Gogtay, N., . . . Giedd, J. (2006). Intellectual ability and cortical development in children and adolescents. *Nature, 440*(7084), 676–679.

Stevens, C., & Bavelier, D. (2012). The role of selective attention on academic foundations: A cognitive neuroscience perspective. *Developmental Cognitive Neuroscience, 2*(Suppl 1), S30–S48.

Stevens, C., Lauinger, B., & Neville, H. (2009). Differences in the neural mechanisms of selective attention in children from different socioeconomic backgrounds: An event-related brain potential study. *Developmental Science, 12*(4), 634–646.

Thomas, M. (2016). Do more intelligent brains retain heightened plasticity for longer in development? A computational investigation. *Developmental Cognitive Neuroscience, 19*, 258–269.

2

Introducing the Habits of Mind in the Early Childhood Classroom

Donna Tobey

There's a lot of talk these days about the need to prepare children for a world vastly different from the one in which they live today. In December 2012, the National Intelligence Council issued its fifth report since 1997 with predictions about what this world might look like. The report suggests "megatrends" for the future, such as an increase in the middle class that will create additional strain on resources such as food, water, and energy; changing demographics with increased mobility; and a change in the structure of those countries influencing the world from one hegemonic power to a coalition of world powers collaborating on issues of importance. The report, titled *Global Trends 2030: Alternative Worlds*, should be of significant interest to those working with young children, as the children in today's early childhood classrooms will be entering the workforce in 2030.

At Palm Beach Day Academy, an independent school in West Palm Beach, Florida, we are preparing our young children today for an adult world that they will enter in 2030. Given the rapidly

changing environment in which we are living, we are always asking ourselves how we can create an environment for learning that remains developmentally appropriate yet addresses the dispositions that will foster the type of "minds" needed in 2030. We have been devoting considerable time to reflecting on this question. Working with experts in the area of developing thinking such as Bena Kallick and Art Costa and participating in professional development opportunities such as Harvard University's Project Zero Classroom (http://www.pz.harvard.edu/projects/making-learning-visible), we have come to realize that the way to address this question is through promoting thinking dispositions. Our experience over the past several years confirms that it *is* possible to expose and instill powerful patterns of thinking in young children that create a foundation for the more complex thinking that will serve them throughout their school years and beyond.

A few months ago, when we were asked to share some of the work we were doing with respect to developing the Habits of Mind in our early childhood classrooms, my reaction was "We'd love to!" followed shortly thereafter by "How can I frame what we do?" It was while tending to my orchid collection and taking a walk through a local botanical garden that I made a connection between my hobby of growing orchids and developing the Habits of Mind in young children. The following sections describe what I learned.

Start with a Sense of Purpose

When I first embarked on my quest to learn more about orchids, I did not realize where it was going to take me. My purpose at the time was simple: I wanted to be able to sustain the life of a beautiful, living organism rather than toss it away. Because I truly knew nothing about orchids, I needed to stick with my purpose to accomplish this goal.

For the past several years, Palm Beach Day Academy has examined what it means to be preparing students for the future. Spending

time in the summer at Harvard's Project Zero has helped us to consider questions such as "What's worth learning?" and "How do we create a culture for that type of learning to take place?" We've created professional learning communities to help us better understand approaches that focus on thinking, such as the work being done in the early childhood centers in Reggio Emilia, Italy. David Perkins, senior researcher at Project Zero, often speaks to the fact that we are "educating for the unknown." Given that idea, we felt it was crucial that we help our students, whatever their age, to develop the ability to think. This then became our purpose—to create a *community of thinkers*.

Become a Student Yourself

I did not grow up in South Florida. Having been raised in the Chicago area, I had no knowledge of how to grow or care for orchids. So I began reading books and magazines and checking the internet for information. Fortunately, South Florida is home to some of the world's best orchid growers, and the smartest thing I did was to visit their nurseries to hear directly from the experts about their experiences and to garner their advice. Because of their passion for the subject, I spent many hours speaking with them and gathering tips that I could use in my backyard.

Learning about the Habits of Mind was not dissimilar. Fortunately, I had read the Habits of Mind books several years earlier and believed that instilling these dispositions would contribute greatly to developing thinkers and the type of culture we were seeking in our school. Working with Bena Kallick and Art Costa as our "thinking experts" allowed us to learn more about ways to implement the habits into the fabric of the curriculum. We became the students. Reading books by practitioners who had implemented the Habits of Mind in their classrooms provided models of successful practices.

Know That Many Things Can Happily Coexist

Although I would say that I have a passion for orchids, I also have an interest in just about anything that grows. Recently I started a raised-bed vegetable garden and a small herb garden. All of these happily coexist in my backyard. In fact, if I were to have all of one or all of another, I would lose the sensory experiences that the diversity of my backyard brings to me.

In our early childhood classrooms, a similar type of diversity exists, and it is the blending of instructional strategies and tools that allows very powerful types of thinking to take place. Several years ago, we began using Thinking Maps (http://www.thinkingmaps .org) in all of our Lower School classrooms, from our preprimary boys and girls (2-year-olds) right up through 3rd grade. All of the faculty members, including special area teachers, were trained in the use of the maps, and students began to use Thinking Maps in developmentally appropriate ways. For example, whereas older children might create the maps on paper, something as simple as a hula hoop became an excellent hands-on tool for our preprimary and primary youngsters to create a circle map to help define a concept.

Thinking routines, particularly the routines made popular through the Visible Thinking project at Harvard, became staples in our teachers' toolboxes. Eventually, when appropriate, the thinking routines and maps were combined to further deepen understanding and make children's thinking visible.

Habits of Mind are a natural fit with this work. Although we are still exploring the most appropriate way to introduce and use the verbiage with the very youngest children as we do with the older students, the dispositions *are* being developed on a daily basis. From time to time a habit is explicitly named, such as when a child *persists* with a task or shows *empathy and understanding*. But we do this in a developmentally appropriate way and, usually, within the context of something that naturally occurs.

Realize That Some Things Develop Quickly, Some Things Take Time

The orchid grower must be patient and realize that not all orchids bloom at the same time and with the same frequency. This reality was something I had to learn and come to expect. While certain orchids are frequent bloomers and produce robust sprays of flowers, others bloom just once a year — and sometimes not even once a year. And although that may be the case, all orchids in my garden get the same attention and care.

The same can be said for developing the Habits of Mind with young children. Some habits can be internalized quickly, whereas the acquisition and understanding of other habits may take more time or require repeated exposures to have the disposition become a habit. Just like various types of orchids, some habits bloom quickly and others take a year or two to get established.

Given that our Lower School campus encompasses children from age 2 through those in 3rd grade, we have been able to watch this development happen naturally with respect to the acquisition of an understanding of the Habits of Mind. Our experience has been that children in our preprimary (age 2) and primary (ages 3–5) classes can begin to develop some of the habits through learning activities that typically occur in the classroom. We became more intentional as our children began to develop print awareness. We displayed the Habits of Mind on bulletin boards, and teachers started to use the language explicitly, such as "I love the way you *persisted* in drawing your illustration!"). Students began to recognize when the habits were being used and started to understand the need for a habit as, for example, when they needed to *think interdependently* as they played a challenging game.

By 3rd grade, the Habits of Mind were deeply rooted in what happened in the classroom on a daily basis. Students now clearly understood what the habits were and could identify *when* they were being employed. This understanding allowed them to monitor their

behavior in a very conscious way as well as use the Habits of Mind to inform their choices as a community of learners working together. Lessons were enhanced, as when characters in literature were analyzed in terms of their use of the habits.

Understand That Culture and Conditions Make a Difference

I now belong to two orchid societies in the Palm Beach area. We meet once a month, and each meeting features a guest speaker as well as "show and tell" by members as they share orchids from their own collections that are in bloom. The beauty of the meetings is that people who are passionate about orchids share their tips about how to grow beautiful specimens. Often conversations take place about the "culture" needed (the material one uses to plant the orchid), proper fertilizing techniques, or how to provide just the right conditions for a particular plant with respect to lighting requirements or water. Culture and conditions make all the difference in having success as an orchid grower.

In much the same way, having the right "culture and conditions" is essential for growing the Habits of Mind in a school. Fortunately, as a faculty, we all saw the benefit to and critical need for developing *thinkers*. Basic skills will simply not be enough for this generation of children. Once that belief was firmly rooted in our decision making, we focused on creating that culture of thinking. Doing so meant training teachers who could then inform students, valuing this type of approach to support the efforts of teachers, providing information to parents, and staying the course with what we were trying to do. The end result was a "thought-full" culture where students were developing patterns of behavior that will serve them now and in the future.

Share the Joy, Reap the Harvest

As any gardener will attest to, the greatest joy is when we reap the harvest of our efforts. Whether it be enjoying food from a bountiful vegetable garden

or arranging flowers from a cutting garden, enjoying the fruits of our labors is rewarding and keeps us wanting to repeat past successes again. While visiting the American Orchid Society headquarters one afternoon, I overheard someone say, "It's like giving birth when you step outside and see an orchid in bloom."

In schools, the joy is seeing what happens with the students as they truly understand the Habits of Mind and begin applying them to their daily lives. Because these are skills that will serve them well not only now but throughout their lives, it's like a gift that keeps on giving—much like the orchid that reblooms and gives great joy year after year.

Recently we have been enjoying an innovative tool for bringing the Habits of Mind to life for our students. The Institute for Habits of Mind, in collaboration with WonderGrove Studios, has created a set of videos that can be shown and discussed with children. The videos use the same set of cartoon characters to help children learn about each habit. These three- to four-minute videos present children with a conflict or problem and the strategies for resolving the problem using a specific Habit of Mind. (For more on the videos, see Chapters 9 and 10.)

Our piloting of the videos has taken place with students in pre-kindergarten, kindergarten, and grade 1. In addition to the videos, teachers are provided with ancillary learning activities that can be used to deepen a child's understanding. As we pilot the use of the videos, we are finding that children are completely engaged while they watch and enjoy the follow-up activities as well. Given the success that we have experienced, we plan to expand the use of the videos to grade 2. We also plan to make the videos available to our parent community, providing another opportunity to strengthen the home-school connection and bridge what's happening at school with the home environment.

Grow a Network, Create a Future

I recently joined a Facebook group called "Newbie Florida Orchid Growers." The group is growing day by day with numerous posts and questions from people new to the art of growing orchids along with very experienced growers. I enjoy checking the site a couple of times a week because it connects me with others who have a similar passion. I have an opportunity to answer questions posed, as well as have my questions answered. There is a congeniality and willingness to support one another that will ultimately benefit all.

That same sharing can take place among educators who believe in the value of developing the Habits of Mind in young children. The internet allows people around the world to connect and establish a network of individuals committed to this shared vision. It behooves all of us to take advantage of every opportunity we can to learn from others and share our collective wisdom. Doing so will ultimately benefit the children in our care and better prepare them for the world we know they will inherit in 2030 and beyond.

3

Implementing the Habits of Mind in an International School in Mexico

Diana Garza

San Roberto International School in Monterrey, Mexico, is a values-focused institution that serves students from prenursery to 9th grade, with instruction provided mainly in English. We began our journey with the Habits of Mind in 2008, shortly after our general director and our Values Department coordinator attended a course in Florida organized by the Teacher Training Center for International Educators. The course, titled "The Heart of Teaching: Beyond Content" and presented by educational consultant and author Jennifer Abrams, introduced them to the Habits of Mind, and they became convinced that it was what the school was looking for to provide our students with the lifelong skills that would enable them to make wise choices. Through the Habits of Mind we could enrich our students' experience in both academics and values and character education.

The school formed a committee of teachers and administrators from different areas, grade levels, and campuses. This committee was in charge of investigating ideas and resources, and it appointed an implementation leader to develop a six-year plan for the school.

During 2009–2010 we began implementing our plan by pro-viding professional development on the Habits of Mind to various stakeholders: parents, preschool teachers, administrators, and staff. We wanted to introduce the adults—especially teachers and administrators—to the habits so they could experience their own development of the habits before teaching them to our students.

During 2010–2011, we began introducing the Habits of Mind to the five divisions of the preschool:

- Prenursery (ages 17–29 months)
- Nursery (ages 2 years, 6 months–3 years, 4 months)
- Preschool I (ages 3 years, 5 months–4 years, 5 months)
- Preschool II (ages 4 years, 6 months–5 years, 5 months)
- Preprimary (ages 5 years, 6 months–6 years, 5 months)

We also continued training teachers at those levels, and we began offering training to parents and all nonteaching personnel.

As an international school, we completed a new cycle in 2016 within our accreditation process, which has included the creation of a new mission and vision statements. Inspired by these, the Habits of Mind Committee developed a five-year plan to ensure our contin-uous growth in the development of the Habits of Mind.

A Closer Look at Implementation

The school followed a sequence of steps to create a program that would lead to fostering knowledge on intelligent behaviors. We agreed that all 16 Habits of Mind would be part of the program and that development of the habits should occur during the students' time at school from Prenursery to 9th grade.

We studied the main characteristics and abilities of people at different stages of development of the habits, and we created student, parent, and teacher profiles to try to define the characteristics that would guide us in determining the Habits of Mind to emphasize

at different age levels. We distributed the habits in developmental stages, shown in Figure 3.1.

Our intent in allocating specific Habits of Mind to the developmental stages was not to suggest that those habits should be the only

Figure 3.1   **Levels at Which Habits Are Taught at San Roberto International School**

HABIT OF MIND	Prenursery–Preschool II	Preprimary	1st–2nd Grade	3rd–5th Grade	6th–9th Grade
Persisting	★	★	★	★	★
Managing impulsivity	★	★	★	★	
Listening with understanding and empathy	★	★	★	★	★
Gathering data through all senses	★	★	★	★	★
Creating, imagining, and innovating		★	★	★	★
Responding with wonderment and awe		★	★	★	★
Finding humor			★	★	★
Remaining open to continuous learning			★	★	★
Thinking flexibly				★	★
Questioning and posing problems				★	★
Applying past knowledge to new situations				★	★
Thinking and communicating with clarity and precision				★	★
Thinking interdependently					★
Taking responsible risks					★
Striving for accuracy					★
Thinking about thinking (metacognition)					★

Source: San Roberto International School, Monterrey, Nuevo León, Mexico. Used with permission.

ones reinforced by teachers with their students, but rather that they be given a special focus. The scope and sequence of the Habits of Mind would ensure that during the span of time spent in the school, from preschool to graduation, students would have developed the 16 habits. Teachers would have the freedom to work on any habit at any time if they considered it appropriate to the academic content and skills being taught.

During the 2013–2014 school year and after three years of implementation, early childhood teachers suggested increasing the number of Habits of Mind to focus on for students in Preschool II and Preprimary. They said they could continue reinforcing the original four habits that they had introduced to students two years before and could introduce two more habits, as Figure 3.1 shows.

Teachers' response to the implementation of the Habits of Mind has been very positive; having teachers in younger grades sharing their success stories with their colleagues has been helpful and motivating. The implementation plan involved our entire student population, beginning with our youngest students in 2010–2011 and continuing with lower-elementary students in 2011–2012, upper-elementary students in 2012–2013, and middle school students in 2013–2014. Since then, we have continued practicing the Habits of Mind at all levels, through high school.

Strategies

The early childhood curriculum at San Roberto International School is based on The Creative Curriculum for Preschool. Teachers have designed and included lessons and activities to introduce and foster the various Habits of Mind assigned to the preschool grade levels. They are expected to include the habits in their lessons and learning targets.

The teachers have implemented the Habits of Mind using a variety of strategies. At the Prenursery and Nursery levels, they

introduce the habits and allocate time to explore the habits' meaning once a week, during whole-group time. They also plan and include daily activities with students.

Using stories to talk about the Habits of Mind has proven to be helpful. Teachers of the youngest students have conducted read-aloud sessions using books such as *The Tortoise and the Hare*, by Aesop; *I Can't Get My Turtle to Move*, by Elizabeth Lee O'Donnell; *No, No Titus!* by Claire Masurel; *Mice Squeak, We Speak*, by Arnold L. Shapiro; *From Head to Toe*, by Eric Carle; and the *Coco and Tula* collection, by Patricia Geis.

Visuals have also helped to encourage our students to practice the Habits of Mind. Posters with pictures of kids climbing a mountain or racing in cars to achieve a goal, for example, have helped to enforce the meaning and practice of various Habits of Mind.

Some strategies have focused on the Habits of Mind vocabulary. Teachers send information to parents in which they share vocabulary, activities, and tips that parents can use at home to promote the use of the habits outside school. These strategies have brought positive feedback from parents. One of our teachers created a Habits of Mind picture album. She asked parents to take pictures of their children using the habit of *persisting*, for example. Involving the parents in this way has fostered the identification of the habit in different activities, as well as the use of the related vocabulary by both students and parents.

Teachers have developed and taught specific phrases and hand movements. Examples include "Stop, Think, Breathe, and Act" for the habit of *managing impulsivity*, and "Try, Try, Try Again" for the habit of *persisting*.

Like their colleagues in the Prenursery and Nursery classrooms, teachers in the Preschool I, Preschool II, and Preprimary class-rooms have used books to introduce and support the development of the Habits of Mind. Popular titles include *Leo the Late Bloomer*,

by Robert Kraus; *Today I Will Fly*, by Mo Willems; *My Friend and I*, by Lisa Jahn-Clough; *A Mindful Garden of Verses*, by Marie Ciota; *No, David!* by David Shannon; and *The Little Engine That Could*, by Watty Piper.

Teachers use short videos, personal anecdotes, role-playing activities, and chants to introduce and reinforce the habits. Constant reinforcement with students and communication with parents have motivated children to practice the habits. Resources such as vocabulary lists, videos, websites, and special activities to practice at home have been shared with parents.

The school has created a compilation of resources available for teachers that they can access electronically.

Celebrating success with the Habits of Mind is an important component of program development. All teachers at San Roberto International School provide continual recognition through charts, "catching" students applying a habit, sending notes home, and other means. At the end of every term, a "Habits of Mind fairy" visits the students in each classroom and congratulates them for their work with the habits. Also at the end of the term, students enjoy a picnic during recess in recognition of their effort.

Parents and teachers understand that developing the Habits of Mind is a continuous process, and teachers look for ongoing use of vocabulary, identification, and application of the Habits of Mind in and out of school. Feedback from parents about their children applying the habits is considered an important indicator of acquisition.

San Roberto International School has made the Habits of Mind part of its institutional Values and Character Education Program. A Habits of Mind committee composed of teachers and administrators has been leading the implementation of the program. Committee members offer regular information sessions to classroom teachers and specialized teachers (physical education, art, music) in all grade

levels, as well as to those in charge of extracurricular activities. Sessions have also been offered to parents and to other school and maintenance personnel. One teacher per grade level is designated as a Habits of Mind Champion, helping to provide the grade-level team with ideas, resources, and general communication to promote and reinforce the program. The school has been persistent in promoting the Habits of Mind with all the members of the school community.

Reflection by a Preprimary Teacher

Preprimary teacher Janette Johnson offers the following reflection on her experience in teaching the Habits of Mind:

> It wasn't until we applied the program in our classrooms that we were able to observe the impact in the social, emotional, [and] academic [areas], and [in] . . . discipline. After working with the habits of *managing impulsivity, persisting, listening with understanding and empathy,* and *gathering data through all senses* and always finding the friendliest and [most] meaningful way to work [on] them with the children, we realized that little by little students easily identified situations in which one or more habits were applied, both in reading aloud and in daily life.
>
> Using the vocabulary to name each habit, we received feedback from parents who mentioned that the children were starting to transfer [their understanding of the habits] to daily situations. [The children] also identified circumstances in which their parents needed to apply a habit!
>
> At first, we thought that [implementing and using Habits of Mind] was going to be a heavy load for teachers, but as we started working, we realized we were already doing many things without using a specific name for such actions. In addition, we noticed that the most meaningful way to internalize the habits is through everyday life situations.

The change in children's attitude has [been] reflected [through fewer] discipline problems and more reflection on what they are doing, a greater understanding of the consequences of their actions, and more effort on achieving their objectives and meeting the goals set. Children also support their classmates, and it is common to hear [them] advising each other on what to do and how to react to different situations.

The teachers and staff at San Roberto International School continue to pursue the objective of developing the Habits of Mind in students and the community. We understand this is an ongoing process, and we ourselves continue to practice the Habits of Mind as we work toward this objective.

4

Small Is Beautiful: A Place to Grow the Habits of Mind

Louise Pon-Barry and Sarah Baker

Some say that small is beautiful, and we agree. In our minds, our small school, Kittredge School in San Francisco, is a beautiful thing. Its small size has allowed our staff to come together as a team and to develop a schedule for studying the Habits of Mind. We decided to cover 1 habit per month, 8 habits per school year; in this way, students will learn all 16 habits over the course of two years. Our long-range goal is to develop the habits in our students so that they are empowered to succeed in life as well as in school. We want them to positively contribute to their community while also working toward personal success. We use the Habits of Mind as a way to create a positive, mindful culture for our school community.

Every month our school holds an assembly to introduce the Habit of Mind we will study. Our school principal leads the assembly and shows a short video clip that demonstrates the habit in action. Kids at all grade levels are now able to identify the habit. The seed is planted, and teachers bring the habit into their classroom for further exploration.

Everyone in our school is learning, discussing, and reinforcing the same habit all month long. This approach allows the habit to be part of the conversations of the entire school at the same time. "Little buddies" discuss the habit of the month with their "big buddies," and kids in various classes can spot the habit as it unfolds, for example, at recess. In this way, we are consistently reinforcing the habit throughout the community. What makes the school culture successful is the consistency we develop by using a shared language as we all focus on the habit of the month. With this common focus, it is easy to strike up a conversation, compliment someone, or remind someone of how to work toward success with the particular habit.

Differentiating Based on Child Development: Kindergarten and 1st Grade

Approaches to teaching the Habits of Mind correspond to our students' levels of development. Here we describe the approaches in kindergarten and 1st grade.

Taking the Habits Through the School Year

When the school year begins, we know that students are concerned with making friends. We introduce the habit *listening with understanding and empathy* as we all get to know each other and form new friendships. Especially with the younger children, learning to share is an important part of living in the social climate of the classroom, and *listening with understanding and empathy* is a key component. It comes into play, for example, when a classmate takes the prettiest pink marker that a child wanted to use for her picture, or when she's been waiting all morning for recess and ran as fast as she could to the swings but her friend got there first. This habit is a good foundation for building interpersonal relationships throughout the school year.

As we make our way through the fall and winter, the sounds of leaves crunching beneath our feet, the smells and tastes of holiday

meals, and the warm hugs of family coming to visit lead us to the habit of *gathering data through all senses*. At school, we share a Thanksgiving feast, decorate gingerbread houses, and have an all-school holiday party. We hear *latkes* (potato pancakes) sizzling in a pan or smell sweet *sufganiyot* (jelly donuts). Every opportunity to see, identify, and use the habit of *gathering data through all senses* reinforces the concept we are teaching.

As the end of winter gives way to spring, Kittredge School gears up for an all-school talent show. Each class performs an act, which means that each student will experience the habit of *taking a responsible risk*. The prospect of standing in front of an auditorium of friends, family, and even strangers makes a young performer think, "What if I trip and fall on my face? What if I sing off-key? What if I forget the steps and freeze?" These are all possibilities. Nonetheless, students get up on stage every year, *taking a responsible risk*. As these fears arise, we remind our students that our community is a safe place. We tell them that anything may happen when they are onstage, and they can't let the possibility of failure impede the opportunity for them to shine.

Soon it is April, a point in the school year when students have become comfortable with each other and the academic expectations. Some begin to feel that they don't have to try as hard as they did earlier in the year. But as a staff we want them to finish the school year strong, to stay focused on their studies, and so we highlight the importance of *persisting*. Because it's basketball season, at our monthly assembly we watch a clip of Stephen Curry of the Golden State Warriors. He wasn't born a basketball sensation; he excels in *persisting*. Even after reaching impressive levels of success, he persists because he knows that is the only way to stay on top. Some students already have a buy-in to this habit because they idolize Curry, who some people think is the greatest shooter in NBA history. Some become interested in persisting because Curry is simply amazing

to watch. He is not the tallest guy on the court, but he is accurate. Watching Curry practice is a great way for students to see that persistence pays off.

As we close the school year, we want our students to understand the importance of *remaining open to continuous learning*. Soon it will be summer, and we want them to continue to keep their minds active and engaged. We want our students to feel a sense of accomplishment but also to understand that there is always room to learn more. Sometimes this means learning a new way to tie a shoelace or taking music lessons for the first time. As they leave for summer vacation, we want them to be engaged in new experiences, and when they return in the fall, we want them to be able to build upon what they already know.

Integrating the Habits into Our Academic Work

In kindergarten and 1st grade we begin the day with a class discussion. We follow up with student work about the habit we are working on, and close by collectively sharing our work as a class.

A variety of jumping-off points can launch the description of the habit. Sometimes we watch a video clip or read a story that captures the habit. Sometimes we just talk about how this habit is present in the children's lives, when they have used this habit, or how they would like to use the habit in the future. When we've come to an understanding of the habit, we ask the students to write a story or illustrate their ideas on paper.

The habit of *creating, imagining, and innovating*, for example, might lead to drawing a "dream house" and describing what is in each room. After teacher modeling, the students design their own dream houses guided by questions such as "Will your house have a pool? A science lab? A salon? A giant trampoline?" Kids let their imaginations run wild. As soon as we post these illustrations on the bulletin board, the students are thrilled to check out each other's houses as well as share their dream houses with their parents.

When studying the habit of *thinking flexibly*, we might give students a piece of paper with a squiggly line running across it and ask them to use the line as the starting point of a picture. Spread out around the classroom, each student has an island of personal space for independent work. Then we meet back together and see how people can interpret the same line in many different ways.

A favorite Habit of Mind to study in kindergarten and 1st grade is *managing impulsivity*. Although it might seem that such "big words" would be difficult for little kids to understand, we find that with visual representation they become quite manageable. We depict *managing impulsivity* with a picture of a stoplight. On the left side of the light is a caption: Red = Stop, Yellow = Think, Green = Go. When students are thinking about *managing impulsivity*, they learn to use this three-step process: *Stop* before they act. *Think* about the outcome. *Go* when they know how to proceed. They illustrate an event that shows them *managing impulsivity*, and as an extension, they write a sentence describing what is happening when they Stop, Think, and Go.

As we learn about the habit of *persisting*, we have our little buddies (kindergarteners and 1st graders) play a game of Capture the Flag with their big buddies (8th graders). They learn that sometimes their team captures the flag, sometimes it doesn't; either way, they have to be persistent for the duration. It always helps (for auditory learning, especially) to add music to a teachable idea. For example, we sang a "Be Persistent cheer" on the sidelines of a game of Capture the Flag.

Weeks after the game, kids were still singing the catchy tune. The kinesthetic learners could connect with the habit as they played Capture the Flag; the auditory learners could connect the habit to the cheer.

When we discuss *taking responsible risks*, we encourage students to step outside their comfort zone. In this exercise, we ask students

to lean back and trust that a friend will catch them. As an extension, we ask students to stand on top of a stool and lean even further back, letting their classmates catch their whole body.

While studying the habit *creating, imagining, and innovating*, we pair the K/1 students with their 8th grade buddies. Each buddy pair is asked to create its own architectural masterpiece out of uncooked spaghetti and marshmallows. These are not materials we use every day, and they require a bit of spatial reasoning. These types of hands-on experiences tend to be memorable because they involve a novel approach. They offer a fun way for students of all ages to create and work interdependently. In this exercise, students are exploring the habit through play. In the younger grades—but truly at any age—these experiences are the ones that students remember.

Differentiating Based on Child Development: 2nd and 3rd Grades

In 2nd and 3rd grades we start the year with the big idea: What are Habits of Mind? Do students know what a *habit* is? What do they think the *mind* is? Once students are clear about the meaning of a habit and the mind, we start a three-week unit to develop understanding around a specific habit. We give students opportunities for discussion, thinking, and generating work. We show them an exemplar of a finished product so they know what they are working toward.

The three-week unit begins with asking students to write what they think the habit means without prior instruction. Students might then listen to a poem or watch a video on the selected habit. We ask them to write examples of times they have used this habit, select one of these examples, and then create a drawing that includes a description. From there, students brainstorm a word splash related to the habit and then read the corresponding word splash from *Learning and Leading with Habits of Mind* (Costa & Kallick, 2008, pp. 118–123).

This activity expands their understanding of synonyms and further deepens their comprehension of the habit by providing multiple forms of expression. We also use this tool to build dictionary and thesaurus skills. After a discussion, we gather in teacher-led small groups to listen to student ideas on ways to represent the habit in a drawing with a personal example. One model is past/present/future. Students can draw an example of how they—or someone they know—have used the habit in the past, are currently using it, will use it in the future—or possibly all three. After adding a descriptive sentence to the drawing, students complete a follow-up assessment to show what they understand about the habit.

Other activities used in teaching these habits include individual, partner, or small-group options. For example, an individual activity might involve answering a series of questions on a worksheet like the one shown in Figure 4.1. Working on their own, with a partner, or as part of a small group, students may create word searches and crossword puzzles with definitions for related synonyms as clues. Individual or group writing activities, such as creating poems and fictional stories, allow students to reflect on their personal use of the habits and stimulate their imaginations to invent whimsical settings in which the habits would be useful. Kinesthetic exercises might include creating story cubes or writing and performing skits, songs, dances, newscasts, and even commercials persuading classmates of the benefits of employing the current habit in their lives.

Finally, student work is displayed on a designated Habits of Mind bulletin board right outside the classroom, where classmates, other grades, staff, and parents can see it. We set aside part of class time for students to view one another's work and express themselves using positive language to support each other, such as "I think," "I notice," "I wonder," "If this were mine . . . ." These dialogues between students encourage speaking and listening skills and foster deeper understanding of a specific habit.

Figure 4.1   **Example of Habits of Mind Work**

Name of Habit: _____
Month/Year: _____

You have studied this habit for two full weeks! Congratulations, you're well on your way to success! Please share your new definition of this habit using key vocabulary words.

_____
_____
_____
_____

Write ways you see this happening at school with yourself or others.

1. _____

2. _____

Write two ways you see this habit happening outside school.

1. _____

2. _____

How will practicing this habit help you become successful?

_____
_____
_____
_____

What are two ideas you can think of to incorporate this habit into your life more?
Ideas: Give an example of a challenge where this habit would help you succeed or solve a challenge. Write about things you can think or do to practice the habit more.

_____
_____

We employ the "I Do, We Do, You Do" model to build confidence in tackling projects. Students view an example of finished work done by the teacher. They then work with the teacher to create an example together, and finally work independently to create their individual project. Students have the opportunity to access habits using reading, writing, listening, speaking, and creating illustrations. We support them in making connections to how a habit relates to themselves, how to see it in others, and how to acknowledge local and world issues in which the habits are being used or could be used.

We use as many modalities of learning as possible—visual, auditory, and kinesthetic. The WonderGrove video animations (HOManimations .com/ascd) are great for lower-elementary grades, delighting the students with their characters and animation; a lively discussion always follows the viewing of a video, with related questions and personal examples. The students recite poetry from *The Mindful Garden of Verses* (Ciota, 2008) for each habit to practice reading as well as listening skills. We also ignite their kinesthetic abilities for fine and gross motor skills by having them use clay to represent the habit with a symbol or other clay structure. On the playground at recess, students have ample opportunities to use the habits for solving problems. Staff who facilitate playground activities support the development of habits by asking students to support one another with the shared language of the 16 habits.

We use Bloom's taxonomy (Bloom et al., 1956) of cognitive thinking as we teach the habits. For example, using Bloom's six levels of thinking for *metacognition* might look like this:

- **Remember**—Students can recall that the habit they are learning is *metacognition*.

- **Understand**—Students can explain the meaning of *metacognition* to a parent.

- **Apply**—A student notices that the way he is approaching a math problem isn't working and begins thinking about the problem in a new way.

- **Analyze**—A student is able to differentiate what is and is not metacognition when given scenarios.

- **Evaluate**—A student can support why she is using a new type of thinking by comparing the old way with a new way.

- **Create**—A student investigates other ways of solving a math problem and comes up with a way all his own, based on researching others. Another example is a student creating a piece of writing that includes a character who used metacognition to solve a mystery.

Making a habit visual—whether on a wall or a board—is extremely effective in promoting student awareness. Whatever draws attention is what the students focus on.

We as teachers model the habits and acknowledge the habits in students and colleagues alike. The more we "catch" each other using the habits, the more the habits seem to be used and the more the students notice them in one another. Students also join conversations in which a teacher comments on another teacher using the habit. In this way, students see that the habits are useful for everyone.

Observing Students as They Develop the Habits, in K and 1st Grade

When students purposefully address and show their understanding of a habit through their daily actions, we know they are internalizing that habit. When they use the habits regularly through their words and actions, we know that these ideas are becoming part of who they are. Sometimes this process can take a few weeks, and sometimes it takes years.

Kids are quick to notice someone using the Habits of Mind. Circle time offers a great opportunity to see if friends are, for example, *managing their impulsivity*. Being able to sit attentively for 15 minutes deserves a class cheer, and we take a moment to recognize the class accomplishment.

Students are happy to recognize their peers as they demon-strate that they are *remaining open to continuous learning* or *striving for accuracy*. This "pat on the back" approach helps students to be cognizant of the Habits of Mind vocabulary, and the fact that they are internalizing these habits and living them is demonstrative proof of their understanding of these ideas. A case in point is the following anecdote a parent shared with us:

> On [the] soccer team that one dad coaches, the kids are adorable and have so much fun but regularly get beaten—terribly. They take it in true Kittredge fashion, however, and chant "Be persistent!" on the sidelines while the other team [not a HOM school] chants "Be aggressive!"

As students progress in their development, they begin to initiate conversations about the Habits of Mind. Sometimes we challenge them to find use of the habits in themselves or in others. In their written assessments, we ask them to use a "before/after" approach, which provides evidence of their perception of growth. As teachers, we enjoy observing the students support and encourage one another as they incorporate our shared vocabulary into their academic and free time. With our scaffold approach of teaching eight habits per year and then repeating the sequence every two years, we see students build on past habits and get excited about revisiting those they previously studied.

Involving Parents

Parents see our Habits of Mind wall displays featuring student work when they drop off their student or attend school or classroom events. The displays enable parents to initiate conversations with other parents to acknowledge the Habits of Mind work of another child.

On the days when the school conducts its monthly assem-blies to introduce each habit, classroom teachers distribute rubber

bracelets featuring the habit of the month (see Figure 4.2). The students are always excited to receive new bracelets and take them to their parents for them to wear too! That is one way that the Habits of Mind vocabulary reaches a broader community. The bracelet is a conversation starter, encouraging people to ask, "What does that mean? What is that habit about?" One parent told us, "If I see a new bracelet on Luke's wrist, I'll ask him [about it]. I think the bracelets are really effective." Another called them "a brilliant idea." We've seen parents proudly wearing the bracelets and enthusiastically initiating or joining conversations with students about the new habit. The conversations also provide an opportunity for the students to demonstrate their knowledge of the habit. Being able to describe the habit to others strengthens their understanding.

Figure 4.2   **Habits of Mind Bracelets**

Source: Louise Pon-Barry. Used with permission.

We know that habits are being internalized when parents tell us how the habits come up outside school. Students are bringing the habits home and unpacking them for their parents—as when one of us heard a student tell his dad, "Manage your impulsivity. Order the salad." In another case, a parent shared this observation: "When we are baking together, she has started to experience things with all the senses—she has pointed out the sound of eggs cracking or the soft feel of flour—instead of just the usual tastes and smells." We've also heard of parents using the Habits of Mind in conversation to support one another's children at sports events and in other situations outside school.

Kittredge School administrators put out a weekly newsletter for parents, highlighting the habits and upcoming events. In addition, each elementary class puts out a parent newsletter that helps to remind parents about what's happening in the classroom and ways to be involved with their child's current learning topics.

A Teacher's Voice

Our friend and colleague Daria Rose shared the following thoughts. They illustrate how the habits have permeated her life and even changed her way of thinking and her behavior:

> On a personal note, I find the Habits of Mind coming up in conversation on a weekly basis. With friends and family, I am often using the vocabulary and then describing where that idea came from. Just like my students, I am identifying the habits as I see them being used, as well as noting when I should have employed them but didn't. As I grow as an individual, I am finding that my understanding of these habits is changing too.
>
> These concepts are floating around my brain, trying to match up to the events of my life on a daily basis. Life with my 2-year-old daughter is a constant reminder to *respond with wonderment and awe*. She looks at the world through a lens of wonderment and

awe. It helps me remember to be in the moment with her and to marvel at the song of a bird singing outside our window. She is *gathering data through all senses* and implores me to do the same as we cook dinner. Who else wants to bite into a big knob of ginger or stick her hand into a bag of dry rice? Using the Habits of Mind helps me to remember that I am not only a teacher, but also still a student of life. In the past, [if] I spilled rice all over the kitchen, I might have expressed [my reaction with] an expletive. Today, I *find humor* in the situation, and I'm happier [because of] that reaction.

Tips for Success

Based on our experience at Kittredge, we can offer some advice in the form of three factors that increase the likelihood of success in implementing the Habits of Mind:

• Addressing one habit per month instead of all the habits together is a manageable way to undertake the effort.

• Working in conjunction with the entire school staff is essential. It is possible for individual teachers to incorporate the habits into their classroom routines; however, taking a whole-school approach and thinking interdependently about the effort will more likely ensure the longevity of the process.

• Extending outreach beyond the school so that everyone in the community is on board will result in much swifter progress.

We have been studying these habits and teaching these habits for a number of years now. We are still learning how to present them best for a variety of learners.

Final Thoughts

As educators, one of the key benefits of the Habits of Mind framework that we appreciate is how it provides a platform for students to

acknowledge the success of their personal growth and development in an otherwise academic setting. These personal successes can be illuminated by teachers, peers, or the students themselves without formal assessment. By using the shared vocabulary, we can support, encourage, and coach our students as they blossom into more well-rounded individuals. Some of the most satisfying moments in teaching are the aha moments of comprehension, and the Habits of Mind provide an opportunity for more of these. They bring confidence and joy to students of all levels and learning styles—and we notice and identify our use of the habits in our personal lives. After "catching kids being good" for so many years, we can honestly say that we have caught ourselves using these tools as well, beyond the classroom.

The Habits of Mind have made us better teachers and human beings by keeping us aware of and working toward our personal best, and they can be used by anyone to enhance the quality of their work. We feel lucky to be able to guide the students at Kittredge School in the visible growth of personal character traits that will help them make positive changes in the world.

Bloom, B., Englehart, M., Furst, E., Hill, W., & Krathwohl, D. (1956). *Taxonomy of educational objectives: The classification of educational goals. Handbook I: Cognitive domain*. New York: Longman.

Ciota, M. (2008). *The mindful garden of verses*. Westport, CT: Institute for Habits of Mind.

Costa, A. L., & Kallick, B. (2008). *Learning and leading with habits of mind: 16 characteristics for success*. Alexandria, VA: ASCD.

Part II: Activating and Engaging the Habits of Mind

Are you somewhat skeptical about young children's capacity to handle the concepts and vocabulary of the Habits of Mind? Prepare to be surprised! You will find that they love learning and using big words, including *metacognition*, *impulsivity*, and *flexibility*. Labels, however, are not enough. They also need to understand the actions that accompany the labels—what it looks like and sounds like to *listen with empathy* or to *think interdependently*, for example. And, this is where they need you, their teachers and caregivers, to model the language and habits.

To help you teach and model the habits for young children, we will supply classroom and personal strategies. This part of the book is filled with tools, resources, and techniques for engaging children in activities that will help them to experience, activate, and practice the Habits of Mind.

visual habits

gather data through senses
take responsible risks
innovating
imagining
creating
impulsivity
meta cognition
flexibility
think interdependently

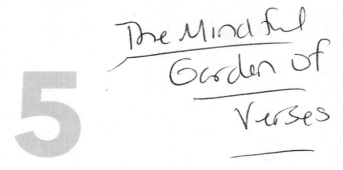

5

Thinking Play:
Honoring the Child

Michelle Scheu

Thinking is integral to everything that my teaching partner and I do with our children, whether they are solving math problems, socializing with friends, or creating a robot. Thinking is embedded in the fiber of each classroom, part of a culture that has been cultivated for many years. High-level thinking is evidenced in the children's language, their confidence in their learning, and their behaviors. Children are highly independent and are respected as thinkers, inquirers, and problem solvers. Conversations with children demonstrate the ways we empower them to co-create their classroom experiences. They join adults in the planning and decision making around the content of what we teach, helping to generate curriculum based on their interests. In addition, they are encouraged to make choices about what they will focus on and how they will pace their own learning. Teachers are a part of the audience for the students' thinking play, and together we celebrate how competent and capable they are becoming as they demonstrate their learning.

Teaching Children How to Learn: A Split-Screen Approach

My teaching partner and I use a "split-screen" concept, with one "screen" being the teacher's focus on the *content and concepts* children need to learn, and the other the focus on teaching them *how to learn* (Claxton, n.d.; Murdoch, 2016). Teaching children how to learn involves developing the Habits of Mind, which are required to become a skillful thinker. For example, while focusing on the content of mathematics algorithms with Year 1 children, the teacher is teaching them how to achieve learning success as a thinker by practicing the habit of *striving for accuracy*. The children come to know that being an effective mathematical thinker requires accurate calculations. But they also need to know that being accurate does not happen instantly, and so they will also need to adopt the habit of *persisting* as they come to realize that with practice over time they will succeed.

Another example involves investigative learning, with children collecting data while doing scientific experiments on movement. The content focus is how things move; the thinking focus is adopting the habit of a researcher by *gathering data through the senses*. In this instance, the children's thinking would also be enhanced by reminding them of their prior learning of a scientific thinking process (wonder > hypothesis > observe > gather data > findings) and the system tool for recording that information. This example illustrates three aspects of thinking being used together—the Habits of Mind combined with what I have termed Processes of Mind and Tools of Mind (see Figure 5.1 on p. 61).

Thinking Play

Although learning to be a thinker permeates our days at Chevallum State School, it is most evident in the practice of Thinking Play, an intellectually rigorous, transdisciplinary, play-based curriculum that operates alongside and interrelates with the more formal learning of

mathematics and language. Implemented for one and a half to two hours every day, it provides learning that reflects real-life experiences that embed child and community partnerships. Through the Thinking Play approach, teachers plan for and facilitate learning that is motivating, memorable, and relevant to the age and stage of the child. Thinking Play involves authentic investigative learning experiences that occur as learners seek to find an answer to a question posed through investigating, applying knowledge and skills, and creating solutions.

In implementing Thinking Play, teachers and students design curriculum together, using the following steps:

1. **Provocation**—Provocation is usually inspired by the children before the initial planning. At other times, teachers might stage a provocation to begin a Thinking Play.

2. **Teacher Planning**—Teachers decide on an appropriate conceptual thread to underpin the unit, keeping in mind related curriculum areas. The design is based on a Thinking Play overview and usually covers 10 to 15 weeks of learning.

3. **Small-Group Thinking**—Although the essential learnings in the plan are nonnegotiable, the shape and direction of the Thinking Play is flexible and open for discussion as teachers and children cocreate the document.

4. **Whole-Group Thinking**—Children's ideas are taken to the whole group, and each child has a say as voting on preferences takes place. Children modify and plan the direction of the Thinking Play and clarify the culmination, or product, of their choice, such as a performance or a community event.

5. **Enacting**—The codesigned plan becomes an exciting, relevant document that is valued by children and teachers alike. These ideas are then enacted in smaller groups, interspersed with whole-group discussion when necessary as they prepare for the culmination.

6. **Culmination**—When the Thinking Play is audience ready, families and friends of the children come to share in the excitement of the presentation. Having family and friends as the audience adds an authentic layer of relevance to the children's learning.

7. **Documentation**—The culmination is a community celebration that is documented and becomes a part of the children's memories, often fondly recalled well into adulthood.

The Thinking Play Map

To ensure that children are informed and in control of their own learning pathways when enacting Thinking Play, the inquiry process of thinking is made visible through a Thinking Play map (see Figure 5.1). The map was developed using inspiration from educational consultant Lane Clark's work on making thinking visible (www.Laneclark.ca). It tailors the original Thinking Play process for children to use in Thinking Play environments and combines both critical and creative thinking. The map is used during Thinking Play learning to keep children aware and informed about the type of thinking in which they are participating. This scaffolds children's thinking and gives them a common language to discuss their thinking. The aim is for children to eventually work independently, thinking and working with minimal teacher support.

The Thinking Play map can be used by children individually in a Thinking Journal; they color in each stage as they come to it and color over the arrows if they revisit a stage. The Thinking Play map supports the development of children's independent thinking and problem-solving skills as they work toward the culmination. Initially children require scaffolding to understand how to use the map effectively. With experience, they can use the map independently in whole-group, small-group, or individual Thinking Play investigations.

FIGURE 5.1   **Thinking Play Map**

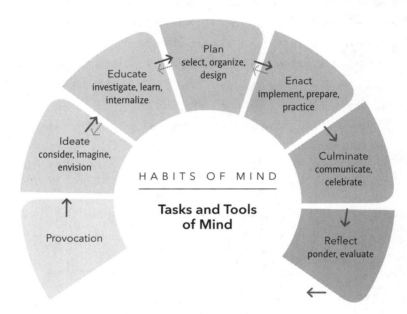

Source: © 2018 Michelle Scheu. Used with permission.

Development Plans

As teachers codesign curriculum with children, they bounce ideas, plans, and decisions back and forth, creating a Thinking Play development plan to clarify the direction and ensure that curriculum learning goals are achieved. The ratio of negotiable to nonnegotiable curriculum varies according to the age group, determining the degree of influence the children have over their learning. Generally, with younger age groups, teachers have more flexibility over sharing control of the curriculum with the children. Teachers identify a reasonable amount of negotiable content as they prioritize the essential learning content, reduce the "nice-to-know" but not essential content, and discover transdisciplinary links.

A conceptual thread permeates the entire unit of work, giving students an intellectual framework in which to store knowledge and

skills as they build understanding of the big ideas of life. These are ideas that are revisited throughout students' lives as they mature and develop deeper understanding. For the Bug Theme Park investigation shown in the development plan in Figure 5.2, for example, the underlying conceptual thread includes the following components:

Deep Understanding: How can I investigate using scientific thinking to help me understand my world?

Habits of Mind: *Questioning and posing problems; gathering data through all senses*

The Thinking Play development plan will be subject to change according to the children's input, but it ensures that the effort is not a rudderless ship. It helps teachers plan for and guide the direction of the Thinking Play.

FIGURE 5.2   **Thinking Play Development Plan for a Bug Theme Park**

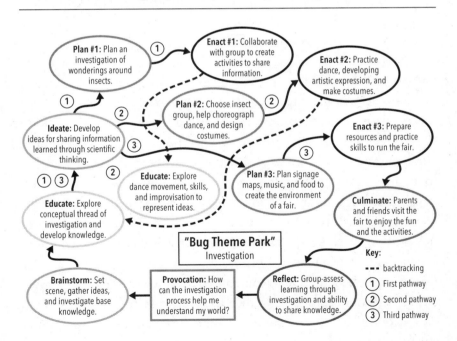

Source: Michele Scheu. Used with permission.

Habits, Tools, and Tasks

The number of Habits of Mind introduced in a Thinking Play experience depends on the age and stage of the children. Teachers use thinking tools such as drawings, diagrams, plans, checklists, step-by-step systems, T-charts, and concepts maps. They include thinking tasks such as comparing, analyzing, and decision making. Each habit, tool, and task is represented by a corresponding card that displays the name and a symbol. These laminated cards are kept in three drawers accessible to children. The appropriate cards are selected and displayed on the wall near the Thinking Play map. This approach helps children to recognize, internalize, and transfer each concept.

Focusing on the Habits of Mind

Although the teaching of the Habits of Mind is most evident in the Thinking Play activities, explicit teaching of the habits begins in separate teaching sessions set aside for this purpose. Longer sessions occur as a new habit is being introduced, followed by regular shorter sessions to scaffold learning of the habits. We want to ensure that the children are developing deep understandings so that they can be confident in discussing and choosing appropriate options for habits to include in a Thinking Play investigation.

To introduce a new habit to the group, teachers use animated Habits of Mind video clips (HOManimations.com/ascd) and character cards. Follow-up usually involves an activity chosen from those suggested in supporting documents associated with the animated videos or a circle-time activity planned around the habit. The video is revisited several times to reinforce learning.

In my teaching I have found that children 4 to 8 years old can learn one or two Habits of Mind deeply in a 15-week unit of work. Although other habits may be mentioned, the children are most likely to retain one or two and be able to transfer them to other learning situations. For example, the habit of *persisting* was the conceptual

thread for our Robotics Thinking Play. Due to the transitionary nature of Thinking Play learning, the habit of *perisisting* was also a focus when a group of students did their perceptual motor skills program each morning and had to persist to reach their rope-skipping or ball-skills goal. It was also mentioned when children were doing a writing assignment and some were working quickly to be "done" rather than persisting to produce their best work. Encouraging them in *persisting* toward their goal of self-regulation became a key factor as children learned their social skills.

By the end of the school year, even though it had been three terms since we had focused on the habit of *persisting*, a child would often be heard explaining to a teacher or another student, "It was hard work. I really had to persist to learn that." This example provides evidence that children as young as 4 can adopt and use the Habits of Mind with deep understanding if the habits are taught explicitly and given relevance in everyday situations, and if the children are given opportunities to practice transferring the skills to a variety of situations.

Final Thoughts

Children in their first three years of schooling thrive academically, socially, and emotionally when they are provided with developmentally appropriate, thinking-rich play that is research-based and that incorporates the highly successful Habits of Mind approach. Including the Habits of Mind in the curriculum gives children a variety of tools as they learn how to think.

Clark, L. (n.d.). Home page. Retrieved September 1, 2017, from http://www.laneclark.ca

Claxton, G. (n.d.). Home page. Retrieved July 7, 2017, from https://www.buildinglearningpower.com/about/professor-guy-claxton/

Murdoch, K. (2016). *The power of inquiry: Teaching and learning with curiosity, creativity and purpose in the contemporary classroom.* Melbourne: Seastar Education.

6

Strategies for Teaching the Habits of Mind to Preschoolers and Primary Students

Michelle Bunder

Although I am committed to the Habits of Mind, I wondered how I, as a primary education teacher in New South Wales, Australia, could incorporate sophisticated vocabulary terms such as *metacognition* and *interdependence* into my teaching in a way that our younger students could understand and grasp. I was not sure where to begin. How might I embed the Habits of Mind into my classroom to help my students solve problems and be successful?

As I pondered this question, I discovered many strategies that you might incorporate into your classroom tomorrow—yes, *tomorrow*! Over the years, I have developed, tried, and tested many teaching strategies, and I have reached conclusions about what has worked with my students and what hasn't. I found that the most important part of implementation is to believe in what you are doing, believe in the Habits of Mind, persist when things may not go as you had hoped, and remain open to continuous learning with your students. When you do, you will find your students are "not

only skillful but they are also inclined, disposed, and compelled to employ good thinking" (Costa & Kallick, 2014, p. 3).

The Classroom Environment

Classroom environment is an essential factor for the successful implementation of the Habits of Mind. I suggest you begin by creating a poster or other wall display that shows all 16 habits. Then create a second display at students' eye level, with elements related to each individual habit, that can be moved and taken on and off the wall as needed.

A cautionary note: When you are creating your displays, it may be tempting to match a particular Habit of Mind to a specific color so that, for example, all of your *striving for accuracy* posters are yellow or those for *finding humor* are red. When I first began my journey with the Habits of Mind, I thought that this was a great idea. I loved that all my Habits of Mind "matched." Then I heard two of my students in the following exchange:

Student A: Gosh, we really need to look at this work again.
Student B: Maybe we should use the blue Habit of Mind. You know the one? The blue one?
Student A: Which blue one, the light or the dark?
Student B: Umm, you know, the blue one!

It was then that I realized that the displays should not match in color. Although it was fantastic that one of my students was able to recognize the need for a Habit of Mind, being able to recognize it only by color didn't help to resolve the situation. Therefore, all my Habits of Mind classroom displays are multicolored, ensuring that my students are not associating a habit with a color but rather are focusing on the imagery on the poster. The focus on imagery creates a deeper link to and an understanding of the habit, as students are embedding and using their knowledge through images as well as words.

Walking the Talk and Talking the Walk

Modeling the Habits of Mind will allow students to see what each habit looks like in action. Throughout the day, "catch" yourself using the habit, and name the action that you were doing that demonstrates the habit. Remember, children learn best through imitation; therefore we educators must both "walk the talk" and "talk the walk" (Costa & Kallick, 2008). For example, if I am jointly constructing a text with my students, I might deliberately leave out a capital letter or a punctuation mark. Once a student has identified the error or you have identified it for your class, you might state, "Oh, my goodness! I'm so glad we checked our work to discover our error! Let's make sure we keep checking our work and *striving for accuracy*, because that's what professional writers do." If your students have not identified the error, you could say, "Good writers always strive for accuracy and check their work again. Let's take the time to reread our sentence." As you walk around your classroom, "catch" students using a Habit of Mind. Name the action they are doing and name the Habit of Mind. For example, "I love the way Ava, Joshua, and Rhys are thinking interdependently. They are listening, taking turns, and sharing their important ideas. Well done!"

Continue this process at the beginning of the year as a way to immerse your students in the Habits of Mind. I have the habits portrayed on small cards attached to a lanyard that is always either around my neck or in my pocket. When I catch a student using a habit, I pull out the corresponding card to help the student link the visual and the language related to the habit with the behavior just displayed. Alternatively, I go to the classroom display and point to the Habit of Mind the student just exemplified and give a firm thumbs-up gesture.

Walking the talk and talking the walk is a form of immersion and a way for younger students to begin to make connections between the language, the visuals, and the definitions of the Habits of Mind. It also provides your classroom and school with a common language of success.

Embedding the Habits in the Curriculum

Once the Habits of Mind are displayed in your classroom and you are embedding the language into your daily conversations with students, it is time to start teaching the habits intentionally. This is when it is essential to look to your curriculum for moments that call for a focus on particular habits. Establishing this practice during the early education years will help students understand, unpack, and embed the habits, and know when they should be using them. Here are some examples of times when I have created intentional teaching moments within the curriculum to incorporate a Habit of Mind:

Mathematics—*Striving for accuracy.* An essential component of mathematics curricula worldwide is following a procedure for completing a word problem. I saw this as a perfect opportunity to teach how to successfully use the habit of *striving for accuracy* at the completion of the problem. We discussed as a class why it was essential to "check our work again" and what other mathematical strategies we could use from our "toolbox" to help with this. We also added a final step—*striving for accuracy*—to our wall display of the procedure for completing a word problem. Each time we revised the word-problem procedure, we also were revising the use and purpose of *striving for accuracy* in that situation.

History—*Listening with understanding and empathy.* Exploring events in the past—particularly those that involve such sensitive topics as war, invasion, inspiring pioneers, or minority groups—offers a perfect time to consider the habit of *listening with understanding and empathy*. The concept of placing yourself in someone else's shoes can be tricky for younger students to grasp, as it involves not only imagining the situation but also understanding the emotions that those involved may have experienced at the time. To help meet the challenge, I create a safe environment for students to role-play and explore *listening with understanding and empathy*. First we establish clear boundaries for the role-play: explicit expectations that

need to be followed. We discuss what it means to be in "someone else's shoes." What would that look like? Sound like? Feel like? To further help, we may watch a video on empathy available from WonderGrove animations (https://wondergrovelearn.net/) or on YouTube. Only then do we begin the role-play, pausing at various times to listen with understanding as the students portray and react to different people within the situation. "What is it like to walk in their shoes?" I ask. "That is empathy!" I encourage students to use specific language as they are sharing: "*I am listening to what you are saying and I understand where you are coming from because you are feeling . . . .*"

Creating intentional connections between the curriculum and the Habits of Mind will ensure that students understand the habits in a way that is purposeful and relevant to their learning. It also means that the next time you discuss a habit, you have a firm foundation on which students can demonstrate the habit of *applying past knowledge to new situations* and use what they have learned.

Classroom Wall Displays

Most classrooms include beautiful displays of student inquiry, discovery, and learning, as well as displays related to classroom expectations. No matter what the display, it can incorporate the Habits of Mind as a way to help students make links to their learning. After intentional teaching moments such as those just described for mathematics and history, you can take a photo of students engaged in the word-problem procedure or the role-play. Then you can add the photo to your Habits of Mind wall display, locating it next to the related habit. Alternatively, any habit that is discussed within the task could be attached to the wall display for that subject or topic. Another possibility—particularly useful for a display related to a specific learning inquiry the students have undertaken—is to have the Habit of Mind that was used highlighted in one color and the thinking tools that were used within the task highlighted in another color.

Having your classroom displays linked to the Habits of Mind helps students draw conclusions about what habit they might need to use to be successful in the future. It provides students with a visual reminder of past examples of successful application.

Habits of Mind Experts

A strategy that employs students as "experts" in a particular habit reinforces the use of the Habits of Mind both inside the classroom and during outdoor learning experiences. Being an expert requires setting the example for classmates and ensuring that they are using the Habit of Mind that is the focus.

Of course, it is important for the experts (and their classmates) to fully understand the habit that they are representing. One way to help accomplish this is with sheets of paper that answer the question "What does an expert look like?" on one side and "What does an expert not look like?" on the other. Establishing these clear guidelines at the outset will ensure that expectations are met and all students feel safe and supported as they develop their understanding. As with any pedagogical strategy, it will take time to establish experts and embed this practice.

A positive aspect of having experts is that you can ensure that each child has a turn. Students love being the expert, and it is a great way to build the confidence of those who are more reluctant and quieter. You can also tailor the expert role to specific students so that they can really shine. In the classroom setting at the beginning of the year, I nominate experts for the lessons. It always makes me smile when, for example, a student approaches a group to talk about how they are *thinking interdependently*, asking what is working for their group and what isn't, discussing how the group could resolve any problems, and offering suggestions.

I like to vary my strategies with the Habits of Mind each day, so I look at my day plans for the week to decide where experts could be

best used. By the end of the year, though, students themselves may remind me that experts need to be chosen.

The "expert" strategy is portable and can be used when we take learning outside. Wherever the learning goes, so do the Habits of Mind! I have a set of the Habits of Mind on cards with a ribbon attached to each one, so that students can wear them when we are out and about. "Wearing" the habits keeps them at the forefront of our learning and teaching. The student who is wearing the card with the Habit of Mind that is our focus becomes the expert in that particular disposition for the lesson. For example, wearing the card for *gathering data through all senses*, the expert might encourage her classmates to share their findings or to explain what they can see or hear as they gather data. This role might then cross over to the expert on *thinking and communicating with clarity and precision*, who may ask the student to communicate his findings in another way to help other students, or the expert may restate the earlier explanation if students did not understand it the first time.

Ultimately, through the "experts" strategy, the students are taking charge of the implementation of the Habits of Mind and empowering their fellow students to achieve success. The strategy helps to create a cohesive culture—provided you make clear that being an expert does not include the right to report a classmate's behavior to the teacher or boss others around. It helps to remind students that experts will always practice the habit of *remaining open to continuous learning* and be humble.

In Their Own Words

Once your students are beginning to feel more confident in using the Habits of Mind, or in one particular habit, you can begin to explore the strategy of "In their own words." As stated previously, I recommend that each classroom have at least two sets of Habits of Mind on

display—one that remains on the wall and one that can be removed or that students can manipulate when working on a particular habit.

Before beginning this strategy, explain that the students are going to be using the habit of *thinking and communicating with clarity and precision* as a way to add discoveries and understandings about the Habits of Mind to the display. When your students have explored a Habit of Mind more deeply, ask them to say "in their own words" what that habit means. What does it look like, sound like, feel like? To further enhance clarity, you may even explore what the habit does *not* look like. Record your students' key phrases and ideas and add these next to the visual of the Habit of Mind on display. With young students, I recommend adding no more than three phrases next to each poster; otherwise it can become visually overwhelming for some. The best way to pool ideas into just a few phrases is to write down, via a brainstorm, everyone's ideas and explain that you would like to add just two or three phrases to the display so you are going to look for the common idea. Have the students jointly negotiate and agree on what the phrases on the display should be. This filtering process further clarifies, deepens, and broadens students' understanding of each Habit of Mind and empowers them to take ownership over their learning and discovering. However, within this process, it is essential that you acknowledge everyone's ideas by writing the students' names beside their contribution. You could even collate all the ideas and turn them into a Habits of Mind "brainstorm book" that students could reflect upon throughout the year. Once the class has agreed on two or three phrases, they can be added to the wall display.

At some point in your implementation journey you will recognize when your students are ready for this strategy. I recommend using it for just one habit at a time. When I first tried the strategy, I intended to tackle three at a time with my students. The experience did not go as planned. They veered off task and became restless. I suggest you try the strategy once and trust your instincts. If you feel the students

are not ready for it, use another strategy. In my opinion, "in their own words" is more suitable for Year 2 students or those in Year 1 who have had prior experience with the Habits of Mind in kindergarten.

Photo Displays

Building a visual display of the Habits of Mind using photos of themselves is an activity that students really enjoy. Their task is to use the habits of *thinking interdependently* and *creating, imagining, and innovating* to come up with new visuals for the Habits of Mind posters. We begin by looking at all 16 posters for the individual habits, discussing what is clear about each one. What makes the poster interesting and the habit recognizable? How do we know that this visual represents this particular Habit of Mind? We then talk about the power of a photo and how their photographic images must clearly identify the Habit of Mind they are interpreting. With this in mind, once they take their photo, they share it with another group to see if their classmates are able to identify which habit it represents.

For this strategy, I organize the students in groups of two to four, except for the habit *gathering data through all senses*, which has a group of five. The groups are then assigned their Habit of Mind in a "top-secret envelope" and go off to explore, discuss, and create their representation.

Students love to see photos of themselves representing the Habits of Mind, and when the task is completed, we always share the photos as a class. We not only *find humor* but also listen to each group explain the thinking behind their photo. The photos are then printed and added to the wall display.

Goal Setting and Reflection

One element that is so compelling about the Habits of Mind is the influential nature they have on the learner and the learning when

used for goal setting and reflection. Here's a closer look at how the habits affect each of these activities.

Goal Setting

When students engage in goal setting, the Habits of Mind arm them with dispositions that will help them orchestrate and refine the bridge to their goal. Earl Nightingale, an American author, speaker, and radio personality, once said that the problem people face is how to "bridge the gap which exists between where you are now and the goal you intend to reach" (https://www.brainyquote.com/search _results?q=bridge+the+gap). The Habits of Mind clear the pathway for students and help clarify the direction to take to achieve success.

Goal setting can be arranged in a number of ways within the classroom. I always try to have multiple methods for goal setting throughout the day, as well as for the long term. Here are suggestions for how to use Habits of Mind for goal setting within the early childhood classroom:

Lesson goal. After introducing a lesson and before students move to consolidate their learning, discuss and negotiate what Habits of Mind the students might need to achieve their goal for the session. Remove the relevant habit posters off the wall display and place them in a prominent position for the duration of the task to keep students' focus on the habits everyone is striving to use and to facilitate reflection at the end of the lesson.

Daily goal. Print the individual Habits of Mind on small cards or pieces of paper and scatter them over the floor in the morning. As students come into the classroom, have them select a habit that will be their focus for the day. It may be one they would like to refine or know they need to develop more fully. This Habits of Mind card sits on their desk until the end of the day (or week, depending on the circumstances), when students can reflect on how they feel about their progress (see the Reflection section below). I also use this strategy for small-group goals.

Term goal. Using the Habits of Mind cards, students can select one or two habits to use for their goal setting throughout the term or semester. As students feel they have effectively used the Habit of Mind, they can add a sticker or symbol to the card or color in part of it to show their success.

Reflection

The true power of goal setting becomes evident in the form of feedback and reflection. To be successful, students must not only behave in ways that exemplify the habits but also come to "own" them. Reflection is essential to engaging students' minds and cognitive processing, thus further embedding the Habits of Mind (Costa & Kallick, 2014, pp. 96–98). When used as a reflection tool, the habits help students define what it is they are looking for, what they were trying to achieve in the lesson. As John Dewey famously stated, "We do not learn from experience, we learn from *reflection* on experience" (https://www.brainyquote.com/authors/john_dewey).   Reflecting on the quality of a piece of writing, for example, taps into the habits of *striving for accuracy* and *managing impulsivity,* as we take the time to check our work again.

After goal setting, students can each create a Habits of Mind Reflection Journal, where they can record their reflections on how they are using their chosen habits. They may convey their reflections through a drawing, an emotive face, or in writing—whatever they please. You might also ask students to reflect on the benefits of using the Habit of Mind or the challenges they experienced. Lane Clark (2009) suggests that students complete a "so what?" exercise, responding to questions like "What are you going to do now that you are aware of what you need to work on? What will you change for next time?" These questions can also be asked within a sharing circle, a small group, or a whole class. A circle is a great setting for sharing and reflecting, as students can observe one another's faces and body language.

Frequent goal setting and reflecting is an effective way to further embed and implement the Habits of Mind with your students, as it provides them with a vision of success, a focus on how they can create a bridge to achieve their goals. Honest reflection fosters a culture of understanding, learning, and discovering, as students share how they worked through their challenges or what they learned from their successes.

The Habits of Mind Bear

Providing each student with a Habits of Mind bear or other mascot that they can take home is another way to embed the Habits of Mind, especially in kindergarten classrooms. This strategy helps students realize that they can use the habits outside school, and it is a delightful way to involve parents in the implementation process and help them to broaden their understanding of the habits. For families new to the school, it is also an excellent way to begin the conversation around the Habits of Mind.

When you send students home with a bear for the first time, include a journal; provide an example of an "adventure" the bear might go on in the home and how the student might reflect on that adventure in the journal. You can also include a poster of the Habits of Mind to enhance parents' understanding. Students love taking home a bear to share their adventures and using the journal to record the discoveries the bear has had. Sharing the bears' adventures with classmates each Monday can become a classroom routine, linking the habits to classroom activities as well.

A variation of the technique is to have one or more Habits of Mind bears for the entire school. Each week one or more families take the bear home, record their adventure using a Habits of Mind, and send the account to the school via e-mail. The accounts can then be featured in the school's newsletter.

However this technique is implemented, the entire school staff should participate. Involving the entire school community helps the effort succeed.

Habits of Mind Awards

Awards are an effective way to encourage students to use their Habits of Mind. Awards can be distributed in various ways: as a whole-school award given each week (or however frequently your school holds assemblies); as a schoolwide, end-of-term or end-of-semester "special" award; or as a classroom-based award. In all cases, awards are a way to *respond with wonderment and awe* and celebrate the achievements and successes students have had and continue to make as they develop the habits. The school where I currently teach gives weekly awards that recognize students' use of the Habits of Mind, as well as end-of-term "special" awards that recognize a student who has found success through the use of the Habits of Mind.

Over the years, I have explored and used different ways to give awards within my classroom. All have their pros and cons, and the best approach requires determining what is right for you and your students. In any year, as the children and cohort change, so does my approach to implementing classroom awards. Here are some examples of strategies I have used:

Student-led awards. Each week I gave each student an award slip on which to write the name of a classmate of their choice. We then came together in a class circle each Friday afternoon to share and distribute the awards. I, too, participated and ensured that each student received an award from me during the term. Whoever collected the most awards became our Habit of Mind Thinker of the Week, and we posted the student's name on our classroom door. When I used this award system, the students were very open and honest. They valued each member of the class and could see which

Habits of Mind their classmates were using. Each student had a turn at being Thinker of the Week at some point. The awards were then collected and stapled together to form a Habits of Mind chain that we wove throughout our classroom as a visual to show how we "weave" the Habits of Mind into our daily discoveries and learnings.

Student-focus awards. At the beginning of the week, I gave each student a Habits of Mind award with a student's name on it. It was their task, over the week, to observe the student and write down which Habit of Mind the student was observed doing, and how that student was successful in using this particular habit. At the end of the week, we came together as a class to share these awards. Sometimes we would have a frenzy of activity, with students moving around the classroom to give their award to the recipient, congratulating that person, and turning around to find themselves receiving an award from a classmate. Like the student-choice awards, the student-focus awards were collected and linked to form a Habits of Mind chain. The beauty of this award system is that the students are acknowledging each other's successes, and each week every student is receiving an award recognizing effort. And yes, the teacher is included in this too. I used this award strategy with a Year 2 class, and they loved having the opportunity to award the teacher—as well as our valuable school support officers, who also participated. Students looked forward to Friday afternoons, when we would celebrate our achievements over the week. It was also an enjoyable way to reflect back, as before distributing the awards we would gather and talk about what hadn't gone so well that week and how we could set goals for the coming week. It was a positive way to end a week of learning and discovering.

Outside apps. A number of apps are designed with classroom management in mind, and many can be set up to incorporate recognition of achievement in the Habits of Mind. One year I had an app on my iPad that linked to my interactive whiteboard. On this

app, I had all the students' names, as well as the 16 Habits of Mind. When I saw students being successful in using a Habit of Mind or even *taking a responsible risk* by venturing to explore a new habit, I could tap their name and the Habit of Mind and give them a point (the points were collated at the end of the week for a prize). Students would hear the tap, look up at the visual on the whiteboard, and see their name and the reason they had received a point. An added advantage was that parents at home or work could log on to their child's account and see what points the child was receiving and why.

These examples illustrate just a few of the ways that awards can be used within the classroom. The important thing to consider when deciding which system to undertake is the students themselves. Each year your cohort will change, embodying different personalities and learning styles. Over three different years, I have used three different methods, each working well for the students in that class at the time. The key point is to know your students well enough so that you can determine whether the awards should be student-led or teacher-led or both, what will work best for your classroom routine and environment, and what can be not only implemented, but sustained.

Habits of Mind Animations

In conjunction with the Institute for Habits of Mind, WonderGroveLearn has developed instructional animations that are an invaluable resource to support implementation of the habits in kindergarten through Year 2 classrooms. The animations unpack the habits and demonstrate what they mean by using relatable characters students love. This resource also contains lessons linked to each video and materials for classroom use. The animations provide a fantastic starting point for a conversation about the Habits of Mind, including social situations students might encounter or how a habit directly relates to the classroom. The supporting lessons help review the habits and provide the repetition that students need to

implement them. My Year 1 students have found the animations incredibly engaging, providing another way—other than teacher instruction—to demonstrate and reinforce the habits. I value the ability to start and stop the animations at any time, allowing for the learning that so frequently comes through powerful conversations. I also appreciate that my students can take charge of their learning and explore the videos themselves if I set the program up as a station within the classroom.

Striving for Accuracy Glasses

One of my favorite classroom strategies for implementing the Habits of Mind is what I call *"striving for accuracy* glasses." The idea came to me a number of years ago when I was teaching Year 1. At the beginning of the school year, I was exploring *striving for accuracy* with my class and reviewing the strategies with them before they went off to finish their guided writing on their own. As they were finishing up and I was conferencing with each student individually, I found myself repeatedly asking the students whether they had strived for accuracy. I felt like a broken record and knew there had to be another way to remind them about this valuable habit. I knew it had to be something different; a poster on the wall just wasn't going to do it. Then it dawned on me: let's make funky glasses! I scoured the party stores and $2 shops searching for glasses that I could use. I bought all sorts of glasses (enough for one pair per student) and removed all the lenses. The next day I excitedly presented a special box to the class with a *striving for accuracy* poster attached. In a procedure I now follow every year, no matter what the grade, I began by explaining that these glasses were magic and amazing; that when you finished your work— any work—you could walk over and carefully place these glasses on and you would be able to strive for accuracy—and any errors, if you reread and searched carefully, would begin to dance off the page!

My students were beyond excited to give these glasses a try. Then one of them asked me if I didn't need to strive for accuracy too. I replied with a firm "of course" and showed the students my own huge and funky glasses, which made them burst out laughing!

My students then began their writing assignment very excitedly, and as they were finishing, they grabbed the glasses from the box. The room was abuzz with gasps, giggling, and wiggling as students reread their work and discovered their errors. Observing the class, I noticed a shift in the room after a few minutes. Students began to look to each other and ask questions about words they might have misspelled; some were moving to the word wall to check their work; others moved to grab a junior dictionary. The conversations around language and English were electric, and the quality of the writing they produced was astounding. I was proud of all the students, and we agreed there was something special about these glasses.

After our writing session, we reflected as a class on the glasses. We discussed their impact on our learning by engaging in a discussion using the S/W/SW (*strengths, weaknesses, and so what?*) model (Clark, 2009). I also held up the larger poster for *striving for accuracy* as a reminder of our goal and focus for the day. I was amazed at how well students were able to reflect on the purpose and relevance of these glasses. Their feedback included comments such as these:

- When I put them on, it was like my little mistakes jumped out at me!
- They really helped me reread.
- I remembered to check my work again.
- These glasses helped me see that striving for accuracy is important because I could see some of my letters were backward.

- I forgot to strive for accuracy, but then I remembered because I saw one of the other kids with the glasses on. It reminded me what I had to do!

- We need to use these glasses for each lesson. Can we find a great place for the box?

Here's a note about that last comment. Because I consider the class-room to be *our* space, not *my* space, I believe it is essential to ask the students where they would like to place their resources for learn-ing and discovering. We negotiate about the placement of word walls, Habits of Mind walls, learning walls, and displays through-out the year. This approach passes the ownership and responsibility regarding the classroom to all of us.

I am frequently asked if the novelty of the glasses wears off or if the students forget to put them on. The answer is simply, no. When the classroom culture and environment incorporate the idea of "three before me" or consulting a dictionary or a learning wall, and other practices and strategies are in place, the glasses are a natural extension. The power of the glasses in implementing the habit of *striving for accuracy* is like a pebble dropped in a pond; the ripples it creates circulate throughout the room. Once one student puts the glasses on, others follow without any direction from me. If, on the other hand, I notice that students are not striving for accuracy, I simply put on my glasses, and once again, without a word, the students follow.

Final Thoughts

The strategies shared in this chapter do not constitute an exhaustive list but rather represent some that I have developed over years of experience with the Habits of Mind. As you explore the habits with your students, you will create your own list. Some may work, and some may not, but remember to never give up. Persist! When embedded

in teaching and learning, the Habits of Mind unlock so much in children's minds. Students begin to be able to see how to achieve goals, to *listen with understanding and empathy,* and *communicate with clarity and precision* exactly what the problem or challenge may be; but also, they are more likely to *take a responsible risk* as they are armed with dispositions to help them know what to do when the solutions "are not immediately apparent" (Costa & Kallick, 2008, p. 88). Providing this core dispositional foundation for our young students through the Habits of Mind helps us to prepare them for the future. One can only begin to imagine where these amazing students will be and what positions they will hold as they grow up and contribute to our rapidly changing world.

———————————

Clark, L. (2009). *Where thinking and learning meet.* Victoria, Australia: Hawker Brownlow Education.

Costa, A. L., & Kallick, B. (2008). *Learning and leading with habits of mind: 16 essential characteristics for success.* Alexandria VA: ASCD.

Costa, A. L., & Kallick, B. (2014). *Dispositions: Reframing teaching and learning.* Thousand Oaks, CA: Corwin.

Wonder Grove Learn. (n.d.). Home page. Retrieved from https://wondergrovelearn.net/

7

Weaving the Habits of Mind into a School Culture and a National Curriculum

Cushla Scott

Katikati Kindergarten in Bay of Plenty, New Zealand, operates under the umbrella of Inspired Kindergartens, a not-for-profit, community-based organization. Situated in a small rural community, the three-teacher kindergarten is licensed to serve 30 children, ages 2 to 5.

The kindergarten is part of the Enviroschools network, and the following guiding principles are interwoven into the kindergarten's entire culture:

- We believe the environment is instrumental in advancing children's learning. Our program supports children in learning about the natural world, sustainable conservation, and healthy eating. We are educating children and their families about the concept of effecting change for a sustainable world. (In recognition of this ongoing commitment and passion, the kindergarten has received Bronze, Silver, Green-Gold, and in November 2017, Beyond-Green-Gold Enviroschools awards, presented by the Enviroschools Foundation of New Zealand.)

• Our philosophical pedagogy encompasses the principles of Habits of Mind, *Te Whāriki* (the New Zealand early childhood curriculum, first adopted by the Ministry of Education in 1996 and revised in 2017), *Te Whatu Pokeka* (the Kaupapa Maori Assessment for Learning adopted by the Ministry of Education in 2009), and Enviroschools guidelines.

• As critically reflective practitioners, we use a holistic perspective to bring an awareness of social justice, equity, and diversity into assessment.

Our History of Implementation

We have been implementing the Habits of Mind in our program since 2004. In our ongoing endeavor to improve our teaching practice, we regularly review, evaluate, and modify our program to ensure that it meets the needs of the children and meets our curriculum goals (thereby exemplifying the habit of *striving for accuracy*). We value the need to have a genuine shared vision with a clear set of principles guiding our teaching. Being introduced to the Habits of Mind through a respected colleague at the local primary school was a defining "light-bulb" moment. The habits complemented our existing philosophy and provided a rich foundation for our national curriculum, *Te Whāriki*.

Our kindergarten environment emphasizes a collective team spirit and recognizes that through dispositions, or habits, children's interests and strengths can be recognized and supported. This setting ensures that we provide for the cognitive, social, emotional, and physical development of the whole child.

How We Integrate the Habits in Practice

The Habits of Mind underpin our instruction and assessment practice. The following sections illustrate how we implement them into our daily routine.

Persisting

Our program supports the habit of *persisting* by providing opportunities and encouragement for children to develop their own interests and curiosity and embark on long-term projects that require perseverance and commitment. We provide a variety of materials and equipment to promote purposeful, creative, and constructive problem-solving strategies (Costa & Kallick, 2000a). Through their projects, the children at Katikati Kindergarten can revisit prior experiences, follow a process, and extend and develop their ideas and responses to learning situations. If we see them becoming frustrated, we encourage them to put their work aside, with an expectation that they will return to it at a later stage.

Guy Claxton (2002), a strong advocate for teaching resilience, talks about children developing their "learning muscles" and refers to having the ability to stick with things as "brain stretching." He also suggests that "it doesn't help a child to tackle a difficult task if they succeed consistently on an easy one. It doesn't teach them to persist in the face of obstacles if obstacles are always eliminated" (2002, p. 20). Similarly, Carol Dweck of Stanford University in California states, "What children learn best from are slightly difficult tasks which they have struggled through. Knowing they can cope with difficulties is what makes children seek challenges and overcome further problems" (cited in Claxton, 2002, p. 20).

As Carr and Claxton (2004) assert,

> Children's persisting, questioning or collaborating can develop in flexibility and sophistication. Whereas at one time "persisting" may simply have meant not giving up on a problem, later it can incorporate more elaborate strategies for mood repair, emotional maintenance or marshalling assistance, and these strategies may become more subtle and more delicately contingent on the sources of support or recuperation that particular environments afford. (p. 90)

Managing Impulsivity

Teaching and learning experiences for 2- to 5-year-old children at Katikati Kindergarten are often integrated with efforts to encourage socially appropriate behavior. *Managing impulsivity* can require lots of practice for young children.

Reframing strategies and language around *managing impulsivity* can cause a shift from what may previously have been perceived as negative behavior or experience, turning it into an empowering, positive learning opportunity for teachers, children, and parents. Costa and Kallick (2000a, p. 23) note that "reflective individuals consider alternatives and consequences of several possible directions before they take action." Knowing the theory that underpins our practice enables us to provide for socio-culturalism within our kindergarten. The guiding principles of our *Te Whāriki* document strongly reflect and emphasize the importance of relationships and also the essential role the community plays. Therefore, our children are developing a self-awareness of how their behaviors affect others around them. We, as a kindergarten, are continually evolving to meet the needs of diversity within our community.

We encourage children to recognize the various sources of distraction or frustration within the kindergarten setting and how to diminish them. We model a "Stop and think before you act" strategy for *managing impulsivity*. Our emphasis on caring for one another and the environment encompasses many opportunities and experiences that use the strategy. When a child has been hurt through his own impulsive action or has hurt someone else, we often use the language of the need to manage impulsivity and think about the outcome. When children were asked at group time what it meant to manage impulsivity, they gave the following answers, among others:

Stop and think.
Don't hurt people.
Be kind and helpful.
Don't break stuff.

Don't smash down people's towers.
Hug a tree!
Don't stand on our plants.
Recycle.
Save the turtles by not using plastic bags.

Listening with Understanding and Empathy

As teachers, we are very conscious of modeling active listening. Costa and Kallick (2000a) state, "Some psychologists believe that the ability to listen to another person—to empathize with and to understand that person's point of view—is one of the highest forms of intelligent behavior" (p. 23). Mat time (or circle time) offers a great opportunity for children to learn to wait their turn, listen, manage impulsivity, and express their feelings and communicate effectively. The New Zealand national curriculum, *Te Whāriki* (Ministry of Education, 1996), refers to the fact that "children gain increasing ability to convey and receive information, instruction, and ideas effectively and confidently by listening, speaking and using visual language in a range of contexts" (p. 97).

We often hear our children saying to one another, "You're not listening to me!" and "You don't understand me!" We support them in building strategies to resolve their own problems peacefully. We approach and first ask, "What seems to be the problem here?" We encourage the children to give an account of what happened and get them to articulate how to solve the problem. We do this by asking open-ended questions—for example, "How would you feel if . . . ?" or "What could you do to . . . ?" Children invariably solve their own problems and feel proud as a result. This approach empowers children and gives them confidence in their play environment.

Thinking Flexibly

The very nature of our kindergarten environment and emergent curriculum provides flexible, adaptive, and responsive opportunities for children to develop that "can do" attitude.

Young children are egocentric by nature, so being encouraged to work together and to resolve conflict by negotiating, listening, turn-taking, and listening to other points of view has a profound effect, both socially and cognitively. Within our program, teachers act as role models for flexible thinking by offering

- Group discussions whereby children hear varying perspectives.
- Games with rules that can be changed regularly.
- Routines that can be tweaked.
- Equipment and furniture that can be moved around.
- Jokes.
- Yoga, mindfulness, and breathing techniques.
- Socio-dramatic play and drama.
- A kindergarten treaty, guidelines created by the children that make the kindergarten a safe and happy place.

Some children are natural leaders and others are happy to follow. We are mindful to encourage the notion of taking turns with leading play and the importance of being flexible, open-minded, and instilling confidence.

We have observed that when children exhibit flexible thinking skills, they are better able to engage in positive interactions with their peers and to solve problems. "Flexibility is the cradle of humor, creativity and repertoire" (Costa and Kallick, 2000a). When children experience change or things don't go to plan, they can instinctively switch gears, show resilience, and find solutions.

Thinking About Thinking (Metacognition) and Striving for Accuracy

We believe that these two habits fit nicely in between *thinking and communicating with clarity and precision* and *questioning and posing problems* (Costa & Kallick, 2000a, pp. 26, 28). The analogy of the woven mat in *Te Whāriki* is very compatible with the Habits of Mind, as many

habits can be interwoven with one another. Bertram and Pascal (2002) refer to the fact that "motivated children expend the necessary energy to achieve their goals . . . they independently become deeply involved and engrossed in activities and challenges" (p. 249).

When children give up easily, our teachers often say, "You need to try; it's part of your learning." Children readily accept this challenge. They reflect on this idea and immediately try again.

Questioning and Posing Problems

The habit *questioning and posing problems* is an integral part of our program. We encourage our children to contribute their strengths and interests and to work effectively with others as they figure things out. We know we need to provide plenty of opportunities for them to have sustained conversations, to question, to make discoveries, and to take the initiative in conversations. Claxton (2002) calls this having the ability to "lock in" to learning (p. 41).

Our emphasis on "education for sustainability" is a perfect example of how we encourage children in posing problems. We use complex language and heuristic questioning, and we encourage the children to self-educate, or learn by doing. Through involvement in the kindergarten setting's many and varied activities, the children are developing their reflective and creative thinking as they contribute their thoughts and ideas to the group. We encourage and reward children who take the risk of asking a question. This behavior is as valuable as giving answers.

Group time is another opportunity for these behaviors to take place. It also provides a good guide for taking note of children's ability to engage and pay attention to what is going on around them, which in turn is a life skill. Through our participation in the BASE (Baby Watching Against Aggression and Anxiety for Sensitivity and Empathy) program, children are encouraged to ask questions. At first, they simply offer information. We reflect on whether their contribution is a question or a statement of information. This process

continues until the children can differentiate between sharing information and asking a question, for which they were seeking an answer. Sometimes we also throw the question back to the child, by asking "What do *you* think?" We find children readily share their working theories of the world around them, if given the chance.

Carr and Claxton (2004) point out that "an 'inviting' environment is one that not only affords the chance to ask questions, for example, but clearly highlights this as a valued activity. Asking questions or working with others is made attractive and appealing to students" (p. 91). Costa and Kallick (2000a) agree that children who know how to ask questions become problem solvers because they want to know the answer and therefore "fill in the gaps between what they know and what they don't know" (p. 29). We are continually reviewing our program and our environment to be sure that they are organized in a way that enables children to initiate problem-solving activities, whereby they can devise their own problems as well as predict, estimate, discuss, and consider alternative theories.

Thinking and Communicating with Clarity and Precision

The *Te Whāriki* curriculum document (Ministry of Education, 1996) states:

> Communication reinforces the child's holistic development of a concept of self, enhancing their recognition of their spiritual dimension and the contribution of their heritage and environment to their own lives. Children are developing increasing competence in symbolic, abstract, imaginative, and creative thinking. (p. 72)

By providing careful support, guidance, and encouragement and provoking curiosity and wonder, we encourage children to do research and come up with their own theories and opinions. The goal is to have children become responsible for their own learning and to reflect upon what is going well and what they need further support with. Teachers use multiple questioning techniques to foster children's inquiry.

Applying Past Knowledge to New Situations

Children love connecting links from home to school, drawing on past experiences, and sharing those links with the group. We are constantly reminding them of some past problem they encountered, how they solved it, and how they can transfer that learning to resolve a current problem or dilemma. Children bring a wealth of knowledge with them. As Don Tolman noted in a 2010 Bootcamp for Brains workshop: "They are the sum total of all the records and books of knowledge of all their ancestors who came before them."

Carr and Claxton (2004) point out that positive learning responses develop as children begin to realize "that the habits of learning that have stood them in good stead in one domain—doing jigsaws, say—are also applicable and useful in another—trying to write a story" (pp. 352–353). The learning response, though it may initially have taken root more strongly in the context of one activity than another, can spread in its application so that it becomes more "across the board."

At Katikati Kindergarten we also provide many opportunities for children to learn from one another. We often tell our children that they too are teachers; they teach one another, as well as teaching the teachers sometimes. This always makes them smile proudly.

Our assessment resource *Te Whatu Pokeka* (Ministry of Education, 2009) refers to the Maori term *mohiotanga* as "what a child already knows, and what they bring with them" (p. 49). This concept has a huge significance in children's development.

Gathering Data Through All Senses

Our kindergarten provides a wonderful environment for inviting children to become involved, for arousing and engaging their interest. Their senses are constantly stimulated as they investigate and discover their world. Creating and maintaining vegetable gardens is just one example of how children at the school experience and observe nature. They develop their knowledge about the

diversity of their living world, how plants grow, and interesting facts about what is required for their well-being. Children are naturally inquisitive, so *gathering data through all senses* is instinctive.

We see the joy on children's faces when they can finally pick the flower or the vegetable that they planted from seed, nurtured, and can now harvest. What better way to engage all the senses than cooking with the vegetables and herbs from our garden? It appeals to the senses of touch, smell, and taste, bringing about a heady engagement of senses on high alert.

Te Whāriki (Ministry of Education, 1996) recognizes the importance of "children developing the confidence to choose and experiment with materials, to play around with ideas, and to explore actively with all the senses" (p. 88). With this in mind, many of our younger children spend much of their settling-in period engaging in sensory data gathering, exploring sand, water, clay, and the natural areas in the playground. This pleasure in discovery assists with their development of a sense of belonging within the kindergarten environment.

Creating, Imagining, and Innovating

"Creativity is characterized by those children who show curiosity and interest in their world. . . . The creative child is imaginative, spontaneous, and innovative" (Bertram & Pascal, 2002, p. 248). With this idea in mind, our program provides multiple opportunities for children to extend their exploration and experimentation through *creating, imagining, and innovating*. Creativity comes naturally to young children, and our kindergarten program provides them with many opportunities to play around with ideas, to experiment, and to learn through play. We know that creative people are wonderful assets— unafraid to try new and challenging things. We seek to nurture this skill and allow children to feel confident to break new ground in a safe environment. As teachers, we are always modeling this notion by trying out new things ourselves.

Our curriculum extends the belief that we do not come with too many preconceived ideas or scripts as to children's learning. We do not formulate the learning in advance, but rather encourage and extend each child's unique strengths and interests. We are mindful to relinquish our own agendas and carefully follow the lead of the child. In doing this, we are building children's self-esteem and the belief that they can do anything.

Early childhood is a fertile breeding ground for encouraging creative solutions to problems. We consider ourselves to be ambassadors of *creating, imagining, and innovating*. We don't ridicule anyone for even the most outrageous suggestions. We encourage children to come up with unique answers.

Responding with Wonderment and Awe

The children at Katikati Kindergarten are given many opportunities to develop a sense of wonder and an appreciation for the beauty and mystery of the natural world. Children are naturally curious and love to express their wonderment at discovering little things that adults might not see. This expression of awe is a wonderful gem of discovery. The peal of laughter that splits the background noise in two, the widening eyes that reflect the unfolding mysteries, the expression of amazement—these are the moments when we acknowledge that some great learning has taken place. The experience may also present itself in the joy of accomplishment, as when a child completes a difficult puzzle and, relishing that moment when the final piece finds a resting place, responds with a shrill whoop and look of awe—the "I did it!" moment. May there be many such moments in a child's life.

Taking Responsible Risks

When did you last venture out of your comfort zone? As adults, we generally try something if we think we will succeed. Most children, on the other hand, need very little encouragement. They will try anything, as failure is not even part of their vocabulary yet.

We encourage children to assess the risk to mind and body and then "go for it!" We encourage those who are hesitant with "Come on, try! You can do it. It's part of your learning!" Once again, by reinforcing the idea that children are responsible for their own learning, we encourage their natural inclination to try. We praise them for their efforts, even if they failed to attain the desired result—"Wow! You tried! Well done! That shows me that you are learning and growing!" The look on a child's face in response is one of sheer exhilaration. We constantly encourage our children to take intellectual as well as physical risks, as the ability to do so will equip them with the tools to succeed in this age of innovation and uncertainty. Risk taking is also incorporated into reports given to parents.

Finding Humor

The teaching team at Katikati Kindergarten values humor, and never a day goes by without some heartfelt belly laugh shared with colleagues or children. Children sometimes come to kindergarten with heavy agendas, and we feel that they are capable of learning to find humor in situations that may ordinarily not be "funny." For example, a child may experience a spectacular accidental fall. The immediate reaction will be to look at the adult for a horrified reaction and then dissolve into tears. We have learned to show a look of exaggerated awe, accompanied with a statement such as "Awesome fall! That was amazing! Do it again, but be careful to not hurt yourself, OK?" The child will look stunned, then smile and pretend to fall again, and we share a laugh at the antics. This response elicits quite a different outcome compared with the response of an adult looking concerned—which will start the child crying.

Instilling a sense of fun helps children relax and feel a sense of belonging. Humor has been found to have "positive effects on psychological functions including a drop in the pulse rate, secretion of endorphins, and increased oxygen in the blood." It has also been found to "liberate creativity and provoke such higher-level thinking

skills as anticipating, finding novel relationships, visual imaging, and making analogies" (Costa & Kallick, 2000a, p. 36).

Te Whāriki (Ministry of Education, 1996) refers to recognizing the need for children "to enjoy nonsense explanations" (p. 90). We regularly have fun with alliteration and rhyming, games, stories, and dramatic and symbolic play activities.

Thinking Interdependently

We agree with the notion that the ability to work interdependently forms the foundation for lifelong skills and satisfying relationships (Costa & Kallick, 2000a). Collaboration with adults and children plays a central role in this development. A raft of research supports the importance of developing social confidence and its long-term positive effects on empowerment.

The early childhood setting provides numerous opportunities for children to interact in a team environment. The ability to work productively with and alongside others produces extraordinary results. Children also have a tendency to pick up the habits of those around them, and so once again, we have a responsibility to be good role models and to expect this of our children, who are, in turn, the "teachers" of their peers. *Te Whāriki* (Ministry of Education, 1996) suggests that "through working with others, children develop respect for differences, and an understanding of their roles, rights, and responsibilities in relation to other people" (p. 96). In this spirit, we model respect for self, others, and the environment.

Remaining Open to Continuous Learning

This Habit of Mind ties in with *taking responsible risks* and *persisting*. We encourage children to try—and then to try a different way if the first way was not successful. This approach encourages openness to continuous learning. When children come with questions for which we have no answer, we join them in a journey of discovery to gather the knowledge, whether it be from a book, the internet, or a parent with expertise in that area.

This practice demonstrates that there are numerous ways to seek answers or information, and it models the notion that we are all life-long learners. "Once children learn how to learn, nothing is going to narrow their minds. The essence of teaching is to make learning contagious, to have one idea spark another" (Marva Collins, cited in Kagan & Kettle, 2005, p. 285).

The Link to the New Zealand Early Childhood Curriculum

Our curriculum, *Te Whāriki,* has a strong emphasis on holistic, active learning and the total learning process. It directly relates to the way in which knowledge, skills, and attitudes combine as *dispositions*— what Costa and Kallick (2000a) call Habits of Mind and Claxton (2002) calls "patterns for learning." According to *Te Whāriki,*

> Dispositions are important learning outcomes that are encouraged, not taught. To encourage robust dispositions to reason, investigate and collaborate, children will be immersed in communities where people discuss rules, are fair, explore questions about how things work, and help each other. The children will see and participate in these activities. . . . Dispositions to learn develop when children are immersed in an environment that is characterized by well-being and trust, belonging and purposeful activity, contributing and collaborating, communicating and representing, and exploring and guided participation. Dispositions provide a framework for developing working theories and expertise about the range of topics, activities, and materials that children and adults in each early childhood service engage with. (Ministry of Education, 1996, pp. 44–45)

Assessment and Documentation

Our assessment and documentation of children's learning is also available electronically. We use Story Park, which provides an e-portfolio for each child. The portfolio helps teachers, parents, and families work together to record, share, and extend children's learning. The software has been customized for our kindergarten

and includes the Habits of Mind, allowing us to weave them into our stories and observations. We use the tool to analyze the growth, progress, and direction of each child's unique learning journey. During our internal reflection and evaluation meetings, we can conveniently go to the report section and notice emergent trends within our curriculum and plan accordingly.

* * *

At Katikati Kindergarten, we provide an environment that responds to the abilities, interests, learning styles, and motivations for children's learning. As kindergarten teachers, we consider whether our behaviors empower or undermine children's dispositions, then alter our practices accordingly. We are committed to continuous learning as we work to deliver a program that always benefits the child as a learner, the child is always at the center of everything we do.

> Habits are not behaviors we pick up and lay down whimsically or arbitrarily. They are behaviors we exhibit reliably on appropriate occasions and they are smoothly triggered without painstaking attention. (Perkins, in Costa and Kallick, 2000a, 2000b, 2000c, 2000d)

Note: On behalf of my colleagues, we acknowledge Inspired Kindergartens, our umbrella organization, for giving us the autonomy to embark on this incredible learning journey. We are fortunate to belong to a dynamic learning organization that is always seeking to be innovative and has a commitment to responding to individual, team, and community needs. Without their values, vision, and strategic plan, we would not have had the freedom to explore this journey of professional growth.

Bertram, T., & Pascal, C. (2002). What counts in early learning. In O. N. Saracho & B. Spodex (Eds.), *Contemporary perspectives in early childhood curriculum* (pp. 241–256). Greenwich, CT: Information Age.

Carr, M., & Claxton, G. (2004). A framework for teaching learning: Dynamics of disposition. *Early years, 24*(1), 87–97.

Claxton, G. (2002). *Building learning power: Helping young children to become better learners*. Bristol, UK: TLO.

Costa, A. L., & Kallick, B. (2000a). *Habits of mind: A developmental series: Book I. Discovering and exploring habits of mind*. Alexandria, VA: ASCD.

Costa, A. L., & Kallick, B. (2000b). *Habits of mind: A developmental series: Book II. Activating and engaging habits of mind*. Alexandria, VA: ASCD.

Costa, A. L., & Kallick, B. (2000c). *Habits of mind: A developmental series: Book III. Assessing and reporting on habits of mind*. Alexandria, VA: ASCD.

Costa, A. L., & Kallick, B. (2000d). *Habits of mind: A developmental series: Book IV. Integrating and sustaining habits of mind*. Alexandria, VA: ASCD.

Enviroschools. (2011). *Enviroschools in the early years*. Hamilton, NZ: Author.

Kagan, S., & Kettle, K. (2005). *Inspirational quotations, inspiration for leaders and learners*. Victoria, Australia: Kagan.

Ministry of Education. (1996). *Te Whāriki; he whāriki matauranga mo nga mokopuna o Aotearoa-Early Childhood Curriculum*. Wellington, NZ: Learning Media.

Ministry of Education. (2002). *Enviroschools kit*. Department of Conservation. Ministry for the Environment. Hamilton, NZ.

Ministry of Education. (2009). *Te Whatu Pokeka Kaupapa Maori assessment for learning, early childhood exemplars*. Wellington, NZ: Learning Media.

8

Habits of Mind with English Language Learners

Aixa Perez-Prado

My first full-time teaching job was as a bilingual Spanish/English kindergarten teacher in Salinas, California. Most of the students in my class were the children of Mexican immigrants, many of them migrant workers. Several families left for months at a time during the school year, following the crops. Most had few resources at home. Some of my 5-year-old students had to stay home from school occasionally to care for younger brothers or sisters. Their families were low-income, somewhat transient, and generally poorly educated. Despite these significant challenges, the children were eager, bright, resilient, and motivated students who taught me much more than I taught them that first year of teaching.

Through my interactions and experiences as a bilingual kindergarten teacher, I began to build on my teaching philosophy and repertoire of ESOL (English for Speakers of Other Languages) teaching strategies and techniques. I didn't know it at the time, but we practiced the Habits of Mind without having an explicit language for teaching them. These habits became an important foundation

for teaching young linguistic- and cultural-minority students. Once I had the names for the habits, I realized the importance of integrating them with learner-centered communicative methods and techniques.

When I was first hired as a bilingual kindergarten teacher, I had no background in teaching children or in teaching bilingually. I was born in Argentina and spoke Spanish. I came to the United States as an immigrant when I was 4 years old. Although I was teaching many immigrant children, my experience as a new-language learner from a privileged family background was significantly different from that of the children I taught. My first year of teaching challenged my Spanish language skills, my presumptions about how children learn languages, and my ideas about how to teach languages effectively.

During several more years teaching English to both young children and older learners in Costa Rica, Morocco, and Florida, I learned as I taught. I am now teaching foreign language–teaching methods to preservice teachers at the university level. I have developed a list of specific actions, or strategies, that are essential for good language acquisition. Creating and adapting activities that infuse these strategies is a worthwhile undertaking no matter the background or the proficiency level of language learners. Every strategy is an important component of how I design my language lessons.

The beauty of these strategies is that they can be applied to any content area, any grade level, and any proficiency level in the target language. Every activity that already exists can be made more ESOL- or second language–friendly simply by applying or adapting these strategies as necessary.

Habits of Mind for Teachers of Language Learners

Although all Habits of Mind have a place in the ESOL classroom, four are particularly important. The ones I have relied on more than any others are *listening with understanding and empathy, thinking*

flexibly, managing impulsivity, and *creating, imagining, and innovating.* Let's look at each of these in turn.

Listening with Understanding and Empathy

Perhaps the primary lesson I learned as a young bilingual teacher was to listen first, ask questions later. I learned a lot about the habit of *listening with understanding and empathy.* It may seem odd to mention listening first when the primary goal of language teaching is not for the teacher to listen, but rather for the students to be able to listen and understand the language and then very quickly produce it. However, I have found through the years that unless I listen first, with empathy and understanding, no matter how many fun activities or techniques I come up with, they may not be effective in the classroom.

Young children need and should be encouraged to express them-selves freely and without judgment. Giving children the necessary tools for personal expression and an environment where expres-sion is welcome, appreciated, and not judged is an essential aspect of a language-acquisition environment. This approach is what we naturally do with babies learning their first languages. We give them time, praise, attention, and the freedom to express themselves in whatever way they can.

Thinking Flexibly

Another Habit of Mind that is essential as a teacher of language learners is *thinking flexibly.* By practicing flexible thinking and modeling it for my students, I encourage them to be flexible thinkers themselves. This habit is especially useful in language classes as students need to be able to express themselves in a language that is not their own and that often does not have the exact words or struc-tures they need. By learning to think flexibly in another language, children are learning an important set of critical-thinking skills, as well as an essential discourse skill: *circumlocution.* Circumlocution is what we do during oral interactions when we are not quite sure of the words we need or how to express ourselves. We use other words

to describe what we are thinking of until whoever is listening figures out what we mean. Circumlocution is a great tool for language learners because it encourages them to think critically, to use more words, and to take responsible risks in learning another language. My students learn that just because they didn't have the exact words or couldn't express themselves perfectly, that doesn't mean that they can't use the target language effectively. They learn to describe what they are trying to say, to use body language, and to employ context clues to understand when they aren't sure.

Managing Impulsivity

As a teacher of language learners and young children, it is also essential to keep in mind the habit of *managing impulsivity*. Many teachers (especially grammar-loving language teachers) are enamored by what is "correct" and what is "incorrect." Although as a language teacher I want to model accepted standard academic language for my learners, I also need to remember that they are in the acquisition process and will necessarily make many errors that I do not need to overtly correct. This realization can be difficult. It is so much easier to jump in with the correct answer than to allow the learner the time and the experience to self-correct. However, overcorrection and a strict focus on form does not seem to benefit language acquisition in any significant way over time. This reality is especially true for young learners who have less meta-knowledge of linguistic structure and who need the time and the space to discover the world around them. While they are playing in a new language, young children are figuring out language rules through natural interaction with the built-in routine and repetition of games, and through the creativity and imagination of unstructured play.

Creating, Imagining, and Innovating

As a teacher of early childhood students, implementing the habit of *creating, imagining, and innovating* is certainly at the zenith of desirable actions. The ability to enter the world of imagination with the children in the classroom is an essential element of structuring an environment

in which language can be experimented with and practiced as it is being acquired. In such an environment, language becomes the vehicle through which imagination is expressed and recounted to others even as it is used to accomplish the tasks of everyday life. The freedom that we allow young children to enjoy by using their imaginations through play in the early grades is an important and valuable component of the rich and supportive environment that allows language acquisition to take place. A teacher who recognizes this and practices creating, imagining, and innovating herself gives her students continuous opportunities to use language in multiple ways.

LAF Strategies: What They Are and How to Infuse Them in Teaching Young Language Learners

The following sections describe a set of language-acquisition-friendly (LAF) strategies that I strive to include in every activity and lesson that I plan for my young language learners. These strategies go hand in hand with many of the Habits of Mind, and I have come to think of them as being ways to incorporate the habits into the lessons I teach while concurrently giving my language learners the best possible preparation in the language they are acquiring. Any existing lesson or activity can be adapted to include most of these strategies and thereby be made more amenable to second-language acquisition. The way to do this depends on the creativity and knowledge of the teacher and her ability and willingness to employ essential Habits of Mind in her lesson planning and teaching.

In addition to having student practice the language described in the activities below through the Habits of Mind, teachers should emphasize and use the actual language of the habits so that children become accustomed to the vocabulary and learn to both understand and use the terms themselves. With English language learners (ELLs), the emphasis should be on exposure to and understanding of the vocabulary rather than on production at the early stages. As the

ELLs build their linguistic repertoire in English, they will naturally begin to use the essential vocabulary of the Habits of Mind as they apply the habits to their learning. We want the children to associate the label of the Habit of Mind with their behavior. So, when the teacher recognizes that the students are using one or more of the habits, she should be quick to use the related vocabulary, as in "You were *persisting* when you kept trying different ways to solve the problem" or "You used *clear and precise language* when you explained how the farmer found his lost sheep."

LAF Strategy 1: Activities Should Be Personal and Meaningful

The way to make activities personal and meaningful is to first *listen with understanding and empathy* to your learners. Once you know what motivates them, what concerns them, and how they feel, you can easily change any lesson into a more personal and meaningful one by making connections to those learners.

When *listening with understanding and empathy*, a teacher comes to know her learners well and is able to design activities and create techniques that work for them. One activity that I have often used to practice listening with my young learners is the "listening story." The story changes every time but is always a very short narrative that the learners listen to while closing their eyes. I ask them to visualize what they are hearing and imagine themselves in the narrative. I then ask them to answer questions based on what they visualized. The questions always have more than one possible right answer. Each student is able to make a personal and meaningful connection to the story through his or her own visualization and to answer the questions based on this personal connection. For example, I have used the following story on many occasions:

> One day, a brother and sister who lived very far away from here went to their cousin's birthday party. They were very hungry when they got there, so they were happy to see all of the food on the table. There were many things to eat, including a very big cake.

All of the children at the party played games outside and had a good time. Their cousin liked all of his presents, and at the end of the party he gave them each a goody bag to take home.

Questions designed to see if they were *listening with understanding and empathy* include the following:

- Where was the party?
- What kinds of foods were at the party, and how did they taste?
- What games were played at the party?
- When were the gifts opened, and what were they?
- Who had the most fun at the party?
- How do you think the children felt after getting a goody bag?

Young learners come up with all kinds of answers based on what they imagined for themselves. These answers are always personal and meaningful because they come from their own background experiences and cultural knowledge of how birthdays are celebrated. Therefore, there are many correct answers to each of the questions, and multiple perspectives are allowed and welcomed so everyone has a chance to succeed and practice language.

LAF Strategy 2: Activities Should Be Interactive

Interactivity is essential to second-language acquisition, as it is to first-language acquisition. Without interactivity there is no language, as the primary function of language is to communicate with others. Another essential function of language is to allow us to think abstractly and to work interdependently to solve problems by sharing thoughts and ideas. The habits of *thinking interdependently, managing impulsivity,* and *communicating with clarity and precision* are naturally applied during interactive activities.

An infinite number of interactive activities can be implemented with young language learners, enabling them to practice these important habits while giving them opportunities to use language in

novel and familiar ways. These activities include role-plays, games, puppet play, information-gap activities, and task-based language activities.

One example of a task-based interactive activity is to put young learners in small groups and give each of them a clue to solve a puzzle, a riddle, or a mystery. The clue may be in the form of pictures or words, depending on the age and abilities of the learners. In one version of this activity, I give my young learners clues only they can see at the bottom of brown lunch bags. They are not allowed to show their clues to others in their small group, but they need to describe the clues and figure out together how to solve the mystery that the clues give hints for. Here is an example: *Who stole the dirty socks from the hamper?* Each child has a clue in the bag to help solve the mystery. I usually try to use the habit of *finding humor* in activities I do with young learners, as it keeps them engaged, encourages them to *take responsible risks* with their language, and reinforces an atmosphere where learning is fun and it is OK to make mistakes.

LAF Strategy 3: Activities Must Include Higher-Order Thinking

By incorporating higher-order thinking skills in teaching, students are met with a challenge from the first day of class, and therefore they are immediately putting into practice the use of language to think and to analyze. All Habits of Mind include higher-order thinking skills, as they are the practices we want to employ when addressing a problem for which the answer is not immediately apparent. I tend to concentrate primarily on the habit of *thinking flexibly* with young learners, though *questioning and posing problems* and *thinking about thinking (metacognition)* are strong second and third featured habits in my higher-order thinking activities.

One of many thinking activities I do with young learners is one I learned way back in my bilingual kindergarten teacher days. The activity is called "I've Got Something in My Pocket." In this activity, which is adaptable to any language level and content area, the

teacher first models by pulling an imaginary object out of her pocket and pretending to use it in some way that makes it obvious what that object is. For example, I have often pulled an imaginary car out of my pocket and mimicked myself driving so that the children could guess the word *car*. In order for the activity to encourage both *thinking flexibly* and *thinking interdependently*—and to also encourage the use of complex language—I usually start with easy-to-guess real objects and move on to more difficult concepts that involve a lot of guessing and imagination. For example, after I pull a car out of my pocket and give each child a chance to pull something imaginary out of his or her pocket for the class to guess, I change the rules by saying something like, "OK, now put your extra-powerful thinking caps on because I am going to pull a past event out of my pocket instead of a thing." Once we all understand what a "past event" is, I can pull a visit to the library out of my pocket, or a holiday party. It can get increasingly complicated with pulling all kinds of things out of my pocket, such as "kindness" or "jealousy." Young children are great at *thinking flexibly*, and during this activity they get to practice this habit along with listening, speaking, and negotiating meaning. They also practice questioning and cooperating skills as they guess what I've pulled out of my pocket and modify their guesses based on other children's guesses and my responses.

LAF Strategy 4: Activities Should Include Graphics, Visuals, or Real Objects

Most good language-learning activities include more than one way of receiving and processing information. By incorporating graphics, visuals, or real objects into an activity, we give language learners a chance to understand what is happening even if they are not very sure of what the language being used means or how to use it on their own. This approach also gives us a chance as teachers and learners to incorporate the habits of *responding with wonderment and awe* and *gathering data through all the senses*.

In TESOL (Teaching English to Speakers of Other Languages), we use the term *realia* to describe real-world objects that we bring into the classroom to give our learners contextual clues for understanding and to use in interactive activities. With young learners, the opportunity to explore with all of the senses in the classroom is essential, and most teachers readily integrate real objects that they bring themselves or that the children bring from home to share with the class.

One language-acquisition activity I have often done with language learners is a sense riddle called "What Am I?" I give the students a basic structure to work with, and then I fill that in with clues so they can guess what it is that I am talking about. Nobody is allowed to guess until I have finished talking and they have consulted with one another in pairs (*thinking interdependently*). I have a picture or the real object in a box that I pull out when they have guessed the right answer. When possible, we all get a chance to look at, smell, taste, touch, or listen to the object. Here is an example of how the activity works:

What Am I? (a tomato)
    I look like: *a red sphere*
    I sound like: *something that doesn't make any noise*
    I feel like: *something smooth and squishy*
    I smell like: *something fresh from the garden*
    I taste like: *something juicy and not sweet*

This activity builds vocabulary while stimulating critical thinking and reinforcing the habit of *gathering data through all the senses*. Other times we "turn off" one or more of the senses, such as sight and hearing, and the students have to guess the object just by feel or smell or taste. I find that children enjoy this type of language-acquisition activity, which takes the focus off of language and on to sensory experiences. Often, I write the words on the board or poster paper as I am speaking to reinforce

vocabulary, and I include body language and gestures to enhance understanding.

LAF Strategy 5: Activities Should Be Cooperative

Good interactive activities are usually also cooperative activities. This point is important because it ensures that everyone gets a chance to interact and has the structure that is needed in order to know what to do. Cooperative activities naturally allow children to practice the habits of *thinking interdependently, managing impulsivity, persisting,* and *communicating with clarity and precision.*

Cooperative activities not only foster language acquisition but also help to encourage and to support peer relationships. Research indicates that meaningful and continuous relationships with peers are among the best indicators of whether children will acquire a second language with relative ease and speed and whether they will remain in school (Sato & Ballinger, 2016). Heterogeneous grouping is recommended and is comprised of learners who are at different levels of language acquisition and ideally includes both native and nonnative speakers of a target language. When setting up heterogeneous groups, it is essential to ensure that these groups require face-to-face interaction, positive interdependence, and individual accountability. Most successful cooperative groups feature a task that needs to be completed or a problem that needs to be solved by the group, with each member having part of the solution or a necessary role to perform in solving the problem. Almost any reading or content-area lesson can include a cooperative activity that reinforces or presents the content material.

One type of cooperative learning structure I have often used with language learners is one I call "Think, Show, Say, Share," or TSSS. I find it a very effective way to foster thinking skills as well as language skills because it includes a designated-thinking component that asks students to think about a question or an issue silently without producing any vocal language whatsoever. Often language

learners need some extra time to think, and this activity gives them that specified time without singling them out. Some students will be practicing the habit of *managing impulsivity* during this portion of the activity by not blurting out their thoughts, while others will need the extra time to put their thoughts into words.

During the "Show" portion of TSSS, young learners who are not yet writing on their own draw their ideas or thoughts on a sheet of paper. During the "Say" time, they join in a small group with other children and recount their ideas to one another. This allows for face-to-face interaction and individual accountability. Students in this interactive part of the activity have the same role—to explain what their thoughts were. Later, I normally have small groups "Share" their information with the whole class. This process involves some negotiation of meaning and plenty of interaction. It also allows them to practice the habits of *communicating with clarity and precision* as well as *thinking interdependently*. In addition, I often ask small-group members during "Share" time to explain one another's ideas to me or to the rest of the class, instead of explaining their own ideas. In this way I can reinforce the value of listening to one another, and if they didn't listen the first time, then they get more language practice in asking and answering questions for clarification to be able to explain what another person is thinking.

LAF Strategy 6: Activities Should Be Multicultural and Include Multiple Perspectives

Second-language learners are generally members of cultures and language groups that are not represented by the target language group. Therefore, they bring with them into the classroom a variety of ideas, perspectives, and experiences that may be different from those of the majority culture. By incorporating multicultural elements into activities in the classroom, the diversity of language learners and all students is valued and appreciated by the whole class.

It is a common misperception that "multicultural education" means that teachers should be talking about many cultures all the time or covering surface-level aspects of numerous nationalities, such as favorite foods, holidays, and celebrations. Although this approach can be fun, it is not what is meant by multicultural education, and it is not particularly helpful to language acquisition. Allowing for and seeking out and valuing multiple perspectives is a more accurate description of what language learners and all learners in the classroom need.

Any activity can include a multicultural aspect simply by allowing multiple perspectives as part of the activity. This approach allows students to readily practice the habits of *thinking flexibly* and *applying past knowledge to new situations*. One way that I try to always integrate multiple perspectives into my activities with young learners is by asking them to acknowledge and understand through our interactions that there is often more than one right answer to a problem and more than one way to see things. When we read a story together or learn about an event in the past, I ask them to imagine the situation from the points of view of different characters or historical figures relevant to the reading selection. We can do this through role-plays in which they take on a different persona, or with puppets or through skits and simulations. I also ask them to imagine themselves in the specific situations and consider how they would have reacted.

To be truly meaningful, multicultural education should go beyond the levels of adding information about different cultures to the curriculum; it should move toward transforming the curriculum through allowing for multiple perspectives and then taking action to think about and act on issues that affect different cultural groups in the society. For small children, this goal can often be achieved through science lessons with an environmental focus, through social studies examinations of immigration and displacement, through language arts activities that include reading selections from many different cultures and points of view, and in math by discovering multiple ways to arrive at the same answer to a problem.

For example, one activity that I have used with young children that integrates multicultural education and the Habits of Mind is called "How Can I Help?" In this activity, I ask children to brainstorm problems in their communities. Because the family is the primary community group for most young learners, this brainstorm usually generates problems that exist in families. Recently, a group of young learners I was working with came up with the following problem: "Parents work too much and don't have enough time to play!" They agreed on this as the biggest problem they faced after much heated discussion that included siblings behaving badly and the lack of daily opportunities to consume ice cream and candy.

Once children agreed on this as a community problem, we had small-group discussions about how each individual could help his or her family with this problem. They quickly realized that they could not work for their parents in their jobs, but they could help parents with work at home. Each child decided what could be done to help alleviate the workload at home. Small-group members worked together to figure out whether the possibilities to help were realistic, and when they weren't, they modified them. Once finished, each child prepared an index card with a drawing on one side of how he or she could help, and a description on the back in the child's own words (getting help with vocabulary and structure as needed). Language learners received help from their native-speaking peers. They carefully copied the descriptions they wanted on their cards and presented these to their families for homework. They put their help into practice every day for one week and then reported back to the whole class on the results.

LAF Strategy 7: Activities Should Be Engaging

It is not difficult to understand that to truly make an impact, a learning activity should engage the interest and participation of the learner. This point is particularly true for learners who have limited linguistic abilities. They are already struggling to understand what is

going on in school, so having activities that they want to participate in gives them the incentive to strive to understand and encourages their second-language acquisition.

We know from research on second-language acquisition that learners need to feel comfortable and free to express themselves without judgment in order to truly be able to fully engage in class-room activities (Krashen, 1987; Lightbown & Spada, 2006; MacIntyre & Gardner, 1991; MacIntyre & Mercer, 2014; Young, 1991). When the classroom environment further features engaging activities and rou-tines, the ideal stage is set for language acquisition to take place. Engaging activities often allow for practicing the habits of *finding humor, thinking flexibly,* and *responding with wonderment and awe.*

Almost any lesson or activity can be made more engaging for young learners by infusing humor or cooperative competition in the mix. I often accomplish this objective through storytelling; infusing art, music, or physical activity into the lesson; or setting up games and little competitions in the classroom. Although I am a strong believer in cooperative learning, I find that creating competition among cooperative groups can actively engage children while not putting too much pressure on any one individual.

One example of increasing the engaging nature of a language activity is to turn it from a receiving activity to a performing activity. I have often done this by using raps and chants in the classroom. First, I teach my learners a language rap or chant that I create on my own, locate in popular culture (such as from a nursery rhyme, song lyric, or jump rope chant), or find in an ESL book such as *Jazz Chants* (Graham & Rosenthal, 2001). After children have an opportunity to learn the chant and practice through choral repetition and call-and-response strategies, I have them create their own silly rap or chant in pairs or small groups with objects or pictures that I provide for them.

By providing learners with guidelines and criteria when asking them to create language, we are giving them some of the structure

they need in order to complete the task without making it too overwhelming. I often also try to include having my young learners incorporate their own names and one of their qualities or character-istics into a chant or rap to make it more personal and meaningful. There is really no need to encourage children to be silly—it comes naturally to them; but I often model for them a silly rap or chant about myself to get the ball rolling.

As an example, I showed a group of young ESOL students working in heterogeneous cooperative groups with native speakers the following chant that I had created. The objective was to learn some aspects of polite speech, encourage both listening and speaking, and have fun in the process:

I want a snack!
Please say please!
Get out of my way!
Please say excuse me!
My bike is fixed!
Please say thank you!
May I have a snack please?
Of course you may!
Please excuse me.
I'll get out of your way!
Thank you for fixing my bike!
That's OK!

After we practiced the chant for a while using repetition, call-and-response, and role-play, the children created their own chant based on the visual prompts of a piece of broccoli, a toothbrush, a grey crayon, a picture of a messy room, and a cookie. Here's what they came up with:

Eat your broccoli!
No way!
Brush your teeth!

They're not grey!
Take a shower!
I took one yesterday!
Clean your room!
I like it that way!
Eat your cookies!
OK!
Play outside!
Every day!
Get dirty!
Whatever you say!
Call your friends!
Yipee-yay!

Final Thoughts

Toward the end of my first year teaching bilingual kindergarten, a student from another classroom came looking for me one day. My kids and I were sitting in small groups on the floor engaged in an activity with interlocking cubes and jars that I had created to practice following directions. I don't recall the specifics of the activity, but I do remember that we were all laughing and having a good time. There was a knock at the door, and I asked one of my little girls, Nicolette, to open it. When she opened the door, I heard an older child ask her a question. Her response has always stuck with me. He asked, "Where's your teacher? I have a message for her." Nicolette replied, "She's that big kid over there" and pointed to me.

At the time, being referred to as "that big kid" bothered me a little bit, even though it made me smile. I wanted to make sure my students knew I was their teacher, and because I was young and also quite short, I knew that sometimes I could be mistaken for a high school student or a not-quite-adult. Now, when I think back on that

day, I feel proud that at least one of my kindergarteners considered me a "big kid," because I think that implies that she thought of me as someone who was her daily companion in the world of learning-through-play that I sought to achieve in my classroom.

As a TESOL professional, Habits of Mind trainer, childhood immigrant, and second-language learner, I have had many experiences and a good deal of education to bring to my understanding of the language-learning process. I believe that the LAF strategies that I have described in this chapter are genuinely helpful for teachers and students alike in promoting language acquisition while concurrently stimulating critical and creative thinking through the Habits of Mind. Although I did not mention this as one of the Habits of Mind I apply to my strategies and practices, *remaining open to continuous learning* is another essential factor in creating supportive and constructive environments for language acquisition. By paying careful attention to my students in every class, listening attentively, and observing their struggles and successes as language learners, I have been able to add to and refine my strategies and add to my repertoire of teaching activities over the years.

If we want to encourage children to keep their first languages so that they can have the advantage of being bilingual, we must ensure that they have the support and the guidance they need to be successful in their second language, and we want to provide the best and most stimulating of environments for language acquisition to take place. We can do this by giving them the opportunity to figure out language through interactive activities enhanced by strategies that encourage and motivate, all housed within an accepting and playful environment. Even those who do not have the ideal circumstances outside school to succeed can be provided with the tools they need in school to become the best and most successful language learners they can be. Through the implementation of LAF strategies housed

within the Habits of Mind, we teachers can ensure that fewer language learners will sink and many more will swim with the support and confidence they deserve.

    Note: To find lists of the Habits of Mind in several languages, please visit http://www.habitsofmindinstitute.org/resources/hom-languages/

Graham, C., & Rosenthal, M. S. (2001). *Jazz chants old and new.* New York: Oxford University Press.

Krashen, S. D. (1987). *Principles and practice in second language acquisition.* Upper Saddle River, NJ: Prentice Hall.

Lightbown, P. M., & Spada, N. (2006). *How languages are learned* (3rd ed.). Oxford: Oxford University Press.

MacIntyre, P. D., & Gardner, R. C. (1991). Methods and results in the study of anxiety and language learning: A review of the literature. *Language Learning, 41*(1), 85–117.

MacIntyre, P. D., & Mercer, S. (2014). Introducing positive psychology to SLA. *Studies in Second Language Learning and Teaching,* 4(2), 153–172.

Sato, M., & Ballinger, S. G. (2016). *Peer interaction and second language learning: Pedagogical potential and research agenda.* Amsterdam: John Benjamins.

Young, D. J. (1991). Creating a low-anxiety classroom environment: What does language anxiety research suggest? *The Modern Language Journal, 75*(4), 426–439.

The Power of Animations as a Teaching Tool

Terry Thoren

Storytelling is a universally powerful human invention, and since the development of language, it has been the way we learn, teach, make meaning, transfer culture, and create values. Animated stories can help design and refine a society's moral compass by instilling awareness and positive examples in the minds of our children. When we are successful at modeling the skills we want our children to develop through engaging animated stories and characters, these skills remain in their imagination and consciousness throughout their lives. Using animation to tell stories creates an emotional connection that makes the characters real enough so that children will want to model their behaviors. I believe that when children are exposed to engaging characters modeling appropriate social and emotional behavior, they will become the leaders (and problem solvers) of a more thoughtful world.

A Personal History

Early in my college days, I knew that I wanted to produce movies for families. I took an elective childhood psychology course and volunteered to work in my first Head Start classroom for extra credit. My primary task was reading storybooks to the class and individually to some 4-year-old boys who did not have dads living in their homes. Those boys were hungry for attention from a male figure in their lives, and my experience there had an impact and inspired me to learn more about children and how they think. More recently my passion for storytelling to young children has been rekindled by researching and testing the power of animated lessons in the classroom.

From 1983 to 1994, I traveled to six of the seven continents searching for the world's best animation to share with U.S. audiences. In 1987 I created *Animation Magazine* to write about the power of animation as a global art form, and in 2017 the publication celebrated its 30th anniversary. In the 1990s I was the CEO of a company called Klasky Csupo, where I oversaw the production of four movies for Paramount and 600 episodes of animated, family-values TV series for Nickelodeon, including the *Rugrats*, *The Wild Thornberrys*, and *Rocket Power*. The experience fueled my vision as I shifted from entertainment to education.

I have always loved animated stories because of the powerful way animated characters connect with us. For one hundred years, cartoon creators have established a cinematic language that is colorful and emotionally powerful. Many people enjoy the cartoon anarchy portrayed in such classics as *Tom and Jerry* and more contemporary series such as *SpongeBob SquarePants*. The irony, however, is that cartoon anarchy shows like *SpongeBob SquarePants* put the *Rugrats* out of business. Network research indicated that cartoon anarchy and action adventure shows sell more merchandise than thoughtful family comedies, and merchandise is considered the pot of gold at the end of the rainbow for Hollywood animation producers.

My father inspired me to leave Hollywood to work with my sister, who has been a teacher of children with special needs in Denver for more than 30 years. My dad said, "Why don't you stop producing TV animation to sell junk food and toys to kids and figure out a way to use animated stories to model appropriate behavior for students in your sister's classroom?" So my new journey began. My sister and I started writing animated stories to address the most difficult challenges in her classroom of 4- to 6-year-old children with special needs. And it worked! We produced 200 animated lessons to teach social-emotional learning skills and develop a culture of positivity, optimism, and mindfulness in the classroom.

Our dad was a Hall of Fame baseball coach at Cornell University. One of the secrets to his success was systematically repeating the fundamentals of all aspects of the game so that when his players were in a game, they kicked into autopilot mode and operated on instinct. His players had a reputation for being fundamentally sound. My sister and I wanted to use this same formula of systematic repetition to teach children social-emotional learning skills in pre-school through 3rd grade, and we are using the power of animated storytelling to strengthen this mission.

Partnering with the Institute for Habits of Mind

When I met Art Costa and Bena Kallick in 2013, I discovered we had a shared vision and mission for the future of our youth and our world. Wonder Media formed a partnership with the Institute for Habits of Mind to teach the 16 essential dispositions to young children through animation. See Figure 9.1 for an introduction to the animated characters that can help young children see, hear, and understand how the habits are useful in their own lives. The Habits of Mind not only addressed the fundamentals and the "Big R's" (Reading, wRiting, aRithmetic, and Reality), Costa and Kallick were also grounded in the same "heart" that had been the center of my work in Hollywood and more recently in education. We agreed

FIGURE 9.1   **Animations to Teach the Habits of Mind**

that when entering 3rd grade, children must be at grade level in reading, writing, and math to survive the long journey to high school graduation. But they also must be fundamentally sound in the ability to handle the changing reality of the world we live in. To do this, they need creative- and critical-thinking skills, as well as social and emotional skills—and who better to deliver this learning than animated characters?

Many early childhood educators ask whether the language and concepts of the Habits of Mind are too sophisticated for young children. However, we saw that the beauty and scope of animation would allow us to express complicated ideas in a simple, easy-to-understand format. Our animated characters are also easy to love—and to trust. And we have seen that the 16 instructional *Habits of Mind Animations* become a game-changer for teachers who want to have a direct and instructive way to introduce the habits. The universality of animated characters allows them to speak to everyone, and we don't question their race, religion, culture, or creed. We immediately connect with the characters' personalities and enjoy their diverse and imaginative personas and the unique content of their animated world.

• Peter is a courageous leader or a loyal sidekick, depending on the day. He's uncomplicated, optimistic, and fun to be around. He's curious, instinctive, and a catalyst for adventure. Peter is the athlete of the group and MVP of the soccer team, the Mighty Lizards. His academics sometimes take a back seat to sports. He excels in PE and gets by in science because experiments tend to be "cool."

• Maria is an artist and is free-spirited, instinctive, and curious. She's outdoorsy and enjoys hiking and climbing; scars and stitches attest to her adventurous nature. She is warm and outgoing—everyone's friend—and always the center of attention.

• Chris is an adventurer, driven by curiosity and spontaneity. These qualities pay off in his schoolwork, where he excels in science

and history (dinosaurs and experiments). He earns good grades, thanks to his intuition, though if a task becomes uninteresting or repetitive, it's likely to be forgotten. Projects can become obsessions.

- Marcus is adventurous and curious—and loves science experiments. He is laid-back and rarely angry. Marcus is a friend to everyone. He is extremely outgoing and is equal parts class nerd and class clown. Marcus loves making people laugh.

- Dee is mature and sensible for a 7-year-old. She tends to be cerebral in activities and play and defers to the schemes of Chris or Maria. Dee is an observer and is sentimental and compassionate, which makes her a good listener and a source of good advice. In school, Dee excels in math and business, evidenced by her logical mind and organizational skills. She loves pink, polka dots, and spring flowers.

- Ms. Flowers is the 2nd grade teacher at WonderGrove. She is young, relatable, and her lessons promote creative learning.

Despite the apparent usefulness of the animations, some educators may have concerns about using them to teach the habits. A debate about children's "screen time"—their exposure to digital devices—is a source of consternation for parents and teachers (Blackwell, Lauricella, & Wartella, 2016).

> [This debate] has not stopped the march of technology in schools. Even in preschool classrooms, the amount of time spent with digital technology has been rapidly growing. In 2015, more than half of preschools surveyed by Northwestern University reported digital devices were available in the classroom. A growing body of research suggests that limiting the number of screens a child sees might be more than unrealistic. It might be unnecessary. That energy might be better spent ensuring that children are accessing high-quality content—no matter the medium. (Dobo, 2017)

Digital learning remains at the forefront of the conversation in education. Until recently, the American Academy of Pediatrics (2011)

recommended no screens whatsoever until the age of 2. The academy loosened those guidelines in 2016, however, allowing for limited time with quality media (American Academy of Pediatrics, 2016); but as any parent knows, this is a major task. A study on digital storybooks is part of ongoing research at New York University (NYU) that is exploring how children can learn (or not) through digital media.

Susan B. Neuman, professor of childhood and literacy education at NYU, conducted a small study of 38 children in a Head Start preschool program (Neuman, Wong, & Kaefer, 2017). She and her colleagues sought to find out whether oral-language comprehension differed if a story was delivered by a digital device or by an adult reading a words-on-paper storybook to the child. The children watched and heard the digital story on an app that uses audio and pictures with action. The researchers also presented the same stories in a book format for the study. The results indicated that the quality of the content matters more than the format it's delivered in. Young children can learn just as much from a story delivered entirely via a digital device as they can from an adult reading a book version of the same story. In an interview, Neuman said, "This should calm family fears that digital media is not necessarily a good thing. It can be a good learning tool, if used properly" (Dobo, 2017).

Animation is highly engaging to children and a valuable tool for early childhood education and young learners. The years before 3rd grade are when children typically form an emotional bond with imaginary characters and want to believe that cartoon characters are real. And children copy what they see. For this reason, and because of our success using animated stories to model behavior for young children, we have expanded our mission to include a variety of areas to connect with children who are at risk or distracted from learning. Long-term studies show that high-quality early childhood education is particularly beneficial to low-income kids, helping them to avoid repeating grades in elementary school, to stay on track to graduate from high school, to earn more money as adults, and to spend less

time in jail or on welfare (Corporation for Public Broadcasting, & PBS, 2011).

It is an honor, a privilege, and a challenge to be a part of and a partner with education. I believe that teachers are the real heroes in the United States. Along with parents and grandparents, they are the caretakers of our youngsters, and collectively they are shaping the citizens of tomorrow. In that spirit, allow me to introduce the authors of the next chapter, members of the talented faculty at the Charles Wyche School in Miami, who are among those I consider to be teacher heroes. They will share case studies that show the power of using the WonderGrove animations in their classrooms to teach the Habits of Mind.

American Academy of Pediatrics. (2011). Policy statement: Media use by children younger than two years. *Pediatrics, 128*, 1040–1045.

American Academy of Pediatrics. (2016). Policy statement: Media use in school-aged children and adolescents. *Pediatrics, 128*(5), 1040–1045.

Blackwell, C., Lauricella, A., & Wartella, E. (2016). The influence of TPACK contextual factors on early childhood educators' tablet computer use. *Computers & Education, 98*, 57–69.

Corporation for Public Broadcasting, & PBS. (2011). *Findings from ready to learn 2005–2010*. Washington, DC: Author. Retrieved from https://www.cpb.org/files/rtl/FindingsFromReadyToLearn2005-2010.p

Dobo, N. (May 3, 2017). Digital storybooks might be just as good as an adult reading to a child. *Hechinger Report* available at http://hechingerreport.org/digital-storybooks-might-just-good-adult-reading-child.

Neuman, S. B., Wong, K. M., & Kaefer, T. (2017). Content not form predicts oral language comprehension: The influence of the medium on preschoolers' story understanding. *Reading and Writing, 30*(8), 1753–1771. Retrieved from https://doi.org/10.1007/s11145-017-9750-4

WonderGrove. (2014). Animations available at www.wondergrovelearn.com/

10

The Habits of Mind and Video Animations: Lessons Used and Learned

Erskine Dottin, Barbara L. Johnson, and Mickey Weiner, editors

In this chapter we share case studies that show how a cross-sample of teachers at different grade levels at Charles Wyche Elementary School in Miami, Florida, are working to enhance student learning by using the Habits of Mind and the WonderGrove animations (https://wondergrovelearn.net/). In each instance, we see the power of animation to help students learn the meaning of the habits and to understand that they have the capacity to manage, monitor, and modify their behaviors to develop the dispositions of an efficacious thinker.

Case Study 1: Habits of Mind in 1st Grade

Teacher: Sonia Reyes

Learning Goal: To integrate the Habits of Mind through video animations in order to help students connect basic mathematics and school etiquette

Learning Outcome

To some, the term *elementary school* brings to mind the old adage "reading, writing, and 'rithmetic," and, of course, counting and adding and subtracting are concepts we must teach and learn in 1st grade mathematics lessons. Recently, however, educators have come to realize that successful school achievement is linked not only to content knowledge and skills, but also to what some refer to as "non-cognitive skills" and others as "critical-thinking habits." According to Fletcher (2013), "These habits include broad, dispositional capacities—such as curiosity, engagement, persistence, flexibility, and metacognition—that support learning within and across disciplinary and instructional contexts" (p. 50). In fact, Fletcher goes on to say,

> We've learned that, just like rigor and joy, academic progress and personal development are symbiotic. Habits of mind uncoupled from academic content devolve into meaningless study skills and platitudes; academic content uncoupled from habits of mind devolves into perfunctory test preparation. (p. 55)

The research literature is also showing that the use of video animations can facilitate authentic learning opportunities for students (Kearney & Schuck, 2006). In my class, I saw the opportunity to link the learning of an element of basic math (following a sequential pattern of skip-counting by 10s) to socially acceptable behavior (learning how to line up and stand in a safe, quiet, and orderly manner by waiting one's turn) by integrating the Habits of Mind and the use of video animations.

Strategies

Students coming to my 1st grade classroom from kindergarten were hyperactive; they had no structure and no learning routines. At the beginning of the year, therefore, every time we were in the room during a lesson and every time we left the room to go to the cafeteria, I had to repeatedly remind them to "stop, think, and act." It was clear that my students needed to manage their impulsivity.

I wondered, should I introduce my students to the Habits of Mind as other teachers were doing? Habits of Mind was something that had been introduced to my school but that I had avoided because I thought it was just being dumped on us. Then one day I walked down the hall and saw how the teachers and students in the 3rd grade were focusing on the Habit of Mind *striving for accuracy*. It occurred to me that *managing impulsivity* must come before *striving for accuracy* because the former helps us to achieve the latter.

I introduced the Habits of Mind to my students and then began using the corresponding WonderGrove animations. I showed the children the videos *Managing Impulsivity, Striving for Accuracy, Persisting, Thinking Flexibly,* and *Finding Humor,* and we discussed the characters and their traits in depth. It became clear that my students were tuning in to and reflecting on the characters in the animations. For example, after I showed the *Persisting* and *Thinking Flexibly* videos, one of my students who does not eat sweets was reminded by another student, "Antoine, you have to think flexibly. Try it—you might like it." I saw evidence of them making connections between the Habits of Mind and the characters in the videos when someone mentioned, "Hey, Dee [the character in the animated video] likes to gather information through all her senses."

Given what I was seeing with the students' take on the Habits of Mind, I moved next to integrate the habits into the acquisition of content matter. I was doing an end-of-year skills review to help get the kids ready for 2nd grade. We would skip-count by 10s and play a listening game in which they would follow the pattern and take turns skip-counting by 10s. Then I had the students engage in a handout activity that required them to carefully cut out figures and glue them to a piece of paper after they solved a math problem. The figures in the handout had outstretched arms and were holding hands, so the scissor work had to be carefully done. In this way, the students needed to *strive for accuracy* to complete the problems correctly and to pay attention to details as they were cutting and pasting.

Next, we practiced *listening with empathy and understanding* as the children had to stand safely and quietly in a line and call out the correct answer to a skip-counting game. For example, I would put the number 10 on the board, and the students would take turns adding themselves to the pattern as we lined up to go to the cafeteria. They had to watch to see when it was their turn, listen to the response of the person before them so they would know which number came next, and then add themselves to the line following a pattern—and this had to be done by *managing impulsivity* if a student took longer to answer than another student. We practiced by starting with a number such as 31 and adding or subtracting 10 or 20 so that the students reviewed skills as they played an interactive game that required them to practice the Habits of Mind in order to succeed. When someone became impatient because thinking and responding took longer for some students than others, I could hear students remind others to practice managing their impulsivity and to wait, stop, think, and act.

Observations of Learning

I can see that the more we practice the Habits of Mind, the safer our classroom is and the more we learn because we can prevent or diffuse conflicts. Using the habits gives us more time to play and learn. Also, because each character in the animated videos has unique traits, my students can identify with one or more characters as they find things in common. For example, if one animated character loves to read and another loves science, my students can relate to the one with a common interest. By providing a strong visual connection along with common interests, barriers to communication are prevented and learning the Habits of Mind is enhanced. For my ESOL students, the videos are a crucial tool for their English language acquisition.

Evidence of Learning

When my students saw me painting the door of our classroom and noticed that I had made a mistake in my depiction of one of

the characters (the animal on her shirt looked like a kangaroo, not a giraffe, as it should have) I painted over it. They then told me that I had *persisted* and was *striving for accuracy*. Yes, *they* told *me* that they saw me practicing the habits when I was painting our classroom door! The repainting took more than one session, so they could see it was done in different stages. They would point out to me and their classmates whenever we passed through the door, "The teacher is *persisting* until her painting is done." They saw that my first painting of what was supposed to be a giraffe was not done well, so I redid it. When I laughed at myself for painting a giraffe that looked like a kangaroo, they told me I was *finding humor*!

In another example, when a student was collecting papers from his classmates, I heard him say, "I cannot collect your paper because you did not *strive for accuracy*. You put your first name on the paper but not your last name." I, as the teacher, can also see evidence of *striving for accuracy* as homework papers are neater. I present authentic situations, so they can see that the Habits of Mind are important for me, for them, and for everybody else. For example, for *managing impulsivity*, I ask them, if I am at the supermarket and I am in a rush, is it OK to say to other people, "Move and get out of my way"? No, the children say; you must stop, think, and act.

Case Study 2: Habits of Mind in 3rd Grade

Teacher: Lindsey Ramirez
Learning Goal: To enhance second-language learners' ability to make associations and connections

Learning Outcome

Charles Wyche Elementary School has adopted the "nested outcome" concept as outlined in Costa and Kallick's book *Learning and Leading with Habits of Mind* (2008). In this model, teachers work to enhance students' acquisition not only of content and skills but also of Habits of Mind.

I became aware that my second-language learners and struggling readers were showing a disconnect between what I wanted them to learn in language arts content and skills, on the one hand, and the ability to make associations and connections to positive behaviors and interactions between and among themselves, on the other hand. I decided to incorporate the use of video animations as a means to integrate Habits of Mind into the learning process.

Strategies

I used video animations as introductions to what the Habits of Mind were and what they looked and sounded like in practice. I showed the videos one at a time, starting with *Managing Impulsivity*. I felt that in order to gain and maintain students' attention in academic matters, I needed them to learn how to focus on what I was trying to teach them. They needed to learn self-control.

Many of my students are not achieving at grade level, and the abstract concepts of the habits are sometimes difficult for them to comprehend. Showing them the short animations allows them to make a connection between what the habits are and what they look and sound like. It has created a more concrete depiction, increasing their understanding of the habits and how to use them appropriately.

As a reading and language arts teacher, one of my goals is to integrate the Habits of Mind into the characters and plot development of many of our reading selections. We talked about the habits as they came up in the stories we were reading. For example, when we read about two inventors, Mary Anderson and Elijah McCoy, I asked students, "What habits did they use? What did the Habits of Mind do to help them with their inventions?" One of the inventors had to go through many different prototypes before finally developing a product that worked, which led to a discussion about the habit of *creating, innovating, and imagining*, in addition to *persisting*. A lesson featuring the folk character Anansi the spider brought up the habit of *managing impulsivity*.

In addition to the Habits of Mind videos, I used several Disney movies to engage the students in dialogue about how the main characters in each movie were faced with a problem and then used a Habit of Mind in working to solve it. In the movie *Finding Nemo*, they saw how Marlin searched the entire ocean to get his son back; *persisting* against all odds, he finally found Nemo. In *Tangled*, they saw how Rapunzel applied the habit of *thinking flexibly* to get out of her tower by using her hair; and in *Brave*, they saw Princess Merida *striving for accuracy* while shooting an arrow. They saw that the main character in *Zootopia* was *taking responsible risks* as she moved away from her family to become a police officer after everyone told her she could never do it. To familiarize the students with the respective Habits of Mind, I had them complete an activity in which they were asked to explain the habit in their own words and to describe what it looks and sounds like.

Observations of Learning

Many of my students are learning below grade level, and these abstract concepts of the habits are sometimes difficult for them to comprehend. Showing them the short animations allows them to make a connection between what the habits are and what they look like. It has created a more concrete depiction for them and increased their understanding of the habits and how to use them appropriately.

Evidence of Learning

I have found that once students become familiar with the Habits of Mind, they recognize the traits in the animated characters and begin to see that the characters' problem-solving abilities are influenced by how much they practice good habits. After watching the Habits of Mind animations, my students make stronger connections with the habits. They can also relate the habits to characters in other animated movies they have seen. Connecting the habits to familiar movies has made the concepts more interesting and more relevant to the students.

Case Study 3: Habits of Mind in Prekindergarten

Teacher: Isabel Garcia, Prekindergarten
Learning Goal: To help prekindergarten students internalize *persisting* in their early literacy language acquisition

Learning Outcome

"As early childhood education moves to front and center in the public policy debate, more attention is paid to early literacy. . . . Early literacy plays a key role in enabling the kind of early learning experiences that research shows are linked with academic achievement, reduced grade retention, higher graduation rates and enhanced productivity in adult life" (Strickland & Riley-Ayers, n.d., para. 1). The literature shows that children from low socioeconomic circumstances who may be at risk for school failure demonstrate a lack of what Paul Tough (2012) calls "grit" and Costa and Kallick (2008) call "persisting." Heckman and Rubinstein (2001) found that one of the critical psychological traits that allowed students to make it through school is an inclination to persist at a boring and often unrewarding task. One of the learning outcomes for my class is to help the students learn how to achieve a goal or complete a task by *persisting* when faced with a challenge.

Strategies

I had my students view the Habits of Mind animated videos to introduce them to each of the characters. I had the students discuss the varying personalities of the characters so that they could relate to them. Next, we viewed the video on the habit of *persisting*, in which a character has to practice playing his xylophone for an upcoming talent show.

To provide the students with an opportunity to practice *persisting*, I connected the animation video to a class performance we were preparing for, entitled "The Number Rock." Students learned they had to practice just like the character in the video because this

was their first stage experience and they had to learn various dance moves, stay on beat, learn stage directions, listen to know when it was their turn to perform, and overcome stage fright. Achieving these things required persistence. When students became frustrated and wanted to give up, I reminded them about the character Chris in the video having to consistently practice and how he ended up having a great show.

Observations of Learning

As they began practicing for "The Number Rock" class performance, I only had to remind the children once about the character in the video who was persisting through his practice. Shortly thereafter, I noticed the students were encouraging each other using the video character as a reference, saying things like, "Hey, remember how Chris persisted in the video? You can't give up just like he did not!"

Outside the performance experience, I have observed my students working persistently to complete tasks such as learning to write their letters and numbers correctly, learning how to write their full names, and learning the seasons of the year, months of the year, days of the week, and names of shapes.

Evidence of Learning

The students have learned that we must persist not only at school, but also outside school. I have work samples in which students say they will persist at out-of-school activities such as riding their bike, riding their skateboard, riding a horse, and doing their homework.

Case Study 4: Habits of Mind in 3rd Grade

Teachers: Mercedes Alvarez and Maria Valarezo
Learning Goal: To use Habits of Mind and video animations to enrich students' global environmental and climate literacy

Learning Outcome

Earth Day Network (2017) contends, "Education is the foundation for progress. We need to build a global citizenry fluent in the concepts of climate change and aware of its unprecedented threat to our planet. We need to empower everyone with the knowledge to inspire action in defense of environmental protection" (para. 1). The organization sees "environmental and climate literacy [as] the engine not only for creating green voters and advancing environmental and climate laws and policies but also for accelerating green technologies and jobs" (para. 2).

We wanted to make certain that our students were prepared for the state reading test and at the same time were engaged in the effort to develop global environmental and climate literacy. We wanted the Habits of Mind to be the thinking skills they would use to be successful in attaining literacy regardless of the content or topic.

Strategies

We were cognizant of, on the one hand, the importance of the children learning Habits of Mind such as *striving for accuracy, managing impulsivity, finding humor, persisting*, and *working interdependently*, and, on the other hand, the use of a specific habit depends on the situation. We have found that there are times when we need to teach a particular Habit of Mind in isolation, times when we want to focus on a couple of habits that interconnect, and times when we need to correlate several or all habits because they stimulate each other. During the school year of 2016–2017, we found ourselves, as 3rd grade teachers, focusing more on *persisting*. Because the Florida Standards Assessment for Reading is a priority in 3rd grade (the reading test score is one of the factors determining whether a student will be promoted to 4th grade), our sticking to the task of teaching our students all the skills they need to succeed in the reading assessment with a score of 3 or higher is

critical. The students also need to stay focused during their lessons, learn the skills being taught, and complete all the assignments that facilitate their success on the exam. Just thinking of the pressure is enough to tempt students to give up, but that is when they need to be more persistent and complete the given task. They are aware that giving up is easy, but a stronger and more mindful person will persist until the end. They are aware of the obstacles they will confront, but they know that giving up is not an option. They understand that remaining focused at all times is the right thing to do in school and in their personal lives.

Besides improving their reading abilities, we also wanted to enrich their environmental and science literacy. We started by using the WonderGroveLearn video animation *Recycle to Help the Earth* to introduce the students to the subject of Earth Day. The video prompted lots of student discussion about Earth Day. To capitalize on their enthusiasm about Earth Day, we decided to use their regular science lesson to help them connect science and recycling to the Habits of Mind. We had them complete some activities that correlated with the habits as highlighted in the video. We found that the children became very verbal and expressed themselves through lots of examples and details while referring to the character or characters that they viewed in the video. They related easily to the characters and compared their situation or life to that of the animated characters.

To infuse the subject matter into their learning, we taught the students the definitions of words such as *environment, recycling,* and *conservation* to build their background knowledge. We discussed conserving resources and what happens to trash after the garbage truck picks it up. We asked students which Habits of Mind would help us conserve Earth's resources, and we heard various answers. One student said, "We must use empathy to really understand that we all share one planet Earth, and if we mess it up, there is not another one." Another student responded that we must all think

about our thinking so that we make decisions that are more "green" and environmentally conscious.

We also viewed some Discovery Channel videos and had a discussion after we viewed the footage of the effects of global warming and glaciers melting. A student posed a question: "Here in Florida, we live on a peninsula. What happens to us if the glaciers all melt?" We created a mural that illustrated the need to pose questions to fill in the gap between what is known and not known by showing examples of how recycling occurs in our school.

Observations of Learning

We see evidence of students demonstrating Habits of Mind in their written work by remaining open to continuous learning. When working in groups, it is evident that students are applying the habits they have learned. They are not frustrated; they speak to everyone in the group, isolating no one; they help each other; they listen; and they talk things out. Students do not argue as much as our previous students. Instead, we see them finding solutions as a group. And in the last three years, our students have not had any behavior problems. In fact, our students point out that the behavior chart hanging by the door never needs to be used.

Evidence of Learning

We have strong evidence of transfer of learning from a survey that we distributed to our students' parents. The results indicate that parents are seeing their children demonstrate the Habits of Mind frequently at home.

Case Study 5: Habits of Mind with Special Needs Students

Teacher: Eida Tumbeiro
Learning Goal: To use Habits of Mind to prompt and reinforce social development in children with autism

Learning Outcome

Benedict Carey (2014) contends:

> Therapists who specialize in autism often use a child's own interests, toys or obsessions as a way to connect, and sometimes to reward effort and progress on social skills. The more eye-contact a child makes, for example, the more play time he or she gets with those precious maps or stuffed animals. (para. 1)

The same author goes on to note:

> But now a group of scientists . . . are suggesting that those favorite activities could be harnessed in a deeper, more organic way. If a child is fascinated with animated characters like Thomas the Tank Engine, why not use those characters to prompt and reinforce social development? (para. 2)

My goal has been to use WonderGrove animations and Habits of Mind to enhance the development of my students, some of whom have autism.

Strategies

I started by explaining to the students in simple terms the meaning of a *habit*. Then I introduced the WonderGrove animated characters Chris, Dee, Marcus, Maria, Peter, and Ms. Flowers. Next, I focused on the Habit of Mind *thinking flexibly* because at the beginning my students did not like to try new things. For autistic children, *thinking flexibly* is extremely important. They like to stick to the things that are most familiar and often do not like to branch out. Their parents are worried about their child having a new teacher in a new grade. Such concerns and reactions are why *thinking flexibly* is essential. I have seen my students show courage in trying something new. One student, for example, did not want to try a donut or a snack chip. Finally, she did try it and said, "It was delicious!" When I asked her why she decided to try something new, she responded, "Because I need to practice my Habits of Mind and think flexibly so I might discover something new and delicious!"

Another important Habit of Mind is *persisting*. In my class, some-times when students find that something is hard to do, they refuse and tend to shut down. Giving up and running away is common until they know how to persist. Now, commenting on the effect of the use of the habits, the mother of one of my students told me, "I am so grateful because what you did with my son is tremendous. He had the same problem at home and at school. He would complain that things are too hard, and he complained that he did not know how to do the task. Now I find that at home he will stick with it until he is finished."

After showing my students all the video animations about the characters, I asked them to choose one character to add to our class. They voted for Chris, because he likes to read, and he likes horses, apples, and science. Because we already have one student in our class named Chris, the class said, "Oh, good! Now we have two Chrises in our class!" Each morning when students arrive to our class, they greet Chris, the animated character, whose image is on our bulletin board. He serves as a constant visual reminder to practice the habits. And when we need a stronger reminder, we play the video again and discuss the habit we need to practice for the current situation.

I tell my students at the start of class every day, "Remember the Habits of Mind." I remind them daily to practice the habits when they are working in small groups, trying something new, making mis-takes, having difficulty solving an assignment, or behaving rudely.

I give each student a desktop image of the animated character Chris, and whenever a student gets stuck or is ready to give up, I remind that student to look at Chris and remember what he would do. This reminder has helped us remember to practice our habits.

Observations of Learning

My students who have autism have commented that after applying the Habits of Mind, they felt more confident and had found another way to solve problems easily. One student is practicing how to *think about thinking*. Previously, when he got stuck on a math

problem, he wanted to give up and say, "This is too hard for me. I need help. Come sit by me and show me how to do it again." Now when he faces a challenging math problem, he has learned how to develop a plan to solve it. He might use his fingers or his favorite glove and use a known strategy to solve the problem. He can think about his thinking and figure out what he must do.

Another student said that practicing *persisting* is why he passed his Florida Standards Assessment Test. When he first saw the test and realized how long it was, he was ready to give up. His teacher reminded him to take his time and to think of the task as a chance to practice Habits of Mind. She also reminded him to remember what Chris did in the animated video, and the student said, "OK! I can do it too!"

Yet another student loved to finish his assignments quickly, jumping up to show that he was the first to finish. He would end up having errors on the assignment because he did not check his work. Now he checks it twice before he turns it in. His mother reports that he checks his homework before he asks her to review it.

The mother of another student told me how the Habits of Mind had helped her with her daughter. The girl was extremely sensitive to food but now is trying new ones. Another example is a boy who used to give up and become frustrated easily when he had to confront a difficult test or when he could not finish an assignment. Now, after practicing the Habits of Mind, he has become a different student. He never gives up, and he passed the Florida Standards Assessment Test. At the beginning of the school year, another student had problems managing his impulsivity, but now he can control himself because he remembers examples of others, including the animations, using Habits of Mind.

A student who had been happy but verbally nonresponsive at the start of the year was speaking unprompted by the end of the year to say hello or ask questions such as, "May I use the bathroom?" The habit of *finding humor* has helped him to gain confidence and believe in himself. Whereas before he was scared to make a mistake, now

if he makes a mistake, he laughs. He is no longer afraid, because we have all learned how to find humor when we make mistakes. In addition to speaking, he can now read and write sentences.

Another previously nonverbal student in my class is practicing the habit of *applying past knowledge to new situations*. On so many occasions in our class, other students and I would speak to him and he would follow directions. He is smart, but nonverbal. Two months ago, I was working with him individually. When I moved away, he called to me, "Ms. T! Ms. T." I heard him say my name for the first time. His verbal comments seemed related to his being excited about learning new things.

At our end-of-year awards ceremony, my students were able to stand at the interactive whiteboard at the front of the class and teach their parents about the Habits of Mind. The novelty of such an activity—standing before an audience and teaching adults— represented a tremendous challenge for them. At first, they were not confident about their ability to meet the challenge, but then they said, "We can do it, Ms. T!" Their newfound confidence showed me how the Habits of Mind can be powerful motivators and help both me and my students reach our goals.

Evidence of Learning

I acquired concrete evidence of how using Habits of Mind are reinforcing the social development of my students with autism. One of my students confessed that she had been reluctant to try new things. However, she divulged that classmates had urged her to try chips. When she did, she found them to be delicious. As a result, she shared that she had demonstrated *thinking flexibly* and *being open-minded* by tasting chips and had changed her mind about a new food.

Learned in Our School

We've learned that the animations allow students to relate to the characters and their behaviors. Once students become familiar with

the Habits of Mind, they recognize those traits in the animated characters and begin to see how their actions and problem-solving abilities are influenced by how much and how well the characters practice Habits of Mind.

In our school, we have learned that every minute we spend teaching students the Habits of Mind is amplified by the many minutes they are attentive to and engaging with the curriculum that we are expected to teach. Habits of Mind are a means, not an end, for developing the capacities of our young students with special needs.

The commercial world took the research lead and ascertained that visual clues help children remember what they see in advertising (Hendrick, 2011). On the other hand, according to Betrancourt and Chassot (n.d.), knowledge from research on how school learners process multimedia information in order to process classroom material is now being taken seriously by educators. It should be noted that few experimental studies have investigated the effect of animated visuals with primary or secondary school students. However, some of the most recent research in this area has revealed, for example, that animation is particularly attractive and motivating to young students, and that graphics benefit learning (Islam, Ahmed, Islam, & Shamsuddin, 2014).

The administrators and faculty at Charles Wyche Elementary have been identified as an international Habits of Mind Learning Community of Excellence by the Institute for Habits of Mind. We continue to explore ways to create a learning environment conducive to acquiring subject matter content, skills, and Habits of Mind. We were invited by Terry Thoren of WonderGroveLearn to integrate the 16 instructional animations for Habits of Mind into our learning environment. Although there are different ways to use animations, at Charles Wyche Elementary we are using them as a simulation in a discovery-learning approach (Schnotz, Böckheler, & Grzondziel, 1999) to provide an interactive learning experience.

Because the use of video animations to enhance students' internalization of Habits of Mind is a relatively new practice, the lessons being learned by our teachers and students may contribute to further development and understanding. In fact, Costa, Kallick, and Sherman (n.d.) have noted that "we are all learning together how best to use animation as an instructional approach that will serve as a springboard to the Habits of Mind for . . . children" (p. 1).

One lesson learned so far is that children relate to the characters in the animations. When they see the characters using the habits, they want to model what they see. Although the use of animation is an enormously powerful way for students to visualize the habits, using picture books, carefully selected movies, or other resources also works well. Developing the language of the habits has been especially important for our English Speakers of Other Languages (ESOL). They can use this language as they work together to solve problems. They identify with the characters in books or the animations and reference the behaviors in their observations. For example, as noted earlier, Ms. Garcia observed a student saying, "Hey, remember how Chris persisted in the video? You can't give up, just like he did not!" The children also become aware of the teacher's behavior as it relates to the habits. For example, when Ms. Williams raised her voice, a student said, "Ms. Williams, you are not managing your impulsivity like Ms. Flowers did in the video!"

Finally, many of the teachers who are using the video animations to facilitate the acquisition of content, skills, and Habits of Mind have gleaned the following common, major insights. They have observed that successfully immersing students in behaviors that exemplify the Habit of Mind requires the entire staff to think flexibly and to have the academic freedom to make judgments and adjustments in their instructional planning. The fact that the entire school is dedicated to the Habits of Mind makes a tremendous difference, as does the presence of a forward-thinking administrator. If a principal understands that teachers are not only covering

prescribed curricular mandates but also teaching students to make lifelong decisions that will allow them to meet and exceed any state's curriculum standards, the use of animations to teach the Habits of Mind will face no barriers.

Betrancourt, M., & Chassot, A. (n.d.). Making sense of animation: How do children explore multimedia instruction? Retrieved from http://tecfa .unige.ch/perso/mireille/papers/Betrancourt_Chassot08.pdf

Carey, B. (2014, April 7). Inside the mind of a child with autism. *New York Times*. Retrieved from https://well.blogs.nytimes.com/2014/04/07 /inside-the-mind-of-a-child-with-autism/?_r=0

Costa, A. L., & Kallick, B. (2008). *Learning and leading with habits of mind*. Alexandria, VA: ASCD.

Costa, A. L., Kallick, B., & Sherman, M. (n.d.). Getting started with habits of mind animations. Retrieved from http://www.habitsofmindinstitute.org /wp-content/uploads/2014/06/Getting_Started_witih_HOMfinal.pdf

Earth Day Network. (2017). What is Earth Day, and what is it meant to accomplish? Retrieved from http://www.earthday.org/earthday/

Fletcher, J. (2013, Winter). Critical habits of mind: Exposing the process of development. *Liberal Education, 99*(1), 50–55.

Heckman, J., & Rubinstein, Y. (2001, May). The importance of noncognitive skills: Lessons from the GED testing program. *American Economic Review, 91*(2), 145–149.

Hendrick, B. (2011, March 7). Cartoon characters influence kids' food choices. *WebMD*. Retrieved from http://www.webmd.com/parenting /news/20110307/cartoon-characters-influence-kids-food-choices#1

Islam, B., Ahmed, A., Islam, K., & Shamsuddin, K. (2014). Child education through animation: An experimental study. *International Journal of Computer Graphics and Animation, 4*(4), 43–52.

Kearney, M., & Schuck, S. (2006). Spotlight on authentic learning: Student developed digital video projects. *Australasian Journal of Educational Technology, 22*(2), 189–208.

Schnotz, W., Böckheler, J., & Grzondziel, H. (1999). Individual and co-operative learning with interactive animated pictures. *European Journal of Psychology of Education, 14*, 245–65.

Strickland, D., & Riley-Ayers, S. (n.d.). Early literacy: Policy and practice in the preschool years. Retrieved from http://www.readingrockets.org /article/early-literacy-policy-and-practice-preschool-years

Tough, P. (2012). *How children succeed: Grit, curiosity, and the hidden power of character*. Boston: Houghton Mifflin Harcourt.

11

The Librarian's Role in Building the Habits of Mind

JoLynn Scott

At Coal Creek Elementary School in Louisville, Colorado, part of the Boulder Valley School District, we have embraced the Habits of Mind since 2003, when our principal, John Kiemele, brought the program to our school. Over the intervening years, the habits have become not just something we *teach*, but something we *live*. They are reflected in our classwork, the students' behaviors, and our everyday vocabulary. We have monthly assemblies that introduce one habit (through a guest presenter, a skit or an activity by teachers and students, or a book talk or speech by the principal) that will be our focus for the month. That being said, the habits are with us all year long, all around our campus. We truly are a *mindful* school in every sense of the word.

Habits of Mind in the Primary Grades

We begin teaching the Habits of Mind in kindergarten, and these lessons and dispositions stay with the students through their elementary career and beyond. For our youngest students, we begin

with the most basic (and necessary) habits for their development—*managing impulsivity* and *persisting*. These are the areas of behavior where our "kindees" need the most help or practice. For many of our students, kindergarten is the first time they are experiencing an extended school day, away from their parents for longer periods of time. That reality, coupled with the barrage of new skills to learn and rigid schedules, means that they can get pretty "pooped," and a tired kindee can become an out-of-control kindee. In any kindergarten classroom, you can hear teachers reminding students to manage their impulses.

Kindergarteners are learning so many new things, and they can be easily frustrated when new skills don't come easily. *Persisting* is a skill we teach all our students, and we, as teachers, model it with our students. This habit is one that serves us well throughout our lives. We learn from our mistakes and move forward. We don't give up.

In addition to *managing impulsivity* and *persisting*, *thinking interdependently* is an important habit that we stress early on at Coal Creek. Our youngest students come from a self-centered world, but when they enter school, they become a member of a community. Working together—at work, at play, in school, and out of school—is an essential lifelong skill that helps them think beyond themselves. They become part of something greater.

As students grow and mature, many more habits are stressed in our school. We revisit old ones, striving for a deeper understanding and capability in using them, while introducing new habits that are more complex. Our Habits of Mind follows no fixed curriculum. Each teacher and grade level can use the habits however and whenever they see fit—and that is most of the time. The habits are not taught in isolation but are ingrained in our instruction and everyday conversations with our students. Students use the vocabulary (as well as the skills) with each other, and not just under direct instructions from the teacher.

Habits of Mind in the Library

The Habits of Mind are so fully immersed in the Coal Creek psyche, it's difficult to write about how I use them in the library. They are a part of all we do, from the specific library and research skills I teach, to the books I read to the students and the kinds of discussions we have about books that they have read. As in all our classrooms, students can see examples of the habits in the library, from the flower pots of the "blooming" habits, to the Habits of Mind poster I use in our story area.

The main function of the library is to help students "find" things. Whether it's researching for a class project, looking for a book on a certain topic, or browsing for a "just right" book to check out, students need the skills to search and find. For the younger students, we start on a very basic level and build upon their skills as they grow and learn.

The Physical Layout of the Library

First, students need to learn how the library "works"—from the physical layout of the bookshelves, to the OPAC (look-up station), and CIRC (check-out station) computers, and the various other areas in the library (quiet reading area, work tables, story area). The signage in the library is pretty straightforward: E = Everyone books (our school's name for picture books); ER = Early Reader; FIC = Fiction; 000–999 = Nonfiction. I go over general information about each of these at the beginning of the year, but as students begin to become more autonomous, navigating the library is all about the habit of *questioning and posing problems*:

- What kind of book do you want?
- How can you find it?
- Where would it "live" in the library?
- What do you know about the book or subject that can help you find the book?

To help our youngest students navigate the library, I employ *gathering data through all senses* in my library layout. Above the shelves in the picture book area, students can see "stuffies" (plush animals and characters) from their favorite books. This display lets them know that the book corresponding to the stuffie is on that shelf. For students who don't read yet or have difficulty understanding the information on the spine labels of the books, this clue is the first step on their road to independence in locating their favorite books.

Similarly, in the nonfiction section, I've placed labels with simple-to-understand graphics representing our most popular topics for younger students. There is a picture (for our nonreaders), title (to help those who can read), and call number (for older students to find the exact location of the book) for each topic. The youngest students quickly memorize where their favorites are. As students mature, I take them from the simplest (graphic) to the more complex (call number) way to locate the exact book they want.

Tools for Student Use in the Library

My goal in the library is for students at every grade level to be as independent as they can be. I make certain that the library is set up for students to *take responsible risks* in their choice of books; to browse as they *ask questions and pose problems* about the book titles and potential content; to spark their curiosity and encourage them to be *thinking interdependently*. We have many tools in place to help students achieve these goals. At our OPAC (Online Patron Access Catalog), or "look-up," stations, there are comfortable chairs and pens or pencils and scratch paper for students to use in writing down their search results. We teach our youngest students how to use this system. Though the youngest may need assistance from one of our parent volunteers or from me, they quickly become more and more independent in this task.

Our district uses the Insignia Library System, and the OPAC search results are easy for the students to use and understand. I teach

our students which items to look at and write down from their search results. The color-coding is helpful. For example, the information in blue, such as title and author, contains links that can be clicked on for further information, such as a summary of the book or other books by that author. Before they write anything down, they look at the information in green, which tells them if the book is available ("Green Means Go!"). If they see a zero, they know the book is not available, and they need to make a new choice (demonstrating the habit of *thinking flexibly*). If they see a numeral *1*, they know to proceed. Next, they write down the call number, which is in red. They must write down all the information, both numbers and letters (using the habit of *striving for accuracy*).

Not all students use the OPAC. Some already know the area they wish to use, and others just want to browse different areas of the library until they find something that sparks their interest. Depending on the student and that student's past experience in the library, I may suggest a certain topic or area to explore (enabling the habit of *remaining open to continuous learning*). I make a particular point of doing this when a student is "stuck" reading the same type of book each week. I encourage students in *taking a responsible risk* by trying something new. For really reluctant students, I suggest they "test drive" a book for me and give me feedback the following week.

Near the story area, where we begin and end our library time, there is a jar of "browser markers" that help students mark the spot on the shelf where they are looking. Before they look for a book, they grab a browser marker and then head to the shelf where their book is located (or where they are hoping to find a book, if one is not already selected). Before pulling a book out to browse, they mark the spot with the browser marker.

I encourage students to find a book that is "just right" for them, using all the resources available (*gathering data through all senses*). For our youngest students, doing so includes "taking a picture

walk" through the book. For our earliest readers (or those who struggle with their reading), I also suggest the ubiquitous Five-Finger Rule:

- Make a fist and begin reading on any page.
- When you find a word you don't know, put up one finger.
- Zero fingers up = too easy.
- Two to three fingers up = just right.
- Four to five fingers up = too hard.

For our older students, I strongly encourage them to read the blurb on the back or inside flap of the book, which gives them a summary of the book. (Reading the blurb is also a great introduction to our "student book talks," in which they have to give a summary of the book to the class. More on that later!)

After browsing the book, students know whether they want to check it out or not. If they do, they return the browser marker to the jar and head to the checkout area. If they don't, they return the book to the correct spot on the shelf where the browser marker is and continue their search. The idea of the browser marker is not new, but it gives students autonomy in finding their own books and helps keep the library shelves organized.

Because I don't want to be stuck behind the circulation desk during library time, I teach students (from kindergarten through 5th grade) how to check out on their own. Again, those in the earlier grades may need assistance, but they quickly learn the correct way to do it. Students have their own library card (made by me, yearly, and color-coded to their grade level) to use when they check out a book. In kindergarten, I use parent volunteers to monitor checkouts at the beginning of the year. By midyear, kindergarteners are able to do it independently. As their expertise improves, students are more than happy to "teach" each other the process (*thinking interdependently*).

Once they have checked out a book, students are expected to find a place to read. For those who want a quiet spot, we have a lovely reading nook, with comfy pillows on which to curl up by themselves. For those who want to share a book, we have comfortable couches in the story area and group tables in the work area.

Library Class Time

I use a fixed schedule in our library but allow for flexibility as needed. Every class comes to the library at a specific time each week. Kindergarten classes (which are half-day) come for 30 minutes, whereas grades 1 through 5 come for 40 to 45 minutes. If I am needed elsewhere (classroom/computer lab) to assist with units of study, classes can come independently or reschedule. We usually begin with a group gathering, which includes a read-aloud story and discussion or activity, for about 20 minutes. Then students choose books, check them out, and read for 20 minutes. Finally, we have a wrap-up session for the last five minutes. Sometimes teachers stay during library class time, and we coteach. Other times, I teach by myself.

In addition to having parent volunteers who assist with check-outs (for most of the younger-grade classes) and shelving, this year I had a 3rd grade student serving as a library assistant and working with a 1st grade class. His teacher was encouraging him to enhance his leadership skills (*taking a responsible risk*) and asked if he could be of assistance with a younger-grade class. What a joy it was to watch the interdependence between this boy and the younger students! It was also a way for him to "show what he knew" about the library (*applying past knowledge to new situations*).

Library Lessons

My lesson planning draws from several different sources. Sometimes I collaborate with teachers to plan lessons that correspond to a particular area of study. For example, when the 1st grade

is studying Japan, I choose books to read that are traditional Japanese stories or are by Japanese authors.

I also plan lessons based on the Habits of Mind. For example, if our Habit of Mind for the month is *persisting*, I find books and lessons that pertain to that particular habit. I will tell the students up front that the book has the specific habit in it, and instruct them to listen for it. After the book is read, they are able to explain where in the story the habit occurred. Often they will be able to make a personal connection to the habit, either within their own life or in another book. If a book illustrates more than one habit, we discuss the others as well.

In addition, apart from planned lessons, whenever we have a book discussion, I always refer to the Habits of Mind, asking students to find evidence of different habits in the text. Sometimes the habit is explicit, and sometimes it is not. Some habits, like *persisting* or *finding humor*, are easy for young students to identify. Others take a little more focus, so I may have to give a specific example from the story ("When the goose tricked the fox, what habit was she using?") to help the students identify the habit. In general, when I read a book to the class, I'll ask at the end, "What Habits of Mind did you see in this book?" They often find things I hadn't even thought of!

A great habit to focus on in any discussion is *thinking flexibly*. It's important, in a group setting, for students to understand there is more than one right answer. The traditional student often has trouble with this situation, but the out-of-the-box thinker often shines. If a student suggests a habit that isn't directly apparent, I ask the student to use *metacognition* to help the group understand the underlying thinking.

Choosing Books for the Library

When I am asked how I choose books with the Habits of Mind in mind, my answer is simple: I don't! I choose quality books that either fit a specific part of our school's curriculum or books I know

the students will enjoy. I read many different library journals and reviews, pay attention to the Caldecott and Newbery Awards, and stay abreast of the latest, greatest books for elementary students. One of the wonderful things about the Habits of Mind is that in any great piece of literature you can find examples of many of the habits. Characters who exhibit the habits are characters that authors love to write about and readers love to read about.

Teachers often ask me to suggest books on a variety of topics, including the Habits of Mind. Even our principal will ask for a book to use during an assembly regarding a specific habit. It's my job to know the books in our collection and be able to suggest ones that match what staff members are looking for.

The Institute for Habits of Mind (IHOM) has published a bibliography of books that correspond with the various habits (http://www.habitsofmindinstitute.org/resources/bibliography-student-books/). I created a spreadsheet of the bibliography, noting which books we had in our library. Then I used the bibliography to annotate book records in our library system, so teachers could "search" for books that exemplify certain habits. For example, if teachers wanted books that relate to *listening with empathy and understanding*, they could search our library system and find a list of books for that habit.

I will continue to ask staff to help me add to this list, as well as have students recommend books that should be included. We will share our work on the IHOM website. As books come and go, this list will continue to evolve, and I hope to expand it to teachers in other schools, especially those who use the Habits of Mind.

General Library Activities Using the Habits of Mind

In addition to formal lessons and book discussions, I engage students in various activities that further enhance their understanding and use of the Habits of Mind. Here are some of my favorites.

Categories

Students in kindergarten and beyond love to play the game Categories at the end of our library class. (The game is often a great carrot to dangle, to encourage the students to finish their checkouts quickly!) Students hold up their books and I find a similarity among them (which is often challenging). I select students with books that have something in common and ask them to line up in front of the class. Then, after looking at the books, the other students guess the category. When I introduce the game to the youngest students, the category is fairly straightforward—for example, all fiction, all nonfiction, all with animals on the cover. As the students become more proficient, I try to make the game more difficult by picking less obvious categories, such as having a series title as well as a book title, the coloring on the book, or the lettering on the title.

When the students get really good at the game, I challenge them to "stump" me. I retreat to my office and put the students in charge of the game. They pick the category and books, trying to come up with something they think I won't be able to figure out. Once they're ready, I come out of my office and try to guess the category. Sometimes I get it, and sometimes I don't. (My favorite student-led "stumper" category? Sky!)

Obviously, there are many habits at play in this simple activity: *gathering data through all senses, thinking interdependently, thinking and communicating with clarity and precision,* and *striving for accuracy,* to name a few. When there is a disagreement, students also need to use *metacognition* and *thinking flexibly.* I love when they find a category that is different from the one I had chosen but that also fits. The concept of "more than one right answer" is difficult, yet important, for the younger students to learn early.

Student Book Talks

Another favorite activity (which I usually use with older students but have adapted for younger students) is the student book

talk. It's easy to talk about a book you've already read, but it's much more challenging to quickly figure out what to say about a book that you just checked out. First, I talk to the students about what a book talk is (and isn't) and what should be included: title, author, short summary ("but don't spill the beans"), why you chose it, and to whom you would recommend it. (For the kindees, I pare this down to title and why you chose it.) This "easy" activity really makes students *think about thinking* (*metacognition*) and helps us work on our school's oracy goal when students have to *communicate with clarity*.

During our school's book fairs, I still conduct library classes, and the middle of our library is turned into a "bookstore." I have students do a version of the student book talk, called "Book Vendor." (I usually do this with 4th and 5th graders, but recently I had the opportunity to expand it to the younger grades.) I explain that book vendors have to convince me to buy the book for our library collection. In addition to the standard information contained in a book talk, they also have to explain why Coal Creek Library, specifically, should buy this book. Students often convince me to buy a book that I hadn't previously considered.

The younger version of this activity came in the form of students choosing a book for their class library. (Because our final book fair was in May, I had a contest to encourage students to get their checked-out books turned in early. The classes that had all their books turned in got to select a free paperback book for their class library.) For grades 1 and 2, students worked in pairs (which required *thinking interdependently*). In addition to the standard information needed for a book talk, they had to explain why their class would benefit from their book—and figure out a way to present so that both partners had an equal part in the presentation. Finally, the classes voted, based on these book talks, for the book their class would receive. It was a simple yet powerful lesson, showing that the younger kids know, and can use, the habits.

Student Input in Weeding the Collection

When I was inspired to pare down our picture book collection in an effort to keep the highest-quality books on our shelves and make it easier for students to find them, I followed standard weeding protocol, looking at the age of the book, the number of recent check-outs, and the physical condition of the book. Some books, however, defied these guidelines, and I just couldn't decide whether to keep or discard them. One of these instances concerned the 21 books by Leo Lionni in our collection. They were once a favorite at our school, but I noticed that they were not currently being checked out, so I asked my 2nd grade classes to become my "weeders."

I began with *questioning and posing problems*: "Why aren't these books being checked out—because they're not good or because kids just don't know about them?" I devised a reading log/check sheet for them to use, and they were to read at least eight of these books, recording the title, characters, and moral or lesson contained in the book, as well as a "thumbs up, thumbs down, or thumbs sideways" reaction to the book, which required *metacognition*. Students spent several library classes reading these books and recording their reactions to them.

We then *gathered the data* and turned the information into graphs, which enabled us to identify which books were the most popular and which books should be weeded. As we discussed the less popular books, students who advocated for them to be kept were able to support their argument with reasons why, or ways the books could be used, displaying *thinking and communicating with clarity*.

I'd like to say this was a well-thought-out lesson design, but it wasn't. My original plan was to just get student feedback on these books to help me make my weeding decision, but the lesson evolved the more we got into it (*thinking flexibly*). I wanted them to be able to gather data and evaluate, just as they would with any other research project. This turned into a very rich, habit-filled activity, and it also gave the students a peek into the decision-making process I use every day when it comes to our collection development. Based on

student input, I ended up keeping all 21 Lionni books, and many of them were eventually checked out—by 2nd graders!

How Do We Know It's Working?

How do I know students are understanding, using, and internalizing the Habits of Mind? I know because I hear, and see, students talking about and using the habits, both in the library and elsewhere throughout the school day. They are better able to discern and discuss the habits during book discussions and library lessons as the year goes on. They often make connections regarding the habits that I hadn't even thought of.

The challenge is to make sure they are not just "parroting" the words but are actually incorporating these dispositions into their everyday life. It's easy for students to use the habits in a classroom setting, but what about when the teacher isn't directly instructing? Do they use the habits when no one is watching? I like to believe they do, but that's a difficult question to answer. Only through anecdotal evidence "after the fact" can we ever know, but I do see evidence in nonclassroom settings, such as the hallway, the playground, and the lunchroom, where the students are more independent.

As they mature, so does their understanding and use of the habits. For me, as well as other specialists, that is the joy of teaching the students from kindergarten through 5th grade. We not only see growth within the school year (as a classroom teacher does), but we also witness the continued growth within the students' six-year career at Coal Creek—and beyond. As students return, we often hear stories of how they continue to use the habits in middle and high school, and even into college. So, yes, we know the Habits of Mind are being used at Coal Creek Elementary, and it all begins with our youngest students.

Note: For library activities and books using the Habits of Mind, visit the Institute for Habits of Mind website at www.instituteforhabitsofmind.com.

Part III: Integrating and Sustaining the Habits of Mind

You now realize that the Habits of Mind are not just kid stuff. They are applicable to all adults, including parents and teachers. And, children are much more likely to embrace the habits when they become not only goals but also the norms modeled by members of the school and community. When this happens, the habits become obvious in the signals in the environment, such as in the vocabulary used among teachers, parents, and students, and in the recognition of achievements, performances, and growth.

Living the Habits of Mind, truly integrating and sustaining them, calls for using them in the culture of the school and the home. Part III of this book is a testament to celebrating those conditions, which take dedication, patience, and leadership. Our mission is to create a more thoughtful, compassionate, and humane world. Please join this crusade by starting children early with the Habits of Mind.

12

Integrating the Habits of Mind into a Bicultural Setting

Tracey Nelson

Ka mōhio koe, ko ahau, ka mōhio koe te ako. (To know me is to teach me.)

Geraldine Kindergarten is an early childhood community serving children ages 2 through 6. Our bicultural curriculum *Te Whāriki* embodies the language, culture, and values of both Māori and Pakeha. Our community is in the town of Geraldine, in a rural area south of Christchurch on the South Island of Aotearoa (New Zealand).*

In this chapter, from the viewpoint of my role as head teacher, I share the story of how the kindergarten has engaged, implemented, and sustained the Habits of Mind. The account draws attention to the value and practical application of the habits in an early childhood setting and our effort to delve deeper into our pedagogy and to personalize the program for our bicultural context, through our bicultural curriculum document, *Te Whāriki: He whāriki mātarunaga mō ngā mokopuna o Aotearoa.* Many people have been involved in the

---

*Aotearoa is the Māori name for New Zealand.

work and commitment to continually improve teaching and learning outcomes for our children, teachers, parents, families, and *whānau* (extended families), and each has been integral to our success and achievements as a recognized International Habits of Mind Learning Community of Excellence.

Getting Started

The Habits of Mind program was already in place at our local high school when Geraldine Kindergarten adopted it in 2005. We appreciated the simplicity of its language and saw the potential for a continuous experience for our students, starting in early childhood. We recognized that the Habits of Mind framework would provide a shared understanding of the language of learning so parents could contribute and children could immediately identify themselves as learners. We explored how we could make this concept meaning-ful for younger children. We began by reading, attending relevant courses, and adapting practical ideas we saw being implemented in other settings. We completely immersed ourselves in the Habits of Mind for five years, supported by the leadership and mentorship of Karen Boyes, the CEO of Spectrum Education and an affiliate direc-tor of the Institute for Habits of Mind.

Developing a Strategy of Slowing, Paraphrasing, and Inquiry

The acronym *SPI* refers to a teaching tool that I developed to guide our practice. It consists of the following three components:

- *S* **is for slowing** down and being mindful of the *silence* as we engage with children. It's about managing our own impulsivity as teachers and seeking to truly listen and understand. It's about observ-ing quietly, without judgment or planning what to do next. It allows the child to be working in an optimal learning moment that includes an openness to problem solving and an exploration of thinking.

- *P* **is for paraphrasing.** When the timing feels right, it may be appropriate to paraphrase some of the ideas being shared to ensure that there is true understanding of what is happening. As teachers, we need to be mindful of the moment when we can add value to play— but only when we have really explored our children's ideas, either through listening and observing silently or through paraphrasing to gain clarity and understanding. This practice reflects key concepts in our early childhood curriculum as it sends a strong message to the children that we are interested and value their contribution.

- *I* **is for inquiry**, or invitational questioning (Costa & Kallick, 2008, p. 143). When timed appropriately, invitational questioning encourages the practice of numerous Habits of Mind. *Metacognition*, for example, which allows children to share and think aloud about their problem solving, may be encouraged by prompting a student with a request such as "Tell me about the thinking that's happening inside your head right now." This approach invites further *questioning* from peers and allows past experiences to be shared (*applying past knowledge to new situations* and *communicating with clarity and precision*). It also opens the opportunity to practice *listening with empathy and understanding*.

This acronym is a simple yet effective three-step strategy. We have found that an effective SPI encourages us to explore children's working theories and ideas without hijacking their thinking, and this process elicits endless possibilities that are true to the origins of the Habits of Mind. As stated in our early childhood curriculum document, "Children are most likely to generate and refine working theories in learning environments where uncertainty is valued, inquiry is modeled, and making meaning is the goal" (Ministry of Education, 2017, p. 23).

To support our assessment practices, we developed a checklist to examine which Habits of Mind we were using regularly in our teaching and documentation. We soon realized that the checklist was

encouraging us to view our children with a deficit lens, checking more for what they were *not* doing. We needed to revisit the vision of *Te Whāriki* "that all children are confident, competent learners and communicators . . . " (*Te Whāriki*, p. 2). Our role was to ensure that children were engaged in an empowering environment where they had agency for their learning and that we were supporting their dispositional growth in meaningful ways. Our review revealed that we needed to shift our perspective to growing the learner instead of growing the habit. We lost sight of who the children were—their language, culture, and identity—the very foundation on which to grow learning.

Using the Habits of Mind as a Pedagogy for Young Children

As we began to consider the connections between the Habits of Mind and our early childhood education pedagogy, we realized that we teachers needed to reflect on the habits in our own practice— slowing down and *managing our impulsivity*! We recognized and trusted the capabilities of young children to *persevere* and to *think flexibly* and creatively as they developed in their own time. In our national curriculum, there is a Māori description for this: *ā tōna wā* (in their own time). *Te Whāriki* (Ministry of Education, 2017) also refers to teachers needing to acknowledge and respect toddlers' rights for increasing agency.

As teachers, we began to see and recognize how the Habits of Mind were intrinsically used, and with this awareness we came to understand and value the importance of giving children time, space, and opportunities to practice them over and over. We gave undivided attention to care routines in which *listening with empathy and understanding* and working together in a partnership—*thinking interdependently*—were imperative. Teachers began to trust the children to engage in their environment alongside others, allowing for

opportunities to problem-solve and negotiate without immediate intervention by an adult. This effort resulted in powerful learning that had a huge impact on our curriculum. The environment was thoughtfully planned with opportunities to allow this practice to happen within the natural rhythm of the child—like finding the perfect dance partner (Gerber, 1980).

These strategies are now embedded in our teaching practice and guide and inform our planning. Resources continue to be used in creative and flexible ways, and we learn each day as our children now demonstrate with competence the Habits of Mind and create their own understanding.

Achieving Excellence: Adapting and Exploring the Habits in Our Cultural Context

Five years into our use of the Habits of Mind, we were recognized for our work and commitment when we received the International Habits of Mind Learning Community of Excellence Award—a first for New Zealand and for early childhood education. Attaining this award was a career highlight for the teachers and very special for our community. However, the award represented only the beginning of our journey. We realized that the key objective of this award is a commitment to a process of growth and development rather than a status to be achieved That commitment is evident in our ongoing journey of adapting and exploring the Habits of Mind in our cultural context, as described in the rest of this chapter. It was from this place of being recognized as experts that the greatest learning occurred for our team. We had a responsibility, and the award was a catalyst for a change in thinking as we were challenged to consider how we could sustain and continue to develop the habits. We began to see a disconnect between our vision and our practice. With feedback from the senior teacher, we were prompted to think critically about our practice and the connection

between the context of our unique bicultural curriculum and the Habits of Mind.

We knew that teachers could articulate the Habits of Mind with knowledge and expertise, the environment was rich with experiences, and we had effective practical ideas to engage and develop children's understanding of the habits. What was more challenging to see was where and how the languages, cultures, and identities of the children were evident—yet these elements were at the heart of our kindergarten philosophy and community. Documentation of children's learning reflected the Habits of Mind and evidence of children using and applying them both in kindergarten and at home, but who the children were and what constituted their learner identity had been foregrounded by an overemphasis on the habits. This realization was an important lesson for us in terms of considering the full promise of our curriculum. *Te Whāriki* requires us to weave our own local curriculum into instruction and ensure depth and breadth based on the touchstones that are our guiding principles and strands.

Through a critique of our practice, we realized that the Habits of Mind appeared to sit in isolation. There was a disconnect between, on the one hand, what teachers were able to articulate as "what *happens* here" and what that looked like in practice, and, on the other hand (and more important), "what *matters* here." Assessment and data related to the Habits of Mind framework, rather than a focus on the child and the child's family, had become the driving force of our practice.

Developing Depth and Authenticity with a Reluctant Decision to Set Aside the Habits of Mind

Following this realization, we made a conscious but difficult decision to set aside the Habits of Mind and take the time to revisit who we were, what our identity and our vision were, and what teaching

and learning could—and did—look like, sound like, and feel like for the children and families at Geraldine Kindergarten and for the children of Aotearoa/New Zealand. We needed to reflect, review, and re-create a shared understanding of who we were.

We began by removing all visual representation of the Habits of Mind in our environment, so that they didn't keep resurfacing and hijacking our direction and focus. We reviewed our way of assessing children's learning, beginning by slowing down and focusing on relationships. We spent the year exploring and inquiring as a team and with our children, families, and community about what was important to us all without any preconceived ideas of how this exploration would develop. We wanted to find out how well we knew our families, and we developed the following inquiry questions to guide our review:

• What were the aspirations of our parents, families, and *whānau* for their children?

• What could these aspirations look like today, tomorrow, or in the future?

• What could our parents, families, and *whānau* bring to our context? What were their strengths and interests and stories from home and their past?

The following questions became the overarching focus for our internal evaluation:

Ko wai koe? Na wai koe i ahu mai koe i hea?/Who are you? Where are you from?

The review process involved a number of different ways of connecting with our children, families, and community to ensure we were offering every opportunity for contribution. For example, we used sticky notes on a wall display with inquiry questions, conducted parent meetings, and communicated through newsletters, Facebook, and one-on-one conversations.

The Outcome: A Stronger Connection to the Habits of Mind

What emerged from our effort was still an emphasis on the importance of the Habits of Mind, but now with stronger connections to our bicultural curriculum and our own context in Geraldine, New Zealand. *Whanaungatanga* (relationships) and *manaakitanga* (care and respect) are key Māori competencies that we aimed to have as the underpinnings of every aspect of our practice. The connections to the Habits of Mind were clearly visible as we explored how the HOM could only be developed and nurtured through caring, respectful relationships based on a real knowledge of and partnership with the child and the family. We worked alongside parents, families, and *whānau* to develop our own language of learning. One outcome was that our documentation of children's learning began to use a language that the child and family could connect with. Our assessment practices and language of learning included the Habits of Mind alongside other key aspects of our philosophy and curriculum.

Next Step: Developing Coherence

The following year we asked, *How do we ensure that the Habits of Mind are relevant and sustainable in our bicultural context?* Our discussions as a team were robust and critical while reflecting a shared understanding of working and being. We decided to explore an idea of using a *piko* (a fern found in New Zealand) as a visual metaphor to represent it, but to adapt it so that it reflected the holistic connection between our vision, our curriculum, and the Habits of Mind (see Figure 12.1).

The soil holding the piko represents our *whanaungatanga*—our relationships with people, places, and things. At every level these relationships are fundamental to our success. The soil needs to be rich and responsive and is the foundation for teaching and learning. The roots represent our core values and curriculum, *Te Whāriki*, which continually nurture and feed the piko. The frond of the fern represents the

FIGURE 12.1   **Ko Wai Tatou: Who Are We?**

Influences and connections on your child's learning and development

The Habits of Mind are evident all around us

Intentional teaching strategies

Core values at Geraldine Kindergarten:

- Respect
- Excellence
- Leadership
- Perseverance
- Accessibility
- Mahi tahi / working together
- Whanaungatanga / relationships

Our piko piko is a metaphor that the teaching team has drafted to depict who we are at Geraldine Kindergarten and how we support children's learning and development. Adapted with permission, Geraldine Kindergarten.

Habits of Mind—the way children engage in our curriculum, which affects the learning outcomes. The frond (habits) unwinds and continues to flourish as long as the soil and roots remain rich and nourished to feed the fern. The curl at the end of the frond, which in time falls and rejuvenates the plant, represents the learning outcomes that progress and change from experiences. This process rejuvenates our work and affects growth and new learning. The weather component of the image represents the external sociocultural factors that differ for each child and family yet have a great effect on the growth of the fern. We need to understand that "weather" well, so we are ready and responsive.

We visit our local forest weekly, no matter the weather. It is a place where we can take responsibility for its sustainability, see connections to our past, *gather data through all senses,* and *respond with*

wonderment and awe. Changes in the environment from week to week offer opportunities for *questioning and posing problems*.

The Habits of Mind are now strongly grounded in our philosophy, as represented by the piko. The habits now reflect the culture of our families and our community.

Depth and Engagement Through Partnership

This review process took almost two years, and the result was displayed in the form of a draft document in the kindergarten so that children, families, teachers, and our community could continually reflect and add to it. We referred to it often, and each of us had a different interpretation. As we used these reflections to guide our decision making, we saw that families' aspirations for their children were emerging at the forefront of planning and assessment. Teachers listened with greater empathy and understanding (*manaakitanga*); the dialogue was no longer guided by one person holding greater power but by a shared partnership. We explored the stories of *mana whenua* (the indigenous people of our place, the history of our area, and the connections our past had with our children today, and those stories started to become visible in our environment.

Although a number of outcomes of our effort had been evident to some extent before our shift in practice, the outcomes now felt more sustainable, culturally responsive, and authentic. We could confidently make the following statements:

- Relationships (*whanaungatanga*) with people, places, and things form the foundation of our practice.
- The practice of teaching and learning reflects what we articulate.
- Children's languages, cultures, and identities are at the forefront of decision making and teaching practice.
- Children's and families' voices, or contribution, is evident in the assessment and planning of children's learning, recognizing an authentic partnership.

The Habits of Mind are now included in our strategic plan, ensuring their sustainability and our commitment to continual growth. The habits are embedded in our cultural context and therefore relevant and meaningful for our children, families, teachers, and community. Our language of learning, which includes the Habits of Mind, is understood by everyone. More specifically,

• Teachers are able to articulate with clarity what teaching and learning looks like at Geraldine Kindergarten, making clear the connections between our vision, our curriculum, and the Habits of Mind.

• Teachers can articulate what the Habits of Mind look, sound, and feel like in our culturally responsive environment.

• Children are able to identify the Habits of Mind they are using in play, set their own goals for learning using the language of the habits, and revisit strategies for next steps.

• The language of the Habits of Mind is used effortlessly by children, teachers, and parents at kindergarten and at home.

Final Thoughts

Early childhood education is the ideal time to introduce the Habits of Mind. The earlier children are able to recognize and start connecting their behaviors and actions with the language of the habits, the greater the opportunities for practice, mastery, and effective use.

To ensure sustainability, the Habits of Mind need to be embedded in the cultural context of the setting. They need to be woven seamlessly through the vision, philosophy, and curriculum. Knowing our families, their cultural context, and their aspirations for their children is crucial for a collaborative partnership that reflects empathy and understanding. It is through relationships that effective engagement and consultation will occur. This component is crucial for educational decision making and will lead to learning outcomes that will prepare our young children for an unknown future.

To sustain and ensure the HOM are embedded, we need to slow down and be responsive to the language, culture, and identity that a child brings to the classroom before we can "assess" or consider how the child is engaging in our teaching and learning environments. That understanding needs to be evident to ensure a strong sense of belonging. It needs to be reflected not only in the environment but also in our way of being and connecting with people. It needs to reflect *listening with understanding and empathy.*

Note: Thanks to the teachers, children, parents, families/whānau, our community, and the members of our Board of Trustees. I am indebted to Art Costa and Bena Kallick for their aspirations for our children and for igniting my passion to share in the effort. Also, thanks to the professional support and guidance of Karen Boyes and my inspiring mentor and editor, Kathryn O'Connell-Sutherland, for making a difference in our children's tomorrow.

Costa, A. L., & Kallick, B. (2008). Using questions to challenge students' intellect learning. In A. L. Costa & B. Kallick (Eds.), *Learning and leading with habits of mind: 16 essential characteristics for success* (pp. 135–148). Alexandria, VA: ASCD.

Gerber, M. (1980). Differences between caregiving and educaring. Retrieved from http://www.magdagerber.org/differences-between-a-caregiver-and -educarer–vol-i-no-2-spring-1980.html

Ministry of Education. (2017). *Te Whāriki; he whāriki matauranga mo nga mokopuna o Aotearoa—Early Childhood Curriculum.* Wellington, New Zealand: Learning Media.

13

Creating a Mindful Schoolwide Culture to Maximize Learning

Bonnie Tabor

As you enter Waikiki Elementary School in Honolulu, Hawaii, the first thing you notice is the love and joy emanating from the campus. You might hear squeals of delight from kindergarten students as they sample the fruit of our miracle berry trees or applause coming from a grade 1 class as a student demonstrates an original organic mixture he has concocted to clean the classroom's whiteboard. Students may be lingering at the worm bin, happily experiencing the feel of the worms that weave through their fingers or harvesting taro from our food farm in preparation for a cooking demo later in the day. A dance-exercise class is in session in one area, while grade 5 students belay their grade 2 "caring and cooperation partners" to the top of our climbing wall in another area. The mouth-watering aroma that wafts through our campus from our award-winning cafeteria enhances the joy of mastery experienced by our lunch club unicyclists. Passing the office at lunchtime, the laughter from our faculty lunchroom conveys the strong bonds the teachers have formed. A typical day at Waikiki makes

you marvel at the joy and possibility of learning in a school setting that really works.

As the principal at Waikiki Elementary School for more than 15 years, I am often asked for suggestions on how to create a school culture supportive of the kinds of learning just described, a culture that can personalize the learning experience to nurture diversity and capture the wonder and joy of authentic learning—not only for students but for all participants. The key to translating these ideals into practice at Waikiki School rests in our *mindful* school culture. This culture, based on the Habits of Mind, empowers everyone by creating standards of behavior and expectations that truly nurture growth for all stakeholders. The habits fuel the pulse of the school. They unite stakeholders into a cohesive learning community connected by a common set of values whose practice contributes to the betterment of each individual and the school as a whole.

Background and Context

Since the early 1990s, Waikiki School has intentionally focused on social and emotional learning in addition to the development of thinking skills and content knowledge. Over the years, the amazing outcomes of our graduates and the tremendous lure of our school have attested to the power of this consistent focus on how the Habits of Mind link the heart, mind, and intention of all stakeholders. They provide the philosophical foundation and the common vocabulary needed to prepare students to do well on the tests they take in school and in life. They guide us all to live lives of greater intentionality and continuous personal growth.

Current research increasingly supports the path Waikiki School has taken. Paul Tough, in *Helping Children Succeed*, finds a young child's capacity to manage emotions can be negatively affected by early childhood experiences, which can sometimes even change the child's DNA (Tough, 2016). By intentionally teaching the Habits of

Mind (such as *persisting* or *managing impulsivity*), we can reverse the damage of early exposure to negative stress and teach children how to successfully regulate their emotions in order to become successful learners. Current research also shows that character traits such as grit, persistence, and empathy predict future success more reliably than IQ (Tough, 2016, p. 24).

Five Key Factors

Reflecting on Waikiki School's journey on its way to incorporating the teaching of these character competencies or Habits of Mind into our educational programming, I see five factors that emerge as key. The next sections describe each of these factors in detail.

1. Creating a Strong Vision Through Grassroots Involvement

In 1992 Waikiki School became one of Hawaii's first "school/community-based management" (SCBM) schools. As one of its first official acts, the school council convened a retreat. Business people, Hawaii State Department of Education personnel, parents, teachers, university professors, and community members worked tirelessly for several days and nights to put together a vision that could capture the hearts and minds of our students. Barriers such as financial concerns, practical considerations, and other roadblocks were put aside as the participants collaborated to envision the school of their dreams.

After lengthy debate, these "pioneers" crafted a vision of a school that would be a "home for the mind," where the process of thinking would be primary, where the Habits of Mind would be the overriding focus, where content would be the vehicle to develop the thinking process. They envisioned a school that would be couched in the harmony of heart and mind, where students would become good thinkers and thoughtful human beings. Focus would be on the whole child, and lifelong learning would be a given expectation

for all. This vision is succinctly captured in our school's vision and mission statements: "Waikiki School is a safe, vibrant, nurturing environment that encourages lifelong learning" and squarely aims "to create 'mindful,' ethical decision makers committed to making the world a more 'thought-full' place."

The retreat also established the following norms of operation for such a mindful school culture:

- Instead of power, the school would seek to empower.
- Instead of control, the school would seek to free the intellect, to enhance creativity.
- Instead of uniformity of practice, the school would seek to evolve a collective vision of excellence.

Over the 20-plus years since its conception at the retreat, Waikiki School has continued to evolve into a mindful school where thinking, collaboration, and thoughtfulness are paramount. The original vision and underlying foundational beliefs, etched out by the school pioneers, continue to guide us. Over the years the vision has been revisited and refined but remains consistent in the strength it draws from its roots in the voice of the community it serves.

The grassroots engineering of the school's vision as a mindful school is certainly a major factor in its success. It answers the question of why we do what we do and is a key factor in the school's evolution.

2. Staying the Course and Deepening the Focus

Over the course of my tenure as principal, public schools have been faced with various changes in directives, from No Child Left Behind, to Race to the Top, to Every Student Succeeds. Each new mandate has presented new challenges. We maintain our focus and are able to accommodate the changes of the times. Instead of a "flavor of the month" mindset, we are strongly anchored by knowing what really matters to us: producing lifelong learners who will contribute to a more thoughtful world.

3. Modeling What We Value and Teach

A quote attributed to Ralph Waldo Emerson expresses a fundamental truth about Waikiki School: "What you do speaks so loudly they can't hear what you say." The Habits of Mind transcend all subject matter. We don't simply teach the habits; we live them. All participants in the learning community continually seek to become less impulsive, more creative, better at problem solving, more persistent, more present, and more flexible in our thinking. Through intentionally modeling these mindful behaviors, we strive to serve as role models for our learners, strengthening our own personal repertoire of mindful behaviors in the process.

We model, teach, talk, integrate, and deepen our connection to the Habits of Mind at every opportunity. We link the habits to real-life situations and intentionally bring these opportunities for learning into our classrooms as often as we can. We honor our mindful focus in all we do—how we teach, how we discipline, how we relate. The Habits of Mind serve as our goal both for learning and for living.

4. Developing an Empowering Culture

The power of our school culture could not exist without the full support and deep commitment of our teachers. Empowered teachers and students are key to this process. When schools focus on what really matters in life, children are willing to work hard to succeed and accomplish amazing things. Content is used to inspire the desire to learn. Students feel that the work they're doing is meaningful and challenging, and that they're able to get better at it when they work hard.

Practice of the Habits of Mind develops a culture that promotes continual growth for both teachers and students. It challenges all to innovate, to stretch, to revise practice to best meet the ever-evolving needs of our students.

As principal, I serve the school by deepening our capacity to live the values we embrace. My task is to promote and support growth

and experimentation throughout the school. I work to block distraction, buffer nonessential crises, and empower staff to use their multitude of talents to create classrooms and schoolwide practices that inspire. I do all I can to provide the tools, resources, and freedom for teachers to use their artistry to inspire learning. My role is one of facilitator within this process.

Through their practice, the Habits of Mind encourage a respect for individuality, creativity, and flexibility in thinking. This respect translates into a lot of good ideas, a faculty that is willing to share their strengths, and a learning community that rises to meet the challenges. I am often humbled by the innovative ideas, creative solutions, and brilliance that emerge. Once again, my role is to support this process, not direct it.

It is especially important for me, as principal, to model the ideals laid out through the Habits of Mind. I listen intently to the staff, honor their strength, and trust in their capacity to find solutions. I actively facilitate opportunities for learning conversations at every turn.

Within a school culture that promotes experimentation, empowered teachers become energized and engaged in their search to find ever more effective ways of reaching their students. Cooperative teaching, collaborative inquiries into best practice, discussion around student work—these all vitalize our teachers' ongoing quest to develop their craft. My job as principal is to provide the time and space for this to take place and to serve as a partner in the process. Again, my role is to invite, encourage, and facilitate, not direct.

5. Recognizing the Importance of Practices

Over the years, Waikiki School has worked hard to create practices in support of a mindful school culture that nurtures both academic and social-emotional proficiencies. We reinforce, model, and create artifacts, curriculum, projects, community events—anything

we can think of—to contribute to the immersion environment with which we want to surround our students. We actively infuse Habits of Mind across our campus and throughout our school day.

This effort becomes obvious to those who visit our school. Wherever they go, they see explicit reference to the Habits of Mind. Classroom bulletin boards, the signs and murals that adorn the campus, and even the T-shirts that students and teachers wear— all of these indicate (and reinforce) the school's commitment to the Habits of Mind and a fuller, more robust vision of what a person can be. Similarly, visitors hear this commitment in the habits-laden vocabulary of all those who are connected with the school. When a committee from the Western Association of Schools and Colleges (WASC) made its initial visit to the school during the 2014 accreditation process, the committee chair commented that "in his 40 years of experience in public education, [he had] never been to a school where so clearly everyone is 'on the same page'" (Anderson, 2014).

All practice is shaped through the lens of our mindful culture. We do not tell students to just memorize for the test or teachers to simply follow the script. Rather, we provide both students and teachers with the time and encouragement that allow them to think flexibly, take responsible risks, create, imagine, and innovate.

Our classrooms and campus are a bustle of creative activity. Students get their hands dirty exploring our gardens and orchards, build drones and solar-powered cars, integrate ambitious art projects into their studies, and combine technology and culture by producing QR codes for tourist landmarks. Confident that our students and teachers know who they are, we trust them to lead the way. Proceeding from their individual passions and needs, we empower all persons to create and recreate, to invent and reinvent, to do and persistently redo, and to continue to ingeniously author the lifelong process of actualizing their potential as a mindful human being.

Converting Ideals into Practice: An Example

Waikiki School's mindful staff at work is evident in the following example:

> **Background:** Fifty percent of Waikiki School's incoming kindergarten students enter without readiness skills; 33 percent enter as English language learners, 38 percent qualify for free lunch, and 40 percent come from single-parent families.
>
> **Challenge:** To restructure our kindergarten program to better address the needs of our early learners.
>
> **Collaborative Process:** After much discussion, reading, and research, we decided to develop a two-tiered kindergarten program. Following their first year in kindergarten, students could opt to either enter a senior kindergarten class or choose placement in grade 1. "Senior K" would not be considered retention, but rather an intervention to address the readiness of our young learners, providing them with the gift of time. In the Senior K class, learning would be paced to match our youngest students' varied developmental needs.
>
> **Impact:** Since its inception, our Senior K class has proven to be an extremely successful reform model. Its focus on addressing readiness has yielded tremendous dividends not only for the individuals involved but for the school as well.
>
> Over the past 11 years, longitudinal school research shows all Senior K graduates have been able to meet or exceed grade-level benchmarks in their successive elementary years. Special education referrals for Senior K graduates have diminished; ELL student progress has been enhanced.
>
> Allowing students to become fully immersed in an environment supportive of and geared to their level of readiness gives all children at Waikiki School the chance to experience success. The establishment of our Senior K class is just one creative way that the mindful school has restructured itself to come up with an innovative solution to solve a problem. There are many others.

The Mindful Learning Center

Remaining open to continuous learning is not only one of the Habits of Mind that drive our school's vision; it also remains a catalyst for our response to current research in early childhood education (ECE) and social-emotional learning. We have learned how critical early childhood education is, and we are meeting this challenge daily in the Mindful Learning Center, which we opened in the spring of 2016.

The center is yet another chamber of the "heart" of our mission and vision. It houses the ECE, special education, and adult ed learners of our community. It also connects our school with the University of Hawaii, our partner in remaining on the cutting edge of research and practice.

Presently, our mindful preschool serves youngsters between the ages of 3 and 5. In the future, we hope to expand our outreach to include families with children from 0 to 3 years of age. This expansion will allow us to be increasingly proactive in preventing early childhood stress, an intervention that has tremendous potential for preventing social-economic group disparities before they occur. As we work with families early in a child's formative years, educating them in using the Habits of Mind as a mindful approach to dealing with life's challenges is an extension of our vision that our school pioneers would definitely applaud.

Critics assert that the Waikiki School culture is built upon a utopian ideal that defies measurement. Yet our scores and proficiencies attest to our strength and speak for themselves, as does our desirability and the continuing success of our students. But how do we measure the Habits of Mind? How do we measure mindfulness in our students? How do we measure character or the joy of learning? These are questions we welcome with excitement. We know that our inquiry will not only contribute to the conversation about

education and social-emotional learning but also fuel the fire of inspired thought and practice that has made our school what it is: a leader in our district and state and an enthusiastic contributor to the global mission of creating a better world for all.

_____

Anderson, J. (2014). Waikiki Elementary: 20 years of Habits of Mind [blog post]. Retrieved from Succeeding with Habits of Mind at https://habits ofmind.org/waikiki-elementary-20-years-of-habits-of-mind/

Tough, P. (2016). *Helping children succeed*. New York: Houghton-Mifflin Harcourt.

14

Gathering Evidence of Growth from Parents and Teachers

Art Costa and Bena Kallick

Observing and recording is one of the most familiar practices that teachers of early childhood education use. We have compiled the vignettes and excerpts presented in this chapter as examples of teachers'—and parents'—observations and anecdotal reports that document evidence of how children are internalizing the Habits of Mind in school and at home. A thread that appears repeatedly throughout this book is recognition of how students are using the habits' vocabulary, recognizing the habits in their own and others' behaviors, and explaining how the habit was used in a variety of situations. These excerpts are additional examples of evidence.

Structured Observations

Schools use a variety of means to record information related to children's use of the Habits of Mind within and outside school. Here are two examples of specific formats used for this purpose.

A Formative Assessment Report to Parents from Katikati Kindergarten

The Katikati Kindergarten in Bay of Plenty, New Zealand, uses a narrative format to document children's progress in a report that is shared with parents. Figure 14.1 shows an example.

A Parent Survey from Charles Wyche Elementary School

School life is enhanced through family engagement, and Charles Wyche Elementary School in Miami, Florida, uses feedback from parents to help teachers improve student performance and holistic success. One way the school accomplishes this is through parent surveys. Figure 14.2 shows an example of data gathered through a survey in which parents were asked to indicate the level of frequency (frequently, sometimes, not at all) they observed their child demonstrating certain Habits of Mind at home.

Informal Observations

Useful information about children's use of the Habits of Mind often comes in the form of informal observations and anecdotes shared by teachers and parents. Here is a sampling of these kinds of accounts.

From Geraldine Kindergarten (Geraldine, New Zealand)

A parent of one of the students at Geraldine Kindergarten reported that when her daughter was opening presents on her 5th birthday and her older sister was struggling to remain calm, the 5-year-old told her "quite clearly and confidently . . . to 'manage her impulsivity.'" During summer break, when this same student was showing some other children how to slide down a water slide on their tummies, she helped a somewhat reluctant participant by patiently demonstrating the proper technique and reassuring her that she needed "to practice and persevere."

Another parent recounted an incident in which her husband was trying to retrieve something from a space underneath the house and got stuck in the process. As the father cursed over his predicament,

**FIGURE 14.1   Formative Assessment on Progress:
A Reflection Narrative for Parents**

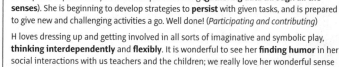

| Assessment Reflection | Date |

Child's Name: H

H really enjoys coming to kindergarten and has made friends easily. It's so lovely seeing her happy face as she gives us all a big hug on arrival. She really enjoys the company of S, K, and C, among others (*relating to others*).

Over the last two terms, it's great to see her playing the Shopping Game, kei a wai, bingo games, and block play, **working interdependently** with others. Her block constructions are fabulous. She now uses lots of other props, such as animals, flowers, shells, and fabric, to make her creations take on a complex dimension (**thinking about thinking** and **striving for accuracy**). At mat-times, she is able to sit and **listen with understanding**, and she enjoys participating in group games, music, and movement. She has many ideas and loves **creating, imagining**, and **innovating**. Her painting techniques have really evolved over her time here. Baking is a real passion; she is always one of the first children to offer to help and is particularly keen to sample the baking (**gathering data through all the senses**). She is beginning to develop strategies to **persist** with given tasks, and is prepared to give new and challenging activities a go. Well done! (*Participating and contributing*)

H loves dressing up and getting involved in all sorts of imaginative and symbolic play, **thinking interdependently** and **flexibly**. It is wonderful to see her **finding humor** in her social interactions with us teachers and the children; we really love her wonderful sense of humor. She is learning to negotiate, take turns, and share with her friends and is a kind and caring girl. She is particularly lovely looking after our younger children and teaching them about the routines and activities here. (*Relating to others*, **Showing empathy**)

She has developed a good understanding of the English language, and we are also mindful to encourage and support her rich and interesting Samoan culture. One of Mum's aspirations is for H to speak more English, which has naturally occurred in this environment. When we made recycled bags, she immediately chose the Samoan flag for the front of her bag, which was awesome. (*Able to communicate clearly with both adults and children/Using language, symbols, and text*; **Thinking and communicating with clarity and precision**)

She **responds with wonderment and awe** when she discovers something interesting to share, particularly in nature. (*Working theories, Thinking*)

We love that she is very happy and settled in this environment, and we look forward to extending her in project work in the areas of her interest, e.g., art and craft projects, dramatic play, music, and movement (**persisting, creating, taking risks**). Mum wants her to be exposed to reading experiences, so we are always reading her lots of books, and she is beginning to recognize some letters and writing her name really well. We will continue to give her lots of opportunities to be involved in our numeracy and literacy program. (**Thinking and communicating, Questioning and posing problems, Striving for accuracy**)

Parent's Aspirations: For H to improve her English, as it is her second language, and for her to have exposure to early reading skills.

Habits of Mind are in bold.
Key Competencies are in italic.

FIGURE 14.2   **Parent Survey Data**

Habits of Mind	Frequently	Sometimes	Not at all
Does your child perceive things from a position other than his or her own? (*Thinking flexibly*)	39/55%	26/37%	6/8%
Is your child thinking before acting? (*Managing impulsivity*)	44/62%	23/32%	4/6%
Is your child sticking to a task until it is complete? (*Persisting*)	40/56%	30/42%	1/1%
Is your child taking time to check over his or her homework? (*Striving for accuracy*)	46/65%	21/30%	4/6%
Is your child acting on the basis of his or her own initiative? (*Taking responsible risks*)	56/79%	12/17%	3/4%
Does your child see the funny side of things? (*Finding humor*)	60/85%	11/15%	0/0%

Note: The data show the number and corresponding percentage of respondents in each category.

his young son told him, "It's all right, Daddy! Keep persisting and you'll find a way out!"

From Katikati Kindergarten (Bay of Plenty, New Zealand)

A parent told a story that illustrated how her 4-year-old demonstrated *creating, imagining, and innovating* and *finding humor* in a challenging situation. He was playing with his older sister, who was being grumpy and impatient, as well as destructive. The boy ran over to a tree and started hugging it. The sister stopped and asked him what he was doing. He replied, "I'm hugging a tree, because they give us oxygen! You should try it! It makes me feel great!" The mother and daughter both went over to the tree and hugged it. They all ended up laughing. The problem was solved, and the youngsters went off to play feeling much happier.

From Kittredge School (San Francisco, California)

Parent comments about the effects of the Habits of Mind include the following:

> We do talk about the Habits of Mind as a family, and I share them with friends because I find them to be pertinent/applicable in many situations.

When the [San Francisco] Giants or the boys themselves are not doing well in sports, *persisting* comes up. Or when the Giants won the World Series, Shane proudly said, "The Giants were definitely *striving for accuracy* when they won the World Series." And one of my favorites is after I made some cookies, I told Zachary he had to wait until after dinner to have one, to which he replied, "I am *managing my impulsivity* for sure."

I love how the Habits of Mind reinforce and emphasize all of the characteristics that we value so highly.

Sometimes [the Habits of Mind] just come up within the context of something we are doing. *Taking responsible risks* is one that often comes up.

Persisting and *striving for accuracy and precision* often come up, within the context of sports or really any time we are talking about something that we have not mastered or something with which we are having trouble.

From San Roberto International School (Monterrey, Mexico)

The mother of a preschool student related how her son observed his sister and his father searching for a book in the girl's schoolbag so she could begin her homework. They said they could not find what they were looking for, but the boy encouraged them to *persist*. On another occasion, he pointed out to his mother that if she said hello to her friends, she was *managing impulsivity*, but if she yelled at them, she was not.

Tracking Internalization of the Habits over Time

Another indicator of internalization of the Habits of Mind is evidence that a student continues to demonstrate them a while after they were initially taught. Here are two examples.

The first account, from parents in New Zealand whose kindergartener had "graduated" from Geraldine Kindergarten and gone on

to primary grades, shows how the habits became embedded in the lives of the entire family:

> Our family loves the Habits of Mind! We first became aware of them through our amazing local kindergarten, where the 16 habits are embedded throughout their whole approach to learning. It made sense to us to adopt this approach at home as well so that our children were receiving a consistent message and could really understand the meaning of the habits and get the most from their use as a development tool.
>
> As parents we found it really useful to have a framework and a vocabulary that we could use to encourage and guide our children as they negotiated new experiences and situations. Some of the habits we still talk about almost daily, such as *persisting, managing impulsivity*, and *striving for accuracy*. We sense that these will be ongoing areas of focus, but the habits also remind us to "catch" the kids *responding with wonderment and awe* or to laugh with them and enjoy it when they are *finding humor* in something. [We] love to see how they glow with pride when we say, "I like your thinking on that topic" or "Wow, that's a great question."
>
> Our children are now well into primary school, and we still use the habits in our everyday parenting. We have heard them use the same phrases we do when they talk with one another and sometimes to their friends, so we know that when our children become parents they too will use the same habits framework to guide and celebrate the development of their children in a positive, holistic way.

The second account is from John Melton, a 4th grade teacher at Waikiki Elementary School in Honolulu, Hawaii:

> Fourth grade students at Waikiki School are well versed in the Habits of Mind. They can define each habit as well as provide real-life examples and non-examples. The lower-grade teachers used the Habits of Mind terminology intentionally in lessons, integrated the habits into the curriculum, and used them spontaneously throughout the day. Teachers hope students will treat the habits as tools, drawing upon the appropriate habit for a given situation.

One of our initiatives is the Waikiki School food farm. The food farm provides a vehicle to teach environmental issues, nutrition, Hawaiian history, and life science. Students are given the freedom to explore various projects and activities, depending upon their interests. On a given day, students might opt to plant seeds, harvest produce, spread mulch, or fix a broken water line. These activities provide opportunities to apply the Habits of Mind in a real-life, meaningful context.

One day a group of 4th graders chose to plant ti leaves (*ti* is a plant brought to Hawaii by early Polynesian explorers). The only instructions given were to plant the ti leaves around the perimeter of a half-circle garden that measured 20 feet in diameter. The ti leaves were in a large pile that included both red and green plants. The teacher instructed the class to make a plan to plant all the ti leaves in a logical, aesthetically pleasing manner.

The group of four boys and three girls began by brainstorming ideas. One boy had the idea to lay the plants out in front of their intended spots. Swiftly both boys and girls spread the plants out in the half circle. Once the plants were laid out, the group observed and began to gather data through their senses. Then one of the girls suggested that they alternate colors to form a pattern—red-green-red-green—drawing upon her prior knowledge of patterns.

Again, the group spread the ti leaves, trading when needed until all the plants were laid out in the intended pattern. At this point, the teacher, who had been observing, said, "How do you know if they are spread out evenly?" The group began to dialogue, thinking interdependently and pondering the teacher's question. They came up with various ideas. One boy said, "Let's use the bricks to measure. There should be two bricks between plants." He drew upon his knowledge in math class, where they were taught to improvise when they did not have a tape measure. The group went back to work spreading the plants and realizing that two bricks were not enough. "Perhaps three would work," one of the girls chimed in. Again, they spread the plants, and this time it worked! They persisted, worked interdependently, and used prior knowledge to solve a meaningful problem.

This called for a celebration of high-fives and cheering before they finished the task by digging the holes for the plants.

Back in the classroom, I gathered the students to debrief their accomplishments. They were asked to share a Habit of Mind that enabled them to accomplish their goal. The ti planting group discussed how they had to work and think together to solve what turned out to be a complicated math problem. A group that had been mulching discussed how they had to persist to finish a job that began as fun and ended up being quite laborious. A group that had been planting seed trays discussed the importance of precision in their task.

In addition to the content that is integrated into the Waikiki School food farm experience, this outdoor classroom serves as a natural laboratory for students to experiment with the various Habits of Mind to solve meaningful problems. Through reflection and probing questions, the teacher is able to guide students along a path of learning and discovery. Ultimately the students realize that the use of the Habits of Mind is beneficial regardless of the context.

Final Thoughts

Internalizing the Habits of Mind may take many years. For some, it's a lifetime endeavor and an elusive quest; others use the Habits of Mind only when reminded; and some seem to be born with the inclination.

Our goal is to start early, during a child's formative, impressionable years, and then continue to strengthen the Habits of Mind over time, until they are used proactively without prompting and with forethought and automaticity. This achievement requires that individuals become situationally alert to cues that signal the need for the habit; it requires them to possess the necessary skills to execute the habit and to be reflective on their effectiveness in employing those skills. Obviously, this does not happen overnight, in one lesson, in one term, in one year, or maybe in one lifetime. But given an early start, we hope to increase the chances that the Habits of Mind will become internalized in all humanity.

15

Leading Schools with the Habits of Mind in Mind

Art Costa and Bena Kallick

> If there is anything that we wish to change in the child, we should first examine it and see whether it is not something that could better be changed in ourselves.
>
> —Carl Jung

Having worked to promote the Habits of Mind for over 25 years, we have learned that to successfully adopt and integrate the habits into the culture of a school and community, quality leadership is a necessary component. Our experience clearly indicates that someone—a teacher, principal or vice principal, department chair, resource teacher, librarian, counselor—needs to be a "cheerleader" to support, model, demonstrate, encourage, remind, and coach staff members in the implementation and infusion of the Habits of Mind, particularly during the start-up years. To illuminate the role of leadership, in this chapter we describe some actions and strategies practitioners have used to succeed in maintaining the focus on the Habits of Mind.

Research indicates that leadership and student learning are inextricably linked. Leadership is about distributing the dispositions, capabilities, and practices that influence student learning (Leithwood

& Seashore-Louis, 2012; Robinson, 2011). These findings suggest that leadership personnel must work with staff to infuse the Habits of Mind into the curriculum, instructional practices, assessment strategies, and culture of the school and its community by doing the following:

- Creating a vision for the habits-infused school and classrooms
- Building a knowledge base about the research and theory supporting the Habits of Mind
- Defining their roles as leaders in realizing that vision
- Developing coaching skills for working with colleagues to infuse the Habits of Mind in lesson planning and the conduct of meetings
- Continuously reviewing, refining, and deepening their understanding of and familiarity with the Habits of Mind

Modeling the Habits of Mind

Robert Fulghum once wisely said, "Don't worry that children never listen to you; worry that they are always watching you." Because we know that much of human learning occurs through imitation of others, it is imperative for leaders (and those who claim to be leaders) to "walk the talk." The Habits of Mind are not just kid stuff. We all can get better at using them. Doing so takes practice, awareness of our own behaviors, feedback from others, self-reflection, and self-talk. Learning to live the Habits of Mind is a lifelong journey that we never fully master; it is always a work in progress.

When staff and community members observe that their school leaders are on a journey of continuous learning, they become more open to and see the benefits of using the habits. When leaders display humility by admitting that they have erred, or should have reacted with greater flexibility when things do not go well, or begin to use more precise language when they are communicating a new idea, members of the school community understand that the habits are to be practiced. They are less fearful of reprisal and see

the value of thinking out loud about their own thinking because they all are taking responsible risks. Everyone in the school is constantly learning and improving their own behaviors to be consistent with the norms, values, and beliefs that the school culture claims in its vision and mission.

Although no one ever fully masters any of these habits, the habits serve as an aspiration for the kinds of behaviors leaders would like to see in themselves, in their staff, and in others. The following are what leaders strive for as they practice the habits:

- *Persisting*—Leaders remain focused. They have a commitment to task completion. They try not to lose sight of their own and their organization's mission, vision, and purposes.

- *Listening with understanding and empathy*—Leaders strive to understand their followers. They devote enormous mental energy to comprehending and empathizing with others' thoughts and ideas.

- *Managing impulsivity*—Leaders think before they act, remaining calm, thoughtful, and deliberative. Leaders often hold back before commenting, considering alternatives and exploring the consequences of their actions.

- *Thinking flexibly*—Agile leaders are adaptable. They can change perspectives, generate alternatives, consider options. They see the big picture and can analyze the parts. They are willing to acknowledge and respect others' points of view.

- *Thinking about thinking (metacognition)*—Leaders are aware of their own thoughts, strategies, feelings, and actions and their effects on others. Leaders "talk" to themselves as they evaluate their plans, monitor their progress, and reflect on their actions, needs, and aspirations.

- *Striving for accuracy*—Leaders are truth seekers. They desire exactness, fidelity, and craftsmanship. Leaders do not accept mediocrity.

- *Questioning and posing problems*—Leaders have intellectual curiosity, a need to discover and to test ideas. They regard problems as opportunities to grow and learn.

- *Applying past knowledge to new situations*—Leaders draw on their rich experiences, access prior knowledge, and transfer knowledge beyond the situation in which it is learned. They learn from their mistakes.

- *Thinking and communicating with clarity and precision*—Leaders articulate their ideas clearly in both written and oral form. They check for understanding and monitor their own clarity when using certain terms and expressions.

- *Gathering data through all senses*—Leaders have highly tuned observational skills. They continually collect both internal and external information by listening, watching, moving, touching, tasting, smelling, and trusting their gut instincts.

- *Creating, imagining, and innovating*—Leaders try to conceive problems differently, examining alternatives from many angles. They project themselves into diverse roles, use analogies, take risks, and push the boundaries of their own limits.

- *Responding with wonderment and awe*—Leaders find the world fascinating and mysterious. They are intrigued by discrepancies, compelled to mastery, and have the energy to enjoy the journey.

- *Taking responsible risks*—Living on the edge of their competence, leaders are courageous adventurers. They dare to take calculated risks.

- *Finding humor*—Leaders have such high self-esteem that they do not take themselves too seriously. They are able to laugh at themselves and with others. They are capable of playfully interpreting everyday events.

- *Thinking interdependently*—Leaders recognize the benefits of participation in collaborative efforts. They seek reciprocal relationships, both contributing to and learning from interaction with others.

- *Remaining open to continuous learning*—Leaders resist complacency about their own knowledge. They have the humility to admit their weaknesses and display a sincere desire to continue to grow and learn.

Creating and Sustaining the Culture of a Habits of Mind School

We are often asked, "How would you know when and if the Habits of Mind have been infused?" We usually respond by saying that we'd know it when there is a "harmony of heart and mind"; when the habits are mindfully infused throughout the curriculum, instructional practices, assessment strategies, and the people and culture of the school; when a school is not just a "Habits of Mind school" but truly a "mindful school" where thoughtful behaviors become a "way of being" rather than a "thing to do." The following are some indicators for you to consider as you assess your school culture (Costa & Kallick, 2008):

- **All members of the school community**—In what ways are the staff, students, and parents
    - Using the Habits of Mind language in their communications?
    - Finding new ways to expand the Habits of Mind in a variety of settings?
    - Valuing the Habits of Mind for all the members of the learning community?
- **Classroom instruction**—In what ways are the classrooms
    - Teaching the Habits of Mind intentionally?
    - Focusing on being alert to situations in which the Habits of Mind can be practiced, valued, illuminated, and reflected upon?
    - Using tools and resources to deepen understanding of the Habits of Mind?

- **Curriculum design**—In what ways is curriculum designed for
    - Weaving Habits of Mind into units and lessons?
    - Building a through-line of how Habits of Mind develop over multiple years?
    - Including the Habits of Mind as stated goals and outcomes for students?
- **School culture**—In what ways is the school
    - Recognizing when the Habits of Mind are performed?
    - Recognizing the Habits of Mind in the environment with signs and signals such as posters, slogans, and other means?
- **Parents and community**—In what ways are parents and community
    - Continuously learning about their student's progress with the Habits of Mind?
    - Revisiting and reorienting themselves to the vision of the school and its commitment to the Habits of Mind?
- **Action research**—In what ways is the school
    - Informing its practices with the Habits of Mind?
    - Collecting evidence of longitudinal growth?
    - Continuing its study of the Habits of Mind?
    - Communicating with others as they learn more about the Habits of Mind?
- **Leading learning**—In what ways is the school
    - Distributing leadership among staff members to support the Habits of Mind?
    - Providing resources such as time, opportunities for collaboration, and finances to support the school's vision?
    - Expecting all leaders to model the Habits of Mind?

Final Thoughts

Leaders lead by example, and the Habits of Mind serve as a guide for developing the best examples for learning and leading. When they are considering new initiatives, they need to set up a process for *thinking interdependently*. When they want to consider changing the report cards, for example, they need to set up a process for *thinking and communicating with clarity and precision*. In other words, they can identify the issues or problems and then ask themselves, which of the habits will we need to practice so that we are thinking most efficaciously? This metacognitive question is then modeled throughout the school by teachers, students, and the community it serves.

———————————

Costa, A. L., & Kallick, B. (2008). *Learning and leading with habits of mind: 16 characteristics of success.* Alexandria, VA: ASCD.

Leithwood, K., & Seashore-Louis, K. (2012). *Linking leadership to student learning.* San Francisco: Jossey-Bass.

Robinson, V. (2011). *Student-centered leadership.* San Francisco: Jossey-Bass.

Index

Note: The letter *f* following a page number denotes a figure.

About the Editors, Authors, and Contributors

Editors

Arthur L. Costa is emeritus professor of education at California State University, Sacramento. He is cofounder of the Institute for Habits of Mind and of the Center for Cognitive Coaching. He has served as a classroom teacher, a curriculum consultant, an assistant superintendent for instruction in the Office of the Sacramento County Superintendent of Schools, and the director of educational programs for the National Aeronautics and Space Administration. Costa has made presentations and conducted workshops in all 50 states as well as Mexico, Central and South America, Canada, Australia, New Zealand, Africa, Europe, the Middle East, Asia, and the islands of the South Pacific.

In addition to many journal articles, Costa is the author of *The School as a Home for the Mind*, and coauthor of *Techniques for Teaching Thinking* (with Lawrence Lowry) and *Cognitive Coaching* (with Bob Garmston). He is editor of *Developing Minds: A Resource Book for Teaching Thinking*, and coeditor, with Bena Kallick, of the four-book series *Habits of Mind; Learning and Leading with Habits of Mind;* and *Habits of Mind Across the Curriculum;* as well as the *Process as Content*

trilogy, with Rosemarie Liebmann. His books have been translated into Arabic, Chinese, Dutch, Hebrew, Italian, and Spanish.

Active in many professional organizations, Costa served as president of the California Association for Supervision and Curriculum Development and was the national president of ASCD from 1988 to 1989. He was the recipient of the prestigious Lifetime Achievement Award from the National Urban Alliance in 2010 and, along with Bena Kallick, received the Malcolm Knowles Memorial Self-Directed Learning Award in 2017 from the International Society for Self-Directed Learning. Costa may be contacted at artcosta@aol.com.

Bena Kallick is a private consultant providing services to school districts, state departments of education, professional organizations, and public agencies throughout the United States and around the world. Kallick received a doctorate in educational evaluation at Union Graduate School. Her areas of focus include group dynamics, creative and critical thinking, and alternative assessment strategies for the classroom. She is the coauthor of *Using Curriculum Mapping and Assessment Data to Improve Student Learning* (with Jeff Colosimo), *Assessment Strategies for Self-Directed Learning* (with Art Costa), and *Students at the Center* (with Allison Zmuda); and coeditor with Art Costa of *Assessment in the Learning Organization*, the *Habits of Mind* series, *Learning and Leading with Habits of Mind,* and *Habits of Mind Across the Curriculum.* Her works have been translated into Dutch, Chinese, Spanish, Italian, Hebrew, and Arabic.

Formerly a Teachers' Center director, Kallick also created a children's museum based on problem solving and invention. She was the coordinator of a high school alternative designed for at-risk students. She is cofounder of Performance Pathways, a company dedicated to providing easy-to-use software for curriculum mapping and assessment tracking and reporting, in an integrated suite. She is currently a program advisor for Eduplanet21, a company that focuses on UbD curriculum unit design and online professional learning.

Her work with Art Costa has led to the development of the Institute for Habits of Mind (www.instituteforhabitsofmind.com), an international institute that provides services and resources to schools that are dedicated to becoming places where thinking and Habits of Mind are taught, practiced, valued, and infused into the culture of the school and community. She and Costa have developed an online course for EduPlanet21.

Kallick's teaching appointments have included the Yale University School of Organization and Management, the University of Massachusetts Center for Creative and Critical Thinking, and Union Graduate School. She was formerly on the boards of the Apple Foundation, Jobs for the Future, and the Weston Woods Institute. She presently serves on the board of Communities for Learning.

Along with Art Costa, she received the Malcolm Knowles Memorial Self-Directed Learning Award from the International Society for Self-Directed Learning in 2017. Kallick may be contacted at kallick.bena@gmail.com.

Authors

Sarah Baker teaches 2nd and 3rd grades at Kittredge School in San Francisco, California. She has taught in public and private schools with students from prekindergarten through middle school since 2000. She has worked in general education, gifted education, and special education, and has also taught creative movement and dance. Baker received her master's degree in teaching from the University of San Francisco and her bachelor's degree in dance from the University of Oregon. She may be contacted at sarahmelissabaker@gmail.com.

Michelle Bunder is a primary education teacher in New South Wales, Australia, who is passionate about purposeful, relevant, and real-life learning with the Habits of Mind at the forefront. She has collaboratively coached and worked with leadership teams and

educators on the implementation of the Habits of Mind in both preschool and primary school settings. As a practicing primary school teacher with a firsthand understanding of the daily pressures facing educators and schools today, she writes, presents, and coaches in a user-friendly and practical manner that leaves educators inspired and armed with ideas they can use immediately. Bunder may be contacted at bunderm02@dow.catholic.edu.au.

Maggie Dent is an educator and a popular author and commentator on parenting, with a special interest in the early years, adolescence, and resilience. Known as the "queen of common sense," she is an advocate for strengthening families and communities, protecting and preserving childhood, and using nature-based play and pedagogy in schools. Her experience includes teaching, counseling, and working in palliative care/funeral services and suicide prevention. A passionate voice for children of all ages, she is the author of 10 books and several e-books and a prolific creator of resources for parents, adolescents, teachers, and other educators. Dent may be contacted at maggiedent4@hotmail.com.

Erskine S. Dottin is professor emeritus and Frost Professor in the School of Education and Human Development at Florida International University, where he initiated a faculty learning community on Habits of Mind and contributed to the decision to focus the preservice and inservice teacher education programs on dispositions (Habits of Mind). He received his PhD in education policy analysis at Miami University of Ohio and was a Fulbright Scholar in Nigeria. He is the author or coauthor of numerous books, including *Dispositions as Habits of Mind: Making Professional Conduct More Intelligent* and *Structuring Learning Environments in Teacher Education to Elicit Dispositions as Habits of Mind: Strategies Used and Lessons Learned* (with Lynne D. Miller). Dottin may be contacted at dottine@fiu.edu.

Diana Garza is an educator whose career has included more than 20 years at San Roberto International School in Monterrey, Mexico, where she has served as a teacher, early childhood principal, and campus director. She was coleader of the project to implement the Habits of Mind on the Monterrey and San Pedro Garza García campuses of the school, including training of all stakeholders. A graduate in chemical engineering of the Monterrey Institute of Technology and Higher Education, she holds a master's degree in education from Framingham State University in Massachusetts. Garza may be contacted at dgarza@sanroberto.edu.mx.

Barbara L. Johnson has been an educator for more than 30 years, serving as a teacher, an assistant principal, and a principal. She is currently the principal at Charles D. Wyche Jr. Elementary School in Miami, Florida, which has been recognized by the Institute of Habits of Mind and the school board of the Miami–Dade County Public Schools as an International Habits of Mind School of Excellence. She has implemented the 16 Habits of Mind schoolwide and believes this contributes to the school's success and continued commitment from its teachers, parents, and the school community. She also serves as an adjunct professor at Nova Southeastern University in Fort Lauderdale, Florida. She received her bachelor's and master's degrees from East Carolina University in Greenville, North Carolina, and a specialist and doctorate degree from Nova Southeastern University. Johnson may be contacted at BJohnson@dadeschools.net.

Tracey Nelson is a kindergarten teacher in New Zealand with more than 30 years of experience. She introduced and led the integration of Habits of Mind at Geraldine Kindergarten, which was the first early childhood center to earn the International Habits of Mind Learning Community of Excellence. Nelson is particularly interested in ensuring culturally responsive engagement so that the Habits of Mind can be successfully integrated all over the world.

She has facilitated professional learning for early childhood educators and primary teachers in New Zealand. Nelson may be reached at traceynelson99@gmail.com.

Aixa Perez-Prado is a writer, homeschooler, and faculty member at Florida International University in Miami, Florida. She has taught English as a Second Language and trained teachers in TESOL methods and strategies and cross-cultural communication both in the United States and abroad, and began her teaching career as a bilingual kindergarten teacher. Her research interests include promoting critical and creative thinking, emotion and language learning, and bilingualism and identity. She is the founder of *The Thinking Café*, a website and series of workshops devoted to thinking as a conscious practice for teaching and parenting. Her thinking blog at the thinkingcafe.org explores thinking, identity, and empathy across cultures. Perez-Prado may be contacted at professoraixa@gmail.com.

Louise Pon-Barry is a teacher at Kittredge School in San Francisco, California, who enjoys working with primary-level children because of their fresh and unique outlook on life. She received her bachelor's degree in liberal studies from Santa Clara University, along with minors in Spanish and art history. She earned her multiple-subject teaching credential and master's degree in education from the University of San Francisco.

Michelle Scheu is an early education teacher in Queensland, Australia. In 2014, she was awarded a National Excellence in Teaching Award from the Australian Scholarships Group (ASG) for her development of a pedagogy known as Thinking Play, which seeks to facilitate learning through quality play. To share her learning and promote quality learning in the early years of formal education, she mentors teachers both locally and internationally, presents

at conferences, and produces YouTube clips. She is the author of *Thinking Play: A Guide for Educators*. Scheu may be contacted at thinkingplayedu@gmail.com.

Cushla Scott has been teaching kindergarten for 30 years and at Katikati Kindergarten since 2003. Her teaching philosophy has evolved over the years, with inspiration from the principles of Rudolf Steiner and Reggio Emilia. She credits Art Costa and Habits of Mind for a powerful dimension to her teaching philosophy, which has aligned with the unique bicultural practice in Aotearoa / New Zealand.

The pedagogy underpinning Scott's teaching encompasses the provision of aesthetic, peaceful, and sustainable environments and communities. By nurturing children's curiosity and love of nature, she provides possibilities and opportunities for their potential. Through these principles, she affirms that lifelong learning is as natural as breathing.

She has three daughters and two grandchildren and lives at Waihi Beach in The Bay of Plenty, New Zealand, with her husband. Scott may be contacted at cushla.scott@ikindergartens.nz.

JoLynn Scott has been teaching for more than 30 years in Colorado's Boulder Valley School District. She began her teaching career in middle school, as a language arts teacher. After earning a master's degree in reading and a library science endorsement, she became the teacher librarian at Coal Creek Elementary School, where she was first introduced to the Habits of Mind. Scott is now enjoying retirement. She can be reached at jolynn.scott@bvsd.org or 4jolynn@gmail.com.

Bonnie Tabor has been involved with Waikiki School in Honolulu, Hawaii, since 1987, initially as a counselor and presently as the principal. She received a bachelor's from Case Western Reserve University, a master's in counseling from the University of Hawaii,

and a master's in special education from the University of California. Throughout her professional career, she has found the Habits of Mind to be inspirational and fundamental to her vision of the purpose of education. As principal of Waikiki School, recently recognized as a State Blue Ribbon winner, she believes the Habits of Mind provide the vision, the direction, and the unity of purpose that have resulted in the school's status as a school of excellence. Tabor may be contacted at bonnie_tabor/waikikie/hidoe@notes.k12.hi.us.

Terry Thoren is the former CEO of Klasky Csupo, Inc., the company that produced *Rugrats*, *Rocket Power*, and *The Wild Thornberrys*. Terry cofounded Wonder Media, LLC, to work with a global team of storytellers to connect with children at risk. Wonder Media uses animated stories to address hunger, child abuse, emergency preparedness, social emotional learning, critical thinking, autism, nutrition, children with disabilities, and children living in a home with an addicted adult(s).

Wonder Media operates four distinct areas of business: it produces a global education website called WonderGroveLearn.com; it produces instructional animation campaigns for large nonprofit organizations; it has a global partnership with the Institute for Habits of Mind to produce instructional animations for the 16 Habits of Mind; and it uses proprietary technology called *AnimationNow* to allow students to create their own animated stories using Wonder Grove Story Maker®.

Wonder Media has worked with Global Institute for Habits of Mind, Head Start, the Betty Ford Center Children's Program, Girl Scouts USA, the Barbara Sinatra Children's Center, the Hero in You Foundation, the Teri, Inc. Campus for Life, the NALC campaign to Stamp Out Hunger, the Festival of Children, the Wyland Foundation, the World Peace Caravan, and Signing Savvy. Thoren may be reached at thoren@wondergrovekids.com.

Donna Tobey has served independent schools in Florida as a teacher and administrator for 30 years. She is currently the Lower School Director at the NSU University School in Fort Lauderdale. A presenter at regional, state, and national conferences, Tobey has contributed to educational magazines and books, sharing classroom strategies and programming that promote the development of critical and creative thinking. She has served on the board of the Florida Kindergarten Council and was a cofounder of ColLABorate South Florida, a consortium of schools dedicated to school improvement through collaborative teacher education and innovation. Tobey may be contacted at dtobey@nova.edu.

Mickey Weiner is a National Board–certified teacher currently working as a mathematics coach at Charles D. Wyche Jr. Elementary School in Miami, Florida. She has taught for more than 30 years in Title 1 schools in Miami–Dade County. She received a bachelor's degree in elementary education from the University of Wisconsin–Madison, and a master's in reading and a doctorate in curriculum and instruction from Florida International University. She enjoys observing how children who learn about the Habits of Mind often take the information home and assist families in decision making and problem solving. Weiner may be contacted at mweiner@dadeschools.net.

Judy Willis is a physician and board-certified neurologist who practiced neurology for 15 years and then received a credential and master's in education from the University of California–Santa Barbara. She taught elementary and middle school for 10 years. She has written six books for educators and parents and now consults with education departments and provides professional development presentations and workshops, nationally and internationally, about learning and the brain. Willis may be contacted at jwillisneuro@aol.com.

Contributors

Mercedes Alvarez was born in Coral Gables, Florida. She attended Florida International University where she acquired a bachelor's in education. After working in the private sector for six years, she began teaching in Miami Dade County and has been teaching elementary school for 23 years. Her hobbies include cooking, traveling, reading, and practicing flexible thinking as she explores new cuisines and restaurants. She may be contacted at mercialvarez@dadeschools.net.

Isabel Garcia is a prekindergarten teacher at Charles David Wyche Jr. Elementary School in Miami, Florida. She was raised in South Florida and attended Charles D. Wyche as a student. She graduated from Florida International University with a degree in elementary education. This is currently her third year teaching and she loves teaching preK. She states that the last two years have truly taught her about the creative expression of the preschool-aged child. She looks forward to continuing her studies and to opportunities to further her knowledge about preschool-aged children. She may be contacted at igarc020@fiu.edu.

John Melton had the good fortune to teach 4th graders for 15 years in Honolulu, Hawaii. His passion for teaching the Habits of Mind is the result of Art Costa's influence at Waikiki School. In addition to teaching HOM, Melton is passionate about Philosophy for Children, a gently Socratic approach to teaching inquiry through children's natural sense of wonderment. Melton has joined the staff at Punahou School in Honolulu and may be contacted at jmelton@punahou.edu.

Lindsey Ramirez graduated from Florida International University with a bachelor's degree in elementary education in 2005. She received her master's degree in curriculum and instruction with a specialization in early childhood from University of Florida in 2015. Ramirez has taught kindergarten, 2nd, 3rd, and 4th grades.

Currently, she is a reading coach. Throughout her career, Ramirez has grown, professionally and personally, with a goal of remaining a lifelong learner. She may be contacted at lramirez01 @dadeschools.net.

Sonia Reyes was born in Aguadilla, Puerto Rico. She attended Inter American University of Puerto Rico and received her bachelor of arts in elementary education. She started teaching in Puerto Rico. In 2000, she moved to Miami and taught Spanish in a private Catholic school. In 2004, she started working for Miami–Dade County Public Schools and has been working at Charles D. Wyche Jr. Elementary since then. She enjoys teaching incoming ESOL students. She exposes them to their new country and traditions incorporating the Habits of Mind. She may be contacted at sreyes@dadeschools.net.

Eida Tumbeiro was born and raised in Isla de la Juventud, Cuba. She attended Enrique Jose Varona University of Cuba and received her bachelor's degree in special education in 2000. She started teaching students with learning disabilities and autism in Cuba. In 2012, she moved to Miami and attained her certification to teach exceptional students. She has been working at Charles D. Wyche Jr. Elementary since 2013. She loves teaching exceptional students and incorporating the Habits of Mind in her daily lessons. She may be contacted at 310665@dadeschools.net.

Maria Valarezo was born in Guayaquil, Ecuador. She attended Barry University and received a degree in elementary education. She earned a master's degree in education with a major of curriculum and instruction from the University of Florida. She has been teaching in Miami–Dade County Public Schools for 17 years. She is creative in the classroom as well as in the worlds of culinary arts and technology. Her hobbies include traveling, cinema, and experiencing new restaurants. She may be reached at mvalarezo@dadeschools.net.

Related ASCD Resources: Habits of Mind

At the time of publication, the following resources were available (ASCD stock numbers in parentheses). For up-to-date information about ASCD resources, go to www.ascd.org. You can search the complete archives of *Educational Leadership* at www.ascd.org/el.

Print Products

Cultivating Habits of Mind (Quick Reference Guide) by Arthur L. Costa & Bena Kallick (#QRG117098)

Developing Habits of Mind in Elementary Schools: An ASCD Action Tool by Karen Boyes and Graham Watts (#108015)

Developing Habits of Mind in Secondary Schools: An ASCD Action Tool by Karen Boyes and Graham Watts (#109108)

Habits of Mind Across the Curriculum: Practical and Creative Strategies for Teachers edited by Arthur L. Costa & Bena Kallick (#108014)

Learning and Leading with Habits of Mind: 16 Essential Characteristics for Success edited by Arthur L. Costa & Bena Kallick (#108008)

Students at the Center: Personalized Learning with Habits of Mind by Bena Kallick and Allison Zmuda (#117015)

Understanding How Young Children Learn: Bringing the Science of Child Development to the Classroom by Wendy L. Ostroff (#112003)

Digital Products

Learning to Think . . . Thinking to Learn: The Pathway to Achievement DVD and User Guide (#607087)

ASCD myTeachSource®

Download resources from a professional learning platform with hundreds of research-based best practices and tools for your classroom at http://myteachsource.ascd.org/.

For more information, send an e-mail to member@ascd.org; call 1-800-933-2723 or 703-578-9600; send a fax to 703-575-5400; or write to Information Services, ASCD, 1703 N. Beauregard St., Alexandria, VA 22311-1714 USA.

WHOLE CHILD
TENETS

1 **HEALTHY**
Each student enters school healthy and learns about and practices a healthy lifestyle.

2 **SAFE**
Each student learns in an environment that is physically and emotionally safe for students and adults.

3 **ENGAGED**
Each student is actively engaged in learning and is connected to the school and broader community.

4 **SUPPORTED**
Each student has access to personalized learning and is supported by qualified, caring adults.

5 **CHALLENGED**
Each student is challenged academically and prepared for success in college or further study and for employment and participation in a global environment.

The ASCD Whole Child approach is an effort to transition from a focus on narrowly defined academic achievement to one that promotes the long-term development and success of all children. Through this approach, ASCD supports educators, families, community members, and policymakers as they move from a vision about educating the whole child to sustainable, collaborative actions.

Nurturing Habits of Mind in Early Childhood relates to the **safe, engaged, supported,** and **challenged** tenets. *For more about the ASCD Whole Child approach, visit* **www.ascd.org/wholechild.**

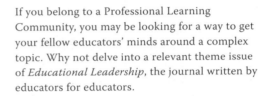